African-American/Afro-Canadian Schooling

BOOKS BY CHARLES L. GLENN

The Myth of the Common School, 1988, 2002. Italian translation 2004; Spanish translation 2006.

Choice of Schools in Six Nations, 1989.

Educational Freedom in Eastern Europe, 1995.

Educating Immigrant Children: *Schools and Language Minorities in 12 Nations* (with Ester J. de Jong), 1996.

The Ambiguous Embrace: Government and Faith-Based Schools and Social Agencies, 2000.

Finding the Right Balance: Freedom, Autonomy and Accountability in Education, I & II (with Jan De Groof), 2002.

Un difficile equilibrio: Europa continentale e mediterranea (with Jan De Groof), 2003.

Balancing Freedom, Autonomy, and Accountability in Education, I–III (with Jan De Groof), 2004.

Contrasting Models of State and School: A Comparative Historical Study of Parental Choice and State Control, 2011.

Native American/First Nations Schooling: From the Colonial Period to the Present, 2011.

African-American/Afro-Canadian Schooling
From the Colonial Period to the Present

Charles L. Glenn

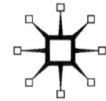

AFRICAN-AMERICAN/AFRO-CANADIAN SCHOOLING
Copyright © Charles L. Glenn, 2011.
Softcover reprint of the hardcover 1st edition 2011 978-0-230-11416-6

All rights reserved.

First published in 2011 by
PALGRAVE MACMILLAN®
in the United States—a division of St. Martin's Press LLC,
175 Fifth Avenue, New York, NY 10010.

Where this book is distributed in the UK, Europe and the rest of the world, this is by Palgrave Macmillan, a division of Macmillan Publishers Limited, registered in England, company number 785998, of Houndmills, Basingstoke, Hampshire RG21 6XS.

Palgrave Macmillan is the global academic imprint of the above companies and has companies and representatives throughout the world.

Palgrave® and Macmillan® are registered trademarks in the United States, the United Kingdom, Europe and other countries.

ISBN 978-1-349-29578-4   ISBN 978-0-230-11950-5 (eBook)
DOI 10.1057/9780230119505

Library of Congress Cataloging-in-Publication Data

Glenn, Charles Leslie, 1938–
    African-American/Afro-Canadian schooling : from the colonial period to the present / Charles L. Glenn.
        p. cm.

    1. African Americans—Education—History. 2. Blacks—Education—Canada—History. I. Title.
LC2741.G54 2011
371.829′96073—dc22   2011001468

A catalogue record of the book is available from the British Library.

Design by Newgen Imaging Systems (P) Ltd., Chennai, India.

First edition: June 2011

With gratitude to Dean Kenn Elmore, Ruth Shane, Mike Dennehy, Reggie Jean, Julianna Gonzalez, and others who are making a difference at Boston University

Contents

Preface ix
Note on Terminology xi

Introduction 1
1 Assumptions about Race 5
2 Enslaved and Free Blacks before 1862 23
3 Equipping the Freedman 45
4 Jim Crow South 79
5 Jim Crow North 109
6 "Uplifting the Race" 127
7 Integration and Its Disappointments 149
8 Have We Learned Anything? 165

Notes 171
References 187
Index 199

Preface

This account of the schooling of Black children and youth in North America over several centuries is written by a specialist in educational policy and administration, not by an academic historian, and it is based primarily on secondary sources. I make no claim to provide new information based on original research, nor do I engage in any of the debates among historians about how to interpret particular aspects of this long and complicated story. My purpose has been to make the story as clear and compelling as possible to the nonspecialist, and to show its whole sweep without neglecting the individuals whose role has been so important.

It is my engagement with the movements for social justice in the 1960s, followed by more than two decades as the state government official responsible for educational equity and school desegregation in Massachusetts, that has informed my reading of the abundant material on the Black experience in Canada and the United States. Perhaps even more, it is some thirty years as associate pastor of a series of Black churches in Boston that has made me want to tell this story.

I wrote this book in parallel with another, also to be published by Palgrave Macmillan, *Native American/First Nations Schooling: From the Colonial Period to the Present*. While the experience of the two groups is different in many respects, it has been marked in both cases by the heavy influence of assumptions about race among the White majority, assumptions that have deeply influenced the manner in which schooling has been provided.

Finally, it is remarkable how seldom Canada is mentioned in histories of education dealing with the United States, and how seldom the United States is mentioned in Canadian histories of education. Remarkable because the parallels are striking, and the differences significant. This is not, strictly speaking, a study of comparative policies of the sort that I have written with my Belgian colleague Jan De Groof, but it seeks to show how much each nation has to learn from the other.

In writing this book—so much out of my usual scholarly concern with comparative educational policy—I have had a sense of discharging a debt to many with whom I have worked over the years in the struggle for racial justice... and to countless others who went before us and will come after.

CHARLES L. GLENN
Boston University

Note on Terminology

Orlando Patterson writes, in the Introduction to his brilliant *Rituals of Blood*, "I refuse to call any Euro-American or Caucasian person 'white,' and I view with the deepest suspicion any Euro-American who insists on calling Afro-Americans 'black.'"[1]

There can be no doubt that we have been bedeviled in dealing with race in North America by the problem of what to call people. When I, as a "Euro-American" (certainly not Caucasian, since I have no ancestors from the Caucasus that I know of) college student, began working with children in Roxbury, in the mid-1950s, it was still common for their parents to refer to themselves as "colored." In 1963, when I spent some time in jail in North Carolina as part of the Freedom Movement, and in 1965, when I was in Selma for the second attempt to cross the Edmund Pettus bridge, we were careful to say "Negro." A couple of years later the rise of "Black" consciousness made it clear that my involvement with racial justice could no longer be as a community organizer in Roxbury; I obtained a state government position with responsibility for enforcing the Massachusetts law forbidding the de facto segregation of what state law referred to as "nonwhite" pupils. Fifty years and more of engagement with racial issues have convinced me, in short, that people have very different ways of thinking of themselves and that there is no way to avoid giving offense to some.

In the title of this book, I have used the awkward phrase "African-American/Afro-Canadian," but in the pages that follow I have simplified matters by using "Black" and "White," despite my respect for Orlando Patterson, and I have capitalized both terms even at the risk of seeming to attribute to skin color more significance than—as will be evident in my final chapter—in fact I believe it has and should have.

I am aware that the same debate about racial labels exists in Canada; "Afro-Canadian" is used by some and rejected by others, as is "Black."

I hope that any readers in either country who are offended by the terms that I have chosen to use will at least give me credit for honorable intentions—and cut me some slack.

In the passages quoted, many from nineteenth-century sources, I have retained whatever racial identifiers were used by the authors without feeling it necessary to add "[sic]" when their prejudices are evident.

On the other hand, I have not capitalized "Southern" and "Northern," except when that is the case in my sources; it seems to me that to do so lends itself too readily to the false idea that racial prejudice and discrimination are and have been uniquely a feature of the states of the former Confederacy.

Introduction

Formal schooling, along the approximate lines of that provided to children of the White majority, of the children of Americans and Canadians of African ancestry has overwhelmingly been provided—when it has been provided at all—in segregated settings. While the curriculum that they followed was commonly adapted in some way from that used at the same period for White pupils, Black children and youth have seldom shared classrooms with White peers. A very rough estimate might be that fewer than 10 percent of Black youth who have received formal schooling over the past two centuries—or indeed four centuries—in North America did so in what we would consider integrated schools and classrooms. After a half-century of school desegregation efforts—often at great cost, both financially and in support for public education—most Black pupils in the United States attend schools with few White classmates.

This book is about how Black children and youth were for many decades excluded from the great enterprise of the "common" public school in both Canada and the United States, and what they received—and have in substantial measure continued to receive—instead.

It asks why policy makers and the White majority in the United States and Canada assumed, at almost all times, that Black children either did not require formal schooling or, if it was provided to them, should receive it in separate schools, and it describes how that separate schooling became institutionalized.

Robin Winks, in the preface to the second edition of *The Blacks in Canada*, acknowledges the justice of a criticism that this had not told "the history of Negro life in Canada" but rather "the history of the Black man as an issue in white Canadian life."[1] The same observation could be made about the account that follows: It is focused primarily on the formal schooling of Black children and youth in North America as a *policy* issue, with all its twists and turns, its ups and downs, and not, except in passing, on the struggle of parents and community leaders to provide adequately for their children by their own efforts.

To a very large extent, it must be said, this is a shameful history, marked by persistent assumptions about the natural inferiority of Black children and in consequence the need to provide them with unambitious forms of schooling if indeed any formal schooling would not be wasted on them. The account has its brighter side as well: Thousands of Black and White teachers who committed themselves, often under great hardships, to educate Black children, and their allies in benevolent organizations and, sometimes though not often enough, in government who supported such efforts.

The eagerness of Black parents, in many cases, to ensure that their children received as much formal schooling as possible is a phenomenon that will often be mentioned but cannot fully be explained. After all, it did not in the great majority of cases actually lead to the hoped-for success of the children in Canadian or American society. All too often, the Black youth who had reached the highest level of schooling offered and achieved everything expected of them by the available schools were then faced with accepting employment that required no such educational attainment.

Yet thousands of parents continued to believe that formal schooling could make all the difference for their children. And for some Black youths, education did open doors; over time it created the "talented tenth" on which W. E. B. Du Bois placed his hope for the future, leaders in the ministry, in other professions, in businesses serving the Black community, and eventually in political life. It was an ironical evidence of this achievement, often against the odds, that one of the most noted "racial incidents" in recent years, involving a Black Harvard professor and a White police officer, occurred in a city with a Black mayor, a state with a Black governor, and a country with a Black president!

If the continued belief of Black parents in the importance of formal schooling, over many discouraging decades, is somewhat of a mystery, a greater mystery is represented by the policy choice on the part of American governments at the federal, state, and local levels; north as well as south, to maintain separate schools for Black children. This long-standing pattern is especially puzzling given the strong resistance in the United States, in the nineteenth and twentieth centuries, to separate schooling for children from immigrant families, which sought the denominational schools they had been accustomed to in Europe. Catholic (and, to a lesser degree, Protestant denominational) schooling was seen as a profound threat to national unity and to the development of loyal citizens.[2]

In Canada, it is true, the political compromises required by the association of Francophone and Catholic Quebec with Anglophone and predominantly Protestant Ontario, as well as the English tradition of denominational schooling, made the "common school" a less potent symbol. We can understand more easily that, in the Canadian context of separate public schools for Catholics and Protestants, for English-speakers and French-speakers, government often provided for separate public schools for Blacks. But why, in the American context of quasi-religious commitment to the "common school," was an exception made so unhesitatingly for Black children?

Why was there so little willingness to see Black pupils sitting on the "long school-bench" on which Horace Mann of Massachusetts, Egerton Ryerson of Ontario, and their many allies liked to imagine the child of the banker and of the working man learning side-by-side? The answer, surely, is that racial segregation is a deeply rooted tradition in American and Canadian education, and that this rested, in turn, on White assumptions about the significance of racial differences that "went all the way down," so fundamental that no education could overcome them. The effect of these assumptions—too often internalized by Black youth themselves with devastating effects on their academic effort and achievement, as the U. S. Supreme Court pointed out in its landmark *Brown* decision of 1954—are with us still, as distinguished Black social scientists have pointed out.

CHAPTER 1

Assumptions about Race

One cannot make sense out of the historical record of the schooling—and often the nonschooling—of Black children and youth apart from the context of changing ideas about the significance and influence of "race." Race is a concept with little scientific meaning but enormous significance, in the United States and Canada, for how individuals and groups are perceived including for how individuals perceive themselves. "Race," in the sense in which the term has been used in North America, is entangled with ethnicity and thus with inherited culture and social networks whose continued significance is to a large extent a matter of individual choice, but it is also frequently taken to refer to an inherent and unchangeable disposition passed on, as we would now say, genetically, to differences that "go all the way down."

Human populations and the differences among them have been classified in many ways, of which perhaps the classic is the five "varieties" identified by Blumenbach in 1795: Caucasian, Mongolian, Ethiopian, American, and Malay. The term "Caucasian" derives from Blumenbach's judgment that it was the Georgians of the Caucasus who represented the purest form of what also would be called the "Aryan" or "Indo-European" racial group. Soon, however, further differentiations were made; among Europeans "one began to hear of Nordic, Alpine, Mediterranean, Baltic, Dinaric, and God alone knows how many other races and subraces."[1]

Much has been written about the assumptions of the White majority about those considered racially different and usually inferior, and no attempt will be made here to repeat or even recapitulate what others have described in detail.[2] There are certain dimensions of this matter, however, that help to explain both the persistent practice of schooling Black children separately and the nature of the debates over the character of that schooling.

In general, it was the White majority, or its policy makers, who determined that Black children would be schooled separately or—in a few cases and belatedly—together with White pupils. It is thus the opinions and assumptions of the White majority about the significance of race that we will be exploring in this chapter.

That should not be taken to suggest, however, that those whose children were being segregated had no views of their own, though often these are less available to us in the form of a written record. There have been many efforts to generalize about the attitudes of illiterate Black slaves, ranging from the perpetual rebelliousness postulated by Herbert Aptheker to the docile and irresponsible "Sambo" described by Stanley Elkins.[3] Kenneth Stampp suggests how psychologically complex the actual situation must have been, and that it grew even more so when emancipation did not lead to equal status. Black writers since W. E. B. Du Bois have explored the "double consciousness" required by accommodation to racial prejudice and discrimination while retaining a sense of self-respect and dignity. Segregated schooling, the Supreme Court pointed out in 1954, was a direct assault on that dignity, and all the more harmful because it was inflicted at a tender age; on the other hand, as we will see, segregated schools were often valued by Blacks themselves as a sphere of control of the education of their children and a refuge from the insults of prejudice.

Although in some cases Black leaders and parents have themselves supported segregated schooling for reasons that had nothing to do with negative assumptions based on race, the significance of such decisions is of course entirely different from that of imposed segregation based on the racial attitudes of the White majority. It is these that this chapter is concerned to describe.

The speculation about the unfitness of Blacks for full participation in American or Canadian society in some cases involved comparisons between Blacks and Indians, to the disadvantage of the former. In one of James Fenimore Cooper's popular novels (1846), an Indian character is contrasted with a Black slave as "vastly superior," since he possessed "the loftiness of a grand nature" developed under "the impetus of an unrestrained, though savage, liberty." The slave, in contrast, "had suffered under the blight which seems to have so generally caused the African mind to wither." The Indian, though savage, is a "gentleman." Similarly, scientist and Harvard professor Louis Agassiz wrote contrasting the "indomitable, courageous, proud Indian" with the "submissive, obsequious, imitative negro" and—by the way—with the "tricky, cunning, and cowardly Mongolian."[4] Thus the popular image of Indians came to be, at worst, that of a treacherous and dangerous enemy, while that of Blacks came to be of a sort of semihuman domestic animal fit only to perform compelled labor.

By the 1830s, a sensitive foreign visitor like Alexis de Tocqueville could conclude (on the basis of what he was told by White informants) that "the Negro hardly feels his misfortune; . . . the habit of servitude has given him the thoughts and ambition of a slave; he admires his tyrants more than he hates them and finds his joy and his pride in servile imitation of those who oppress him. His intellect has been debased to the level of his soul."[5] One should note, however, that Tocqueville's observation is about the *effects* of slavery, not about an inherent inferiority.

Even many strong opponents of slavery insisted that the United States was a "White man's country," and there was no permanent place in it for Blacks. Many believed that just as the Indians (they thought) were doomed to extinction, so were Blacks as a "weaker race" in competition with Whites, and some hoped for such an outcome. "We should so far yield to the evident designs and purposes of Providence," wrote one southern White in 1867, "as to be both willing and anxious to see the negroes, like the Indians and all the other effete and dingy-hued races, gradually exterminated from the face of the whole earth."[6] The year before, a newspaper editor in Wilmington, North Carolina, expressing his regret that Blacks showed no sign of moving to the North, conceded that southern Whites would have to tolerate their presence until "by the mandate of that great natural law which forbids the co-existence of superior and inferior races in a condition of freedom, they shall become extinct."[7]

Nor were such views expressed only in the South. In 1868, a book by a northern White physician argued that science demonstrated that education would do irrevocable damage to the brains of Blacks.[8]

Such judgments and theories have been advanced many times over the centuries, though more frequently in the late nineteenth and earlier twentieth centuries, with the rise of Social Darwinism and scientific racism, than in earlier periods when assumptions about racial differences were strongly influenced by the biblical teaching that all mankind descended from Adam and Eve.

The biblical teaching about the essential unity of humanity—even if it was a unity under the curse of Adam's and Eve's Fall, and the later trespass of Noah's son Ham (the supposed ancestor of Black people)—was already under attack during the colonial period. It was the "enlightened" thinkers of the eighteenth century who, with their rejection of the biblical understanding of an essential God-created human nature, pioneered the idea that Africans were fundamentally inferior. Voltaire wrote that "the negro race is a species of men as different from us as the breed of spaniels is from greyhounds...if their understanding is not of a different nature from ours, it is at least greatly inferior." Similarly, philosopher David Hume wrote that "I am apt to suspect that the negroes and in general all other species of men...to be naturally inferior to Whites. There never was a civilized nation of any other complexion than white, nor even any individual eminent either in action or speculation. No ingenious manufactures amongst them, no arts, no sciences."[9]

Thomas Jefferson wrote, in his *Notes on the State of Virginia*, that in his judgment Blacks were equal to Whites in memory but "much inferior" in reason and "in imagination they are dull, tasteless, and anomalous." Nor did he attribute these qualities to slavery, arguing that ancient Roman slavery had been much harsher than that of slaves in Virginia, yet slaves in Rome "were often their rarest artists.... But they were of the race of Whites. It is not their condition then, but nature, which has produced the distinction." His conclusion, therefore, was "that the Blacks, whether originally a distinct race [which would contradict the biblical account of a single creation], or made distinct by time and circumstances, are inferior to the White race in the endowments both of body and mind.... It is not their condition [as slaves] then, but nature, which has produced the distinction."[10]

Those who believed that observed racial differences rested on fundamentally different natures were implicitly—sometimes explicitly—rejecting the biblical account of a single creation of humanity. These "pluralists" argued that "the various human species were not blood-kin at all. Each species in its geographical home had a separate bloodline back to the beginning [its prehuman origins], which never connected to any other species." Samuel Morton, professor of anatomy at Pennsylvania Medical College, published *Crania Americana* in 1839, with descriptions of the skulls of more than forty Indian peoples. Morton argued that they had been created in their homelands: "His twenty-two great families of man consisted of nations that were initially unique and created on the spot." Others who studied the issue of race claimed to identify up to sixty-three distinct species of humans. These "scientific" theories proved very convenient for those who wanted to deny any common humanity to which appeal could be made for abolishment of slavery or just treatment of Indians or Blacks. The scientifically minded mocked those still clinging to the "religious dogma of mankind's Unity," to which a "trembling orthodoxy clutches like sinking mariners at their last plank."[11]

While Jefferson argued that Indians had the potential to become like Whites, given enough time and the right education, he denied that possibility to Blacks. In effect, Indians were different from Whites because of the environment in which they had lived for many generations; Blacks were different by their fundamental nature, and that could never change sufficiently.[12] In view of this long-standing tradition of denying to Blacks the respect accorded to Indians, it became very common for educated Blacks to claim a measure of Indian ancestry, a fashion satirized by author Zora Neale Hurston when she wrote that "I am the only Negro in the United States whose grandfather on the mother's side was *not* an Indian chief."[13]

Lyons notes that "the Enlightenment produced a number of tracts which complemented the disparaging pronouncements of many natural scientists.... Those writing contributed to a growing feeling that the African was mentally inferior to the European. Of course, churchmen, humanitarians, and abolitionists...would have little to do with such speculations."[14]

Indeed, Catholic and Protestant theologians, during the early modern period, insisted that Africans possessed immortal souls and an irreducible human dignity, even if degraded by the conditions of their life in Africa or in slavery in the Western Hemisphere. As one Massachusetts minister insisted in 1703, Black slaves were "members in a [human] Family...therein equal in that they have Souls equally capable of being saved or lost: And the Soul of a Slave is, in its nature, of as much worth as the Soul of his Master, having the same Faculties and Powers."[15] The following year, a publication in London asserted confidently that Blacks would be participants in the resurrection of the dead at the "Last Day," though it suggested that, since their color was "an accidental imperfection," they would leave it behind "in the Darkness of the Grave, exchanging it for a brighter and a better" color; in other words, they would be resurrected White![16]

These religiously based views about the essential unity of humanity persisted even as Enlightenment ideas spread in educated circles in North America. One of the central tenets of Enlightenment thought, indeed, was the need to disperse the influence of "prejudices" (which included revealed religion) on the human mind; and some did not fail to point out that judging persons by their color was a form of prejudice—a meaning that, in our own time, has tended to crowd out the broader significance of the term in the eighteenth century. A New

Jersey Quaker, for example, wrote in 1772 that it was to the "power of prejudice" that should be attributed the belief that it was lawful to keep Blacks enslaved. "The low contempt with which they are generally treated by the whites, lead children from the first dawn of reason, to consider people with a black skin, on a footing with domestic animals, form'd to serve and obey." Similarly, a leading Congregationalist minister wrote, in 1776, that "our education has filled us with strong prejudices against" Blacks.[17]

Other defenders of the essential humanity of Blacks on religious grounds like John Wesley insisted that their apparent degradation and "stupidity...is not natural; otherwise than it is the natural effect of their condition." Slavery, others pointed out, "has a mighty tendency to sink and contract the minds of men."[18]

In 1787, at the annual meeting of the American Philosophical Society of Philadelphia, the professor of moral philosophy and theology and later president of the College of New Jersey (which became Princeton) delivered an oration on "The Causes of the Variety of Complexion and Figure in the Human Species." Refuting recent proposals by Voltaire and others that there was no common humanity, Samuel Stanhope Smith pointed out that, if this were the case, "the science of morals would be absurd...no general principles of human conduct, or religion, or of policy could be framed."[19]

The movement to abolish slavery in the British colonies and in the United States grew out of the evangelical ferment of the late eighteenth and early nineteenth centuries, as exemplified most notably not only by the British parliamentarian William Wilberforce but also by hundreds of Americans who made this the central cause of their lives.[20] "The abolitionists' belief in interracial fraternity, like their doctrine of immediate emancipation to which it was so closely related, was part of a general radicalization of reform that took place in the 1830s, under the stimulus of religious developments that suggested a higher valuation of the moral capabilities of the individual and that pointed, by implication, to the perfectibility of society as a whole." In contrast with this fundamentally religious impulse, the socially radical but secular workingmen's movements of the same period "went out of their way to emphasize that their "democracy" was for Whites only."[21]

If Blacks possessed human dignity, and their souls deserved the attention of those committed to proclaiming the Gospel, then educating them was important. While one concerned White minister conceded that "indeed their Stupidity is a Discouragement. It seems unto little purpose to Teach, as to wash [white] an Aethiopian," he insisted that this condition derived from the fact that "they are kept as Horses or Oxen, to do our Drugeries [*sic*]" and their souls "are Destroyed for lack of Knowledge.... Are they dull? Then instruct them." And the evangelist George Whitefield, who was very much interested in the education of Blacks, asserted that, with the same education as Whites, Blacks "are naturally capable of the same improvement."[22] A Massachusetts legislator (and future governor) urged, in 1795, that

> the children of the slaves must, at the public expense, be educated in the same manner as the children of their masters, being at the same schools, etc.... we do not know but what giving them the same prospects, placing them under the force of the same motives, and conferring upon them the same advantages for the space of time in which 3 or 4 generations shall rise and fall, will so mend the race, and so increase their powers of perception, and so strengthen their faculty for comparing ideas, and understanding the nature and connexion of the external things with which man is surrounded on this globe, as that they may exceed the White people.[23]

The "enlightened" view that Blacks were inherently inferior did not go unchallenged by Blacks themselves. In his famous *Appeal to the Colored Citizens of the World* (Boston 1829), David Walker charged that "Mr. Jefferson...has in truth injured us more, and has been as great a barrier to our emancipation as anything that has ever been advanced against us." Southern slave owners "beat us inhumanely, sometimes almost to death, for attempting to inform ourselves, by reading the *Word* of our Maker, and at the same time tell us, that we are beings *void of intellect!!!!*... If it were possible for the Whites always to keep us ignorant and miserable, and make us work to enrich them and their children, and insult our feelings by representing us as *talking Apes*, what would they do?"[24]

It was a considerable embarrassment to those advocating the abolition of slavery that the behavior of the free Black population in the North and in the South seemed sometimes to argue that they were incapable of using that freedom wisely. "In 1798 a group of New Jersey abolitionists reported that many free Blacks were 'given to Idleness, Frolicking, Drunkenness, and in some few cases to Dishonesty.' In 1806 a leading Pennsylvania abolitionist described most Philadelphia Negroes as 'degraded and vicious,' and two years later the New York Manumission Society announced that it viewed 'with regret the looseness of manners & depravity of conduct of many of the Persons of Colour in this city.'" An explanation lay close at hand, however, in what Frederickson calls the "environmentalism" adopted during the Enlightenment.[25] This derived in part from Locke and Condillac and was originally directed against orthodox Protestant and Catholic belief that human nature was inherently "fallen" and requiring a Redeemer. It served as the basis for proposals for promoting unlimited human progress (and liberation from religious "superstition") through education. If human beings could be made profoundly better through education, presumably they could be made profoundly worse through the degrading conditions of slavery. Education for the proper use of freedom was the answer.

However, "the environmentalist philosophy was beginning to erode by 1810; by then, increasing doubts were being expressed about the naïve eighteenth-century theory that differences in pigmentation were a comparatively short-range result of climate and over environmental factors,"[26] or that the "depravity" of free Blacks was caused by social influences and could be removed by schooling of an appropriate sort.

Tocqueville noted that there was more racial prejudice in the North—directed at free Blacks—than there was in the South, "and nowhere is it shown to be as intolerant as in states where servitude has always been unknown." He was convinced that "slavery contracted to a single point on the globe, attacked by Christianity as unjust, by political economy as fatal; slavery, in the midst of the democratic freedom and enlightenment of our age, is not an institution that can endure," but he did not see a solution to the massive presence of enslaved Blacks in the South. "The South, if it had to," Tocqueville noted, "could well abolish servitude; but how would it relieve itself of Blacks?" In fact, he warned, "the most dreadful of all the evils that threaten the future of the United States arises from the presence of Blacks on its soil,"[27] since the races were fundamentally incompatible and racial prejudice on the part of Whites would only increase with emancipation.

The conviction that Blacks were incapable of benefitting from more than the most basic instruction received apparent scientific validation over the course of the nineteenth century. Georges Cuvier, the pioneer of comparative anatomy and paleontology, noted in his *Le Règne animal* (Paris 1817, London 1827–1835) that "the Negro race" in appearance "manifestly approaches to the monkey tribe" and "have always remained in a state of complete barbarism." Sir Charles Lyell, the foremost geologist of the age, was more optimistic, believing that through the beneficent influence of slavery, Blacks could eventually be brought "up to the Caucasian standard. Such optimism was dismissed, in 1850, by Dr. Josiah Nott, based on observations during his medical practice in Mobile, Alabama, that the "races of men, like animals, in a wild, uncultivated state, may, if docile, be tamed, educated, and vastly improved, but there are limits set to each by nature, beyond which no advance can be made."[28] It was the inevitable destiny of the White race "to conquer and hold every foot of the globe where climate does not interpose an impenetrable barrier. No philanthropy, no legislation, no missionary labors can change this law; it is written in man's nature by the hand of his creator." The "inferior races," having served their temporary purposes, would eventually become extinct.[29]

Famed Harvard scientist Louis Agassiz was physically revolted when, on a trip to Philadelphia, he was confronted with Black waiters, and wrote to his mother back in Switzerland that he could not "quell the feeling that they are not of the same blood as us." In 1847 he would write that "the brain of the Negro is that of the imperfect brain of a seven months infant in the womb of a White."[30]

It was with the mid-Victorian challenge to religion in the name of science that "the religious underpinnings of the humanitarian enterprise" of educating Blacks were assailed. Charles Darwin concluded that the "mental characteristics [of the various races] are...very distinct," and in general "the era of evolutionism witnessed something of a revival of the persistent notion that Black Africans...occupied a place in the evolutionary scale just above that of the ape." Late in the century, with the enormous influence of Herbert Spencer on thinking about public policy, in the United States as well as in Britain, it came to be widely accepted in circles that prided themselves on "advanced thinking" that "nothing could be done to improve the lot of the inferior races, and any attempt to lend assistance would simply run counter to the course of nature."[31]

The inherent inferiority of Blacks was an article of faith to southern leaders, just as it was an unquestioned assumption on the part of many or most White people in the North. As the Confederacy declared its independence, its new vice president, Alexander Stephens, announced that its government "is founded upon...the great truth that the negro is not equal to the white man; that slavery, subordination to the superior race, is his natural and moral condition. This, our new Government, is the first, in the history of the world, based upon this great physical, philosophical and moral truth."[32] Similarly, after the collapse of the Confederacy and of the northern-controlled Reconstruction that followed, Charles W. Dabney, president of the University of Tennessee, pointed out that "the negro is in the South to stay—he is a necessity for southern industries—and the southern people must educate and so elevate him or he will drag them down... [But] we must...recognize in all its relations that momentous fact that the negro is a child race, at least two thousand years behind the Anglo-Saxon in its development."[33] Or, as a professor at Tulane wrote in 1905, when the reaction against Reconstruction was turning both North and South against equality of the races, Whites should guard "against the emotion of sympathy, of pity for the unfortunate race...which the unfeeling process of Nature demands in sacrifice on the altar of the evolution of Humanity."[34]

There were eloquent voices protesting such assumptions, including southern as well as northern religious leaders. Richard Fuller of South Carolina, though a defender of slavery against its northern critics, insisted that "the whole human family have sprung from common parentage," and that Christianity "requires of a master the moral and intellectual improvement of the slaves." Despite the laws against educating slaves—which he insisted should be and were largely ignored—the effect of the slavery system upon those who had been rescued from the darkness of Africa was beneficent: "The condition of the African has been vastly improved, physically, intellectually, morally, and religiously, by his transportation to these shores."[35]

Distinctions based upon race were rejected directly by Charles Sumner, arguing in 1850 in the *Roberts* case for the integration of the Boston public schools. The school committee had contended that the distinction on the basis of which Negro children were required to attend separate schools "is one of races, not of colors merely. The distinction is one which the All-wise Creator has seen fit to establish; and it is founded deep in the physical, mental, and moral natures of the two races. No legislation, no social customs, can efface this distinction." Such thinking, Sumner charged, quoting an English author, was "founded on the doctrine of an essentially distinct origin of the different races, which are thus unalterably separated." Policy based on such an assumption, he insisted, was unworthy of a city "set on a hill." After all,

> a school exclusively devoted to one class must differ essentially in spirit and character from that Common School known to the law, where all classes meet together in Equality. It is a mockery to call it an equivalent.... Who can say that this does not injure the Blacks? Theirs, in its best estate, is an unhappy lot. A despised class, blasted by prejudice and shut out from various opportunities, they feel this proscription from the Common Schools as a peculiar brand. Beyond this, it deprives them of those healthful, animating influences which would come from participation in the studies of their White brethren. It adds to their discouragements. It widens their separation from the community, and postpones that great day of reconciliation which is yet to come.[36]

But such arguments did not prevail, in the *Roberts* case or generally in educated opinion; opposition to slavery did not commonly translate into readiness to accept the intellectual and social equality of Blacks. Those who disagreed with the common assumption about the innate inferiority of Blacks "had little empirical evidence and no scientific evidence to support their belief—nothing, in fact, but faith. Their faith was derived mainly from their religion; all men, they said, are the sons of Adam and equal in the sight of God. And if Negroes are equal to white men in the sight of God, it is morally wrong for white men to withhold from Negroes the liberties and rights that white men enjoy."[37]

The effect of Darwinian thought pushed into the impossibly remote past the factors that had influenced the separate evolution of the White and Black "races," thus reducing the possibility that a few decades or even centuries could reduce the differences between them. This led quite naturally to the prediction that Darwin made in *The Descent of Man* (1871): "At some future period, not very distant as measured by centuries, the civilized races of man will almost certainly exterminate and replace the savage races throughout the world." In contrast with the biblical view held by Christians, "Darwin's application of the concept of a 'struggle for existence' to human types was natural and inevitable; he recognized no distinction between the factors which made for human survival, development, and differentiation, and those which accounted for 'the preservation of favoured races' in the rest of animate nature." The fact that Darwinism rejected the permanence of species "made it possible to argue that Blacks and Whites had diverged in their evolution to such an extent that their differences could now be considered" in the nature of constituting separate species, though Darwin himself did not go that far. His popularizer and defender, Thomas H. Huxley ("Darwin's bulldog" Can the quotes be removed,) argued in 1865 that "no rational man, cognizant of the facts," could deny that the Negro was inherently inferior. Consequently,

> it is simply incredible that, when all his disabilities are removed, and our prognathous [with a projecting jaw] relative has a fair field and no favor, as well as no oppressor, he will be able to compete successfully with his bigger-brained and smaller-jawed rival, in a contest which is to be carried on by thoughts and not by bites. The highest place in the hierarchy of civilization will assuredly not be within the reach of our dusky cousins, though it is by no means necessary that they should be restricted to the lowest.[38]

The allegedly scientific belief that Blacks were fated for defeat in the future competition, as they had been predisposed for enslavement in the past, seemed to receive confirmation by the conclusion of the 1890 census, indicating that their numbers were increasing more slowly than those of Whites. Conveniently ignoring the fact that the White increase was in large part caused by heavy immigration, this was taken as evidence for "the impending disappearance of the American Negro." Statistician Frederick Hoffman attracted wide attention, in *Race Traits and Tendencies of the American Negro* (1896), with his conclusion that "the time will come, if it has not already come, when the negro, like the Indian, will be a vanishing race." Although Blacks had been in good physical condition under slavery, he argued, "the tendency of the race has been downward," and religion and education had not contributed to "the moral progress of the race," since they could not affect the inherited characteristics that doomed Blacks to inferiority.[39] Similarly, eminent Harvard scientist Nathaniel Southgate Shaler published an essay on "The Negro Problem" in the *Atlantic* in 1884, supporting the disenfranchisement of Blacks in the South and arguing that their uncontrollable immorality made them "unfit for an independent place in a civilized state." Fortunately, Shaler concluded, they were fated to die out eventually.[40]

Twenty years later, an economist at Massachusetts Institute of Technology (MIT) addressed what he and others considered alarming predictions that the Black population would grow at a rapid rate. One professor had estimated that there would be 200 million Blacks (192 million of them in the South), or three-eighths of the population of the United States, while a more sober prediction called for 60 million Blacks by the end of the twentieth century. Professor Walter Willcox assured his readers that the actual number would be less than 24 million (in fact, the number of Black Americans at present is about 40 million). Willcox based this estimate on a falling birthrate and almost stationary death rate, which he attributed to "a growing competition between negroes and whites, and a decrease in the relative efficiency of negroes compared with whites." Analyzing employment distribution (and ignoring the discrimination that, as we will see in chapter 4, was driving Blacks out of many occupations that they had held under slavery), Willcox concluded that increasingly Blacks were confined to jobs requiring muscular effort and little skill, while replaced by Whites in jobs requiring skill or work without close supervision. It seemed inevitable that Blacks would continue to fall farther and farther behind.[41]

It is in this context of ideas about race and the capacities of Blacks that the post-emancipation efforts to educate African-Americans developed, especially after the original religious impulses were replaced by Spencerian reliance upon the unguided operation of economic forces. After all, "if the Blacks were a degenerate race with no future, the problem ceased to be one of how to prepare them for citizenship or even how to make them more productive and useful members of the community."[42] This view was popularized in the North by Columbia history professor William Archibald Dunning, who provided intellectual authority for the ideas that slavery had been a successful social and economic system precisely because it was founded on the reality of fundamental racial inequality, and that Reconstruction had been a disaster because it failed to take the incapacity of Blacks into account, since formal "freedom in no way altered racial capacity."[43]

During the debate over enactment of the Fifteenth Amendment to the Constitution, in 1869, a Democratic senator from Indiana pointed out, as a matter of common knowledge, that "there is a difference morally and intellectually [between the races]; and I do not believe that the two races can mingle successfully in the management of government." Protection of the right of Blacks to vote was futile, since they would not "add to the common intelligence of the country when we make them voters." After all, he continued, "that race in its whole history has furnished no evidence of its capacity to lift itself up.... While the tendency of the White race is upward, the tendency of the colored race is downward; and I have always supposed it is because in that race the physical predominates over the moral and intellectual qualities." Even some of those who supported voting rights did so on the grounds that "we ought to give to this weaker, this inferior race, the means of self-protection."[44]

Scientific racism became increasingly entrenched late in the nineteenth century, as the authority of the Bible, in turn, grew weaker. Tremendous ingenuity was devoted to identifying the ways in which the different "races" differed, and it was often asserted that these differences were not the result of historical experience or cultural norms alone, but were fundamental and unchangeable. French social psychologist Gustave LeBon, for example, insisted that each race possessed "a mental constitution as unvarying as its anatomical constitution," and that this, "the synthesis of its entire past, the inheritance of all its ancestors, the motives of its conduct," constituted its "soul," passed on by parents to their children and unchangeable through education or environment.[45]

The racial inferiority of Blacks was not only a scientific theory but also widely believed among Whites. In the popular 1902 novel *The Leopard's*

Spots, by Thomas Dixon, Jr., of North Carolina, made into a hit on Broadway, a character states as an established fact that "one drop of Negro blood makes a Negro. It kinks the hair, flattens the nose, thickens the lips, puts out the light of intellect and lights the fires of brutal passion."[46] Dixon's novels about Reconstruction and heroic resistance to Black equality by southern Whites became the first smash hit on film, *The Birth of a Nation* (1915). Despite scattered protests by the NAACP, the film gave the White public what it wanted and believed: that Black people had to be kept in their place, and were incapable of rising out of it.

In view of this widespread and persistent assumption, on the part of Whites, that it was futile to provide advanced instruction to Blacks, the insistence of Black church leaders and their White allies among northern evangelicals upon making a classical education available was an act of defiance and an assertion that "the race is rising." Senator John C. Calhoun of South Carolina had said that "if he could find a Negro who could parse a Latin verb, or write the Greek alphabet, he would be disposed to grant his claim to full human capacity."[47] Calhoun's implication was that such an individual would be an unnatural freak, but, as we will see, hundreds and then thousands of Black men and women, in the later nineteenth and early twentieth century, were determined to demonstrate their capacity to "rise," including, in many cases, through study of the classics.

Sometimes it seemed, indeed, that no matter how much progress Black men and women made, how painfully "respectable" they became, they would not be treated with respect by the White majority. The achievements of Booker T. Washington, the most highly regarded Black man in North America in the late nineteenth and early twentieth centuries, were dismissed by a Mississippi senator who declared, "I am just as much opposed to Booker Washington as a voter with all his Anglo-Saxon reinforcements as I am to the coconut-headed, chocolate-colored, typical little coon, Andy Dotson, who blacks my shoes every morning. Neither is fit to perform the supreme function of citizenship."[48]

Supporters of the Progressive Movement became convinced, toward the end of the nineteenth century, that their political goals could be achieved only in alliance with the emerging southern White leadership. The *Atlantic Monthly* proclaimed "the universal supremacy of the Anglo-Saxon."[49] This view was endorsed by leading northern journals of opinion like *The Nation* and *Century*, which "waged consistent campaigns to explain the conditions which made necessary in the South a discipline over the colored man." The editor of *Century* wrote in 1883 "that the negroes constitute a peasantry wholly untrained in, and ignorant of, those ideas of constitutional liberty and progress which are the birthright of every white voter; that they are gregarious and emotional rather than intelligent, and are easily led in any direction by white men of energy and determination." As a result, the editor of *Nation* agreed, "I do not see...how the negro is ever to be worked into a system of government for which you and I would have much respect." A scholarly study, *The Plantation Negro as a Freeman* (1889), demonstrated to the satisfaction of informed opinion that "the Negro's mental, moral and physical traits" meant that he was "unfit for self-government, needed direction, and should confine himself to the lower occupations."[50]

Such gloomy views were still being expressed well into the twentieth century. H. L. Mencken wrote, in 1910, that Blacks would need fifty generations "to be brought to acceptable standards of efficiency and purposefulness," while in 1920 publisher William Randolph Hearst referred to Blacks as the missing evolutionary link between man and ape. In his book *White Capital and Coloured Labour* (1929), the former governor-general of Jamaica argued that Blacks were incapable of efficient work without the discipline of "the Driver and the whip." Acknowledging this hostility, native Jamaican Marcus Garvey, the charismatic founder of the Universal Negro Improvement Association, warned that, in North America, Blacks would soon be "dying out...as completely...as the North American Indian, or the Australian Bushman."[51]

Racialist thinking was encouraged by the anxiety, among Progressive elites, about the "debasing" effect of immigration from southern and eastern Europe. Polemics on this theme, of which perhaps the best known is Grant and Osborn's *The Passing of the Great Race* (1916), almost casually used what was taken to be the obvious Black inferiority to argue for the importance of excluding other undesirable "racial" groups.

> Thus the view that the Negro slave was an unfortunate cousin of the white man, deeply tanned by the tropic sun and denied the blessings of Christianity and civilization, played no small part with the sentimentalists of the Civil War period and it has taken us fifty years to learn that speaking English, wearing good clothes and going to school and to church does not transform a Negro into a white man....Americans will have a similar experience with the Polish Jew, whose dwarf stature, peculiar mentality and ruthless concentration on self-interest are being engrafted upon the stock of the nation.[52]

And again, "Negroes have demonstrated throughout recorded time that they are a stationary species and that they do not possess the potentiality of progress or initiative from within."[53]

It should be pointed out that there was a more hopeful—but perhaps equally mischievous—explanation of racial differences, as expressed in the *Freedmen's Record* in an 1865 editorial:

> While we do not admit the absolute inferiority of any race...there can be no question that races, like nations and individuals, have their peculiarities. All elements are present, but they are blended in various proportions. In the negro race we believe the poetic and emotional qualities predominate, rather than the prosaic, mechanical, and merely intellectual powers.[54]

As in Howard Gardner's theory of "multiple intelligences," we can find in this categorization both a well-meaning intention to celebrate human diversity and an implicit acceptance of different outcomes of schooling, with inevitable implications for life-chances. Oddly enough, the finally discredited nineteenth-century scientific theories about essential differences between Black and White ways of thinking, theories that were long used to justify exclusion of Blacks from government and other positions of responsibility, have reemerged among "Progressive" opponents of efforts to hold Black students to high academic standards. Thus we are told as an established fact that standardized tests "are inescapably biased because they involve 'linear thinking' alien to black culture." The Board of Regents, responsible for education in New York State, published a booklet in 1987 noting that Blacks have a "preference for inferential reasoning rather than deductive or inductive reasoning" and a "tendency to approximate space, number and time instead of aiming for complete accuracy," while a researcher for the Atlanta public schools argued that "any tests that emphasize logical, analytical methods of problem-solving will be biased against minorities," and suggested that gifted students should be identified on the basis of their "athletic ability, 'street smarts', and interpersonal skills."[55] But, of course, linear thinking, analytical methods, accuracy, and all the rest are essential to a whole range of desirable occupations; such definitions of "Black intelligence" seem to point to careers as athletes or entertainers, not as lawyers, doctors, scientists, or indeed presidents.

Orlando Patterson has been an especially eloquent opponent of such racial essentialism, arguing that "the distinction between 'race' and ethnicity is only meaningful if we wish to reinforce the racist belief that Euro-Americans and Afro-Americans are...biologically and immutably different." He finds it a sad irony that "having demolished and condemned as racist the idea that observed group differences have any objective, biological foundation, the liberal intellectual community has revived the 'race' concept as an essential category of human experience with as much ontological validity as the discarded racist notion of biologically distinct groups." After all, he points out, "most of what the typical Afro-American does in daily life has little or nothing to do with being Afro-American. There is no specifically Afro-American way of being healthy, sick, or dying; of falling in and out of love; of doing a good job or making a mess of it; of being happy or being depressed; of being victimized or being a victimizer; of being nice or being just another mean son of a bitch."[56] All this is certainly true.

But, of course, it is not as easy to dismiss the lingering effects of *assumptions* about race as it is to argue that the differences are just in the eye of the beholder. These assumptions continue—though to a decreasing extent, certainly—to influence how the White majority in North America feels and behaves toward those who are perceived as racially, and not just ethnically, different. They continue also to influence how millions of Black Americans and Canadians feel about themselves and understand themselves and their place in a society in which they are a visible minority group. And in no sphere of life have these assumptions, on the part of majority and minorities alike, been more profoundly influential than in formal education.

The persistence, in the twenty-first century, of a troubling "achievement gap" between Black and White pupils (a gap affecting both Indian and Latino pupils as well) has produced an enormous scholarly literature. With genetic explanations excluded from the discussion a priori since the controversy over Herrnstein and Murray's *The Bell Curve* (1994) and, indeed, Arthur Jensen's 1969 article on race and intelligence, it has seemed obvious that if scholars could only identify, once and for all, the cause of the "gap," it would be a simple matter to develop policies and commit resources to eliminate it once and for all. This has proven an elusive goal.

> In the 1960s, racial egalitarians routinely blamed the test score gap on the combined effects of black poverty, racial segregation, and inadequate finding for black schools. That analysis implied obvious solutions: raise black children's family income, desegregate their schools, and equalize spending on schools that remain racially segregated. All these steps still look useful, but none has made as much difference as optimists expected in the early 1960s.[57]

Other proposed explanations for the achievement gap have also led to attempted remedies. Was the problem a "cultural mismatch" between home/community and school? Then an "Afrocentric" curriculum and the use of what was awkwardly baptized as "Ebonics" would be the answer...but they were not. Or was it the powerlessness of Black communities in relation to the public schools, affecting in turn the expectation of success on the part of pupils? Then community control, as at Ocean Hill-Brownsville, should produce outstanding academic results...but it did not. Or was the problem (and this had to be put very delicately) the parenting style in homes from which the pupils came? Then ever-earlier early childhood education should do the trick...but the results, though encouraging, do not seem to persist with sufficient power. And we could go on to instructional methods and whole-school strategies that indeed have demonstrated considerable promise to produce solid results.[58]

The point is not to dismiss any of these remedies (though I believe that they are of very uneven value), but to suggest the importance of modesty and an experimental spirit in addressing this very complex and troubling issue. It is also to suggest that we listen more carefully to what individual Black parents say about their hopes and goals for their children, and not be so quick to prescribe one-size-fits-all solutions. Above all, to avoid the assumption that "race" is a difference that "goes all the way down." It is in that spirit that this historical overview of the schooling of Black Americans and Canadians has been written.

CHAPTER 2

Enslaved and Free Blacks before 1862

It was in part because the justification for North American settlement included the opportunity to bring the Gospel to native peoples who had never heard it that frequent, though usually ineffective, efforts were made to provide Western-style schooling to different Indian peoples. No such geopolitical rationale existed in the case of slaves and free Blacks, though similar efforts were not altogether lacking, mostly by initiatives from England. Anglican clergyman (later bishop) and philosopher George Berkeley complained, in 1731, about the resistance of the colonists to his own efforts to that end because of their "ancient antipathy to the Indians... together with an irrational contempt for the Blacks, as creatures of another species, who had no right to be instructed."[1]

In 1790, there were fewer than 700,000 Blacks (the vast majority slaves) in the United States, less than 5 percent of the population of the new nation, including almost 4,000 slaves in New England, mostly in Connecticut, and 45,000 in the mid-Atlantic states. The first U.S. census found the following percentages of Blacks in each state as shown in table 2.1.

The enslaved Black population of the United States tripled over the next thirty years and, with emancipation legislation in most northern states, came to be heavily concentrated in the South. By 1860, shortly before their emancipation as a result of the Civil War, however, there were nearly 4 million African-Americans, some 12.5 percent of the national population, heavily concentrated in the South. This change occurred primarily through natural increase, in contrast with Latin America and the West Indies, where the conditions of slavery were less favorable to the birth and raising of children. No slaves remained in New England and only a handful in the rest of the North, apart from Delaware.[2]

Table 2.1 Percentage of Blacks in each state as per the first U.S. census

Maine 0.6	Pennsylvania 2.4
New Hampshire 0.6	Delaware 21.6
Vermont 0.3	Maryland 34.7
Massachusetts 1.4	Virginia 40.9
Rhode Island 6.3	North Carolina 26.8
Connecticut 2.3	Kentucky 17
New York 7.6	Tennessee 10.6
New Jersey 7.7	South Carolina 43.7

During the eighteenth century, a certain amount of schooling was provided to slaves by religious organizations, notably the Anglican Society for the Propagation of the Gospel (SPG) with Thomas Bray providing significant leadership for[3] this mission "during a time of renewal for the Anglican church, when it could turn its resources and energies away from political conflicts and into humanitarian and social reforms at home and abroad." This missionary society sought to develop literacy so that slaves "could participate in a book-based liturgy and catechism" characteristic of Anglicanism. "It produced few converts, but had an important impact on literacy,"[4] and "by emphasizing the desirability of converting slaves to Christianity, the S.P.G. underlined the existence of the blacks as people rather than property."[5]

In 1705, the first SPG school for Blacks was opened in the American colonies by Elias Neau, who, discouraged, "asserted that slavery caused moral and intellectual bankruptcy in the blacks." In 1711, a wealthy planter in Barbados left his lands as an endowment for Christian education among slaves, and a number of schools were started in the islands and on the mainland, but "the SPG had trouble establishing schools in which it could produce examples of educable blacks."[6] For most of the century, "over 300 missionaries of the SPG, far more secure than the local lay-controlled ministry and often well-educated and dedicated men, vigorously preached to the slaves."

Despite these efforts, "the SPG missionaries experienced only limited success in converting Blacks, in part due to the White attitude toward educating Blacks. A 'catechizing school' was opened in New York City in 1704. It functioned well until the exposure of a Black rebellion in 1712 placed the school in jeopardy, a situation indicating the white sense of the power of Christian education.... With the support of the governor, the mission weathered this period and continued to function throughout the colonial era."[7] An early history of the SPG, in 1730, reported optimistically that most of the slaves were "very capable of receiving instruction. Even the grown Persons brought from *Guinea*, quickly learn *English* enough to be understood in ordinary Matters; but the Children born of *Negroe* [sic] Parents in the Colonies, are bred up entirely in the *English* Language."[8]

There were missionary efforts in the South to educate free Blacks as well, often through catechetical classes held at different hours than those for White children. It has been noted that "the principal agency concerned with conversion of Negroes [in the English colonies] was English, not American," at a time when at least one SPG representative warned that White colonists in South Carolina "were making near approach to that heathenism which is to be found among negroes and indians."[9] Quakers maintained a school for Blacks in Alexandria, Virginia by 1764,[10] as well as a number of free schools for Blacks in the North. Several of the schools supported by Quakers in Baltimore served both Black and White pupils, as occurred also in the Anglican schools in Nova Scotia.[11]

In Charleston, the Anglican SPG purchased two slaves, trained them to teach, and built a schoolhouse where, from 1744 to 1764, they taught children during the day and adults in the evening. "It is likely that only free African-Americans attended this school, since in 1740 South Carolina had passed a law prohibiting the teaching of enslaved students, and this school was run openly; but it remains unclear if Harry and Andrew were manumitted or if the SPG kept them enslaved. Harry, at least, was apparently paid only with some clothing provided by the vestry."[12]

The SPG and other Anglican efforts, and those of the Quakers and the Presbyterians, were strongly oriented toward developing literacy and a fairly extensive catechism-based knowledge of essential Christian teachings before incorporation into the church through baptism. It was thus an extended process, and depended upon being able to arrange regular attendance by enslaved and free Blacks at instruction in church or in a schoolhouse.

> Quakers were too exclusive and their communities too removed from the great body of American colonists to serve as a model for the larger society. Instead, it was the Anglicans, the Presbyterians, and members of the "popular" churches who provided slaves with a minimal amount of religious instruction and education while supporting the slave system and who marked the direction for slave evangelization and education during the outbreak of religious enthusiasm which converted thousands of the free and unfree during the Great Awakening.[13]

The movement—really a series of movements—of spiritual fervor known as the Great Awakening in the middle of the eighteenth and again in the early and mid-nineteenth centuries, with evangelistic preaching by Methodist or Baptist preachers calling for an immediate response of commitment and change of heart, did not require a prolonged period of instruction. As English evangelist George Whitefield wrote in a 1740 pamphlet directed to slave owners, "Blacks are just as much, and no more, conceived and born in Sin, as White Men are. Both, if born and bred up here, I am persuaded, are naturally capable of the same [religious] improvement."[14]

There is extensive evidence that both enslaved and free Blacks responded eagerly to this message; and paradoxically, the abandonment of the Anglican and Presbyterian strategy of developing literacy as a prelude to conversion, under the influence of the Great Awakening, led to a greater eagerness to learn to read on the part of Blacks *after* conversion, as a means of studying the Bible and devotional works.

Some slave owners were eager to have their slaves taught the elements of Christianity, though on their own terms. "Southern society was not disposed to withhold the consolations of [religion] from its slaves. But the conditions would have to be laid down not by the church as an institution, not even by planters as laity, but by the planters simply as masters.... It was a state of things deplored by the Southern churches."[15] The SPG experienced considerable difficulty arranging such instruction, since slave owners allowed time off only on Sundays, when SPG missionaries were busy conducting services for Whites, and many forced their slaves to provide for their sustenance and that of their families by growing their own gardens during their free time. Similar problems were experienced in New York, where slaves could be instructed only in the evenings after work, when "their Bodies were so fatigued, that their Attention could not be great."[16]

Inevitably, we have only indirect glimpses and surmises about the instruction, and the education in a broader sense, which Black slaves received. One historian contends that "the education acquired by each slave was remarkably uniform, consisting largely of lessons in survival and accommodation—the uses of humility, the virtues of ignorance, the arts of evasion, the subtleties of verbal intonation, the techniques by which feelings and emotions were masked, and the occasions that demanded the flattering of white egos and the placating of white fears."[17] By contrast, analysis of the "spirituals" and folktales that have survived from the time of slavery and the decades that followed convinces Levine that "even in the midst of the brutalities and injustices of the antebellum and postbellum racial systems black men and women were able to find the means to sustain a far greater degree of self-pride and group cohesion than the system they lived under ever intended for them."[18] Surely the answer to this apparent contradiction lies in what W. E. B. Du Bois described in *The Souls of Black Folk* as "two souls, two thoughts, two unreconciled strivings, two warring ideals, in one dark body, whose dogged strength alone keeps it from being torn asunder."[19] The defensive mask of stupidity and passivity did not, surely, penetrate to the core of those who wore it. The consciousness that it *was* only a mask is expressed in the slogan that became popular in the Freedom Movement in the 1960s: "I'm America's New Black Joe: I ain't laughing when it ain't funny, and I ain't scratching where it don't itch!"

Another historian suggests that the nature of the plantation system, far from suppressing all autonomy of those enslaved, required the development of significant skills on the part of at least some slaves, and that the economy of the South depended greatly upon Black skilled craftsmen, both slave and free. As evidence is cited the 1848 census of employment in Charleston, South Carolina, that found that "free Negroes were employed in all but eight of the fifty occupations composing the skilled group, and slaves were employed in all but thirteen. Negroes were fairly dominant as carpenters and joiners, barbers, hairdressers, and bankers. Slaves represented between 47 and 67 percent of all such employed workers." Bullock suggests that the collaboration of owners with the more able of their slaves in the business of operating plantations and other enterprises and the personal intimacy that inevitably arose in many cases helped the latter to develop the psychological characteristics, the feeling of worth, which prepared them to become leaders after emancipation.[20]

Others gained their freedom earlier, either through manumission by their owners (in some cases their natural fathers) or through purchase of freedom with the earnings from their hired labor. While in 1790 there were 32,523 free Blacks in the South, their number—despite many barriers put in their way—had grown to 258,346 by 1860, an increase from 4.7 to 6.3 percent of the Black population in the region.[21]

Some White southern church leaders were convinced that they had an obligation to promote the religious instruction of slaves, and that this could be done without danger to the slavery system. In 1823, an Episcopal clergyman in South Carolina published a pamphlet "to show...that slavery is not forbidden by the Divine Law: and at the same time to prove the necessity of giving religious instruction to our Negroes." A few years later, two associations of Georgia planters undertook to promote such instruction. One of the arguments for such instruction was that it would deprive northern critics of one of their chief charges against the institution of slavery.[22] Some, at least, of the slave holders had twinges of guilt about that institution, and pacified them by showing a concern for the souls of their slaves. "To have heard them talk, indeed, you would have thought that the sole reason some of these planters held to slavery was love and duty to the black man, the earnest, devoted will, not only to get him into heaven, but also to make him happy in this world. He was a child whom somebody had to look after."[23]

Apart from sporadic efforts by missionary societies and by the churches organized by free Blacks—of which there were some seven hundred, South and North, by 1820[24]—there was almost no provision for the formal instruction of slave children, and the situation grew even less favorable in the nineteenth century, in reaction to slave revolts and northern abolitionist criticism. A study that sought to identify members of "the Negro vanguard" during the antebellum period found only one, John Chavis, known for being a teacher, and in that case a teacher of White pupils, with a separate class for Blacks at night.[25]

A few racially integrated schools serving free Black as well as White children were established after the Revolution, but "by the turn of the century, the ebbing of Revolutionary equalitarianism and the rising fears of servile revolt forced the few remaining integrated academies to close their doors or segregate their classrooms."[26] In 1800, the Virginia governor was warned that "many free Negroes had come in from Maryland, that abolition societies were educating Negroes and filling them with ideas of equality, and that this was a patently dangerous combination."[27]

Some states (Mississippi in 1823, Louisiana in 1830, North Carolina and Virginia in 1831, Alabama in 1832, South Carolina in 1834) forbade teaching slaves to read and write, since this—as the North Carolina law explained—"has a tendency to excite dissatisfaction in their minds, and to produce insurrection and rebellion, to the manifest injury of the citizens of this state."[28] The Mississippi law went so far as to forbid the teaching of "free negroes" as well. "Everything must be interdicted which is calculated to render the slave discontented," explained a justice of the Georgia Supreme Court. The journal *Southern Presbyterian* asked, "Is there any great moral reason why we should incur the tremendous risk of having our wives slaughtered in consequence of our slaves being taught to read incendiary publications?" Nor was this to deny them the Gospel, since "millions of those in heaven never owned a bible."[29] Such laws, while not as universally applied as is often suggested by present-day accounts, were also seconded by the direct opposition of the White population to schooling for Blacks; for example, in 1823 a White Methodist pastor in Charleston was mobbed for establishing a school for Black children.[30]

"The laws against teaching slaves to read and write," Genovese comments, "grew out of a variety of fears, the simplest of which concerned the forging of passes by potential runaways. The argument expressed with greatest agitation concerned the dangers of incendiary literature.... Alabama's harsh legislation grew directly out of the postinsurrectionary panic of 1831–1832."[31] Similarly, the circulation of David Walker's *Appeal to the Colored Citizens of the World* led to "new laws for the quarantining of all Black sailors entering Georgia ports, punishing with serious penalties the introduction of seditious literature into the state and tightening laws against slave education."[32] In his autobiography, Frederick Douglass explained that this fear was justified. As a young slave, he had heard his owner say that " 'learning would spoil the best nigger in the world.

> ... It would forever unfit him to be a slave.... It would make him discontented and unhappy.' These words sank deep into my heart ... and called into existence an entirely new train of thought.... From that moment I understood the direct pathway from slavery to freedom," one which he himself followed a few years later.[33]

The experience of Douglass was by no means unique, and indeed some slave owners found it advantageous to ensure that some of their slaves could read. "A house servant learned through necessity how to distinguish among the different newspapers his master ordered him to select, and slaves who served as foremen had to learn enough to keep a daily record. Slaves trained as artisans to meet the many needs of the largely self-sufficient plantations, or hired out in towns, often needed to have some basic reading and arithmetic skills to do their work. As one former slave told an interviewer, "Dey try not to let de chilluns come up so ign'nant. Den dey could use 'em better for dey own purpose."[34]

More generally, however, some slave children gained literacy through the "play schools" that grew out of the sociable relations maintained with their owner's children. The subsequently famous Grimké sisters, daughters of a South Carolina Supreme Court judge, "defied the laws of South Carolina" by teaching their father's slaves secretly.[35] Perhaps "the most common avenue to literacy for Blacks was instruction by a White person who considered it their religious duty to teach their slaves how to read Scripture...the Scotch-Irish and Huguenot Protestants of the South Carolina upcountry fought a losing battle in the early 1830s...to prevent passage of a law prohibiting slave literacy. Nevertheless, they regularly violated these laws privately, as did other White evangelicals throughout the South."[36] Some Whites "expressed libertarian outrage that the state would dictate how they were or were not to treat their slaves."[37]

There is in fact considerable evidence that the laws against teaching slaves to read were often ignored, losing their force as the original panic caused by slave uprisings subsided and as the vigor of northern abolitionism waned after the 1830s. "As with the formation of the African church, black persistence seemed to wear whites down until the proscriptive laws fell into disuse."[38] This was especially the case for Blacks living in cities and towns, where they had frequent interaction with free Blacks. Indeed, "a search of judicial decisions on slavery issues finds little to support the idea that those illegally teaching slaves to read were prosecuted."[39]

The difficulty for many slave owners, as the northern visitor Frederick Law Olmstead noted, was "how, without quite destroying the capabilities of the negro for any work at all, to prevent him from learning to take care of himself." There was an economic interest in making slaves more capable of doing skilled work and doing it semi-independently rather than, as on the great rice plantations, in gangs marshaled by overseers. Slave artisans could be hired out, could be sent to work in towns, where they inevitably were exposed to ideas that tended to undermine the slavery-based system. Above all, they were free to join Black churches where they mingled with free Blacks. One of the White "gentlemen" with whom Olmstead talked in the 1850s claimed that slaves "have much greater educational privileges" than had been the case a generation before. In response to Olmstead's surprise at the phase, he was told "I mean preaching and religious instruction. They have the Bible read to them a great deal, and there is preaching for them all over the country. They have preachers of their own, right smart ones they are, too, some of them." Some of what Black slaves were learning through their churches no doubt would have startled Olmstead's "gentleman." On the other hand, other slave owners whose plantations Olmstead visited took care that "all natural incitements to self-advancement had been studiously removed or obstructed, in subordination to the general purpose of making the plantation profitable,"[40] and it was Blacks who had been subjected to such limitation of their human potential who had most difficulty taking advantage of their eventual emancipation.

There were, as noted, some schools for Blacks in the South before emancipation, with the greatest number in Washington, D.C., with "at least seventy-two teachers for black people in the city in the antebellum nineteenth century."[41] Often the initiative was taken by pious Presbyterians, like the wealthy benefactor who opened a school for Blacks in Charleston in 1740, and those who opened others in Virginia by 1755.[42] The advertisement for a private school in Raleigh, North Carolina, in 1808, states that it will teach "Children of Colour" in the evenings, after the White children have left the premises. The autobiography of Daniel Alexander Payne describes how, in the 1830s, he painfully acquired knowledge, and then passed it on to his pupils in Charleston; he boasts that "my school increased in popularity, and became the most popular of five which then existed. It numbered about sixty children from most of the leading [Black] families of Charleston." In 1834, however, the state legislature passed a law forbidding anyone to teach "any slave or free person of color to read or write," and Payne was forced to close his school.[43] He soon relocated to the North, where he eventually became one of the leaders of the African Methodist Episcopal Church, an activist in the abolitionist movement and, at Wilberforce University, America's first Black college president.

It is not as though the South provided adequate public education for White pupils, though there were a considerable number of private academies and other arrangements for the children of the elite. Cash attributes this to "the heritage of the frontier: that individualism which, while willing enough to ameliorate the specific instance, relentlessly laid down as its basic social postulate the doctrine that every man was completely and wholly responsible for himself."[44] North Carolina had done the most, and by 1860 around 150,000 White children attended more than 3,000 public schools. More characteristic of the southern states was Florida, which "tried in 1850, with little success, to start a public school system from the taxes received from the sale of certain slaves."[45] Southern education reformers, in fact, sometimes justified their efforts by the need to maintain White supremacy; as one wrote in a leading review in 1856, schooling was not required "for the great bulk of [a slave state's] laboring class," but "it *is* required to afford that degree of education to every one of its White citizens which will enable him intelligently and actively to control and direct the slave labor of the State."[46]

Despite the lack of schools serving Black youth, there is evidence of clandestine schooling at least to the extent of basic literacy. An article about "slavery times" published in 1883 on the basis of interviews with former slaves described how "the plantations of a parish or township would be canvassed, and those in whom they could confide, were invited to attend a 'School' in any location where Secresy [sic] could be secured. Sometimes these schools were held in remote swamps and canebreaks, where, perhaps, the foot of the white man had never trod." Jenny Proctor, a former slave, told an interviewer: "None of us was 'lowed to see a book or try to learn. Dey say we git smarter den dey was if we learn anything, but we slips around and gits hold of dat Webster's old blue back speller and we hides it 'til way in de night and den we lights a little pine torch and studies dat spellin' book. We learn it too."[47] Olmstead recorded a conversation with a slave owner in Mississippi who told him proudly that "there ent one of my niggers but what can read; read good too—better'n I can at any rate." "How did they learn?" Olmstead asked. "Taught themselves. I b'lieve there was one on 'em that I bought, that could read, and he taught all the rest." These slaves, the owner told Olmstead, liked religious books, which they bought from peddlers.[48]

Some free Black teachers managed to maintain clandestine schools, typically by pretending to be teaching sewing or other skills that were not forbidden. In several cases, we are told that White women were hired to sit in a corner and sew in case of suspicious visitors. "A woman named Deveaux taught a clandestine school in Savannah between about 1835–1865. Deveaux was still teaching in the same room in 1865 when she was interviewed by a visitor. Deveaux is reported to have said that after the war she was teaching to children of a 'better' class of African-Americans." Others were not so fortunate:

> In Augusta, Edwin Purdy taught a clandestine school for enslaved students. Purdy was a Methodist preacher who taught his school for boys and girls in his backyard. Eugene Wesley Smith, who was born in 1852 in Augusta, told an interviewer: "Going to school wasn't allowed, but still some people would slip their children to school. There was an old Methodist preacher, a Negro named Ned Purdee, he had a school for boys and girls going on in his back yard. They caught him and put him in jail. He was to be put in stocks and get so many lashes every day for a month." According to other sources, Purdy paid a fine of fifty dollars, and received sixty lashes, and then was sent to prison for an undisclosed amount of time.[49]

More formal schooling was available in New Orleans, with its tradition of a "respectable" mixed-race class from the period of French and Spanish rule and no legal prohibition against teaching Blacks. Catholic orders for Black women, like the Oblate sisters, founded in Baltimore in 1829, taught schools for Black children in several cities.

> In 1842, the Congregation of the Sisters of the Holy Family was founded in New Orleans by three women of color, descendants of wealthy and well-established free African-American families. They opened a home on Bayou Road for African-American orphans and elderly, and instructed the young in reading and writing, sewing, cooking, housekeeping and laundry.... Similarly, on April 20, 1847, with a bequest from Mme.
> Couvent, a free African-American woman (and later support from... Creoles of color) a group of free African-American men founded a free school under the name of the Catholic Society for the Instruction of Indigent Orphans.... The students were taught to be fully literate in French and English, as well as arithmetic. When the students reached a certain age, and presumably were suitably bi-lingual, they were placed in jobs in New Orleans as clerks in stores and warehouses. Girls and boys were taught separately, boys on the first floor, and girls on the second. The reputation of the school drew children who were not orphans, and they paid a tuition fee to attend.[50]

As a result of such religiously motivated efforts, the 1850 census showed more than a thousand free Blacks attending schools in New Orleans, with another two hundred attending rural parish schools.[51]

In other parts of the South, where free Blacks and (to a growing extent) enslaved Blacks were Protestant and had formed their own independent churches, these did much to develop literacy and a perspective beyond their immediate circumstances among their members. Sunday schools, for example, might teach the elements of literacy to read the Bible, and indeed the Sunday School movement had started in England and spread to the United States as a means of instructing in literacy as well as religion among the poor who could not afford to attend school during the week.

> The American Sunday School Union founded Sunday schools for blacks in the North and in the border southern states in which children and adults were taught to read and distributed instructional materials in reading to northern black churches. The American Bible Society made grants to northern black schools, to black emigrants to Liberia, to African-American colonies in Canada, which included numbers of escaped slaves, and to slaves in St. Croix and St. Thomas. The Tract Society printed material exclusively for the use of black groups.[52]

John B. Adger, a former missionary to the Armenians, directed a Presbyterian mission to slaves in Charleston; in 1852 he ordered 31,500 pages of religious tracts to use among his congregation, indicating both that many must have been literate and that he was not barred from providing them with "safe" reading material.[53]

In addition, Black churches supported day schools when not prevented from doing so by local White opposition.[54] Of equal significance with the provision of basic literacy was the opportunity to exercise a measure of leadership, and thus to undergo a form of adult education as well as to set an example for children who otherwise would see their parents only in subordinate and humiliating roles. As political scientist Sidney Verba and his colleagues found in their study of voluntarism in American politics, "the churches that African-Americans attend have special potential for stimulating political participation... they belong to churches whose internal structure nurtures opportunities to exercise politically relevant skills."[55] This seems to have been as true two centuries ago as it is today, and occurred to some extent even in those White churches that allowed Blacks to attend their services, though sitting in a gallery or other segregated area; one such church in Virginia painted some of its benches black so that Blacks would have no doubt about where to sit![56] Despite segregation, "emotions and ideals... united poor whites and blacks in evangelical churches" and produced at least a measure of respect for Black "brothers and sisters."

> Baptists, precisely because of their independent church polity, offered more opportunity than any other denomination for black members to exercise a measure of control over their church life. In some mixed churches committees of black members were constituted in order to oversee the church order of black members. These committees listened to applicants relate their religious experience and heard the replies of those members charged with breach of discipline... committees of the "brethren in black"... conducting business, and reporting their recommendations to the general meeting, gave to black church members experience in church governance, and so laid a foundation upon which freedmen would rapidly build their own independent churches after emancipation.[57]

In the same manner, among the Cherokee Indians, the full-bloods (often excluded from power by the English-speaking mixed bloods), "had learned political organization from the congregational nature of evangelical churches; choosing their own leaders derived both from tradition and from the Baptist emphasis on developing a native ministry. For many Cherokees, Christianity (as understood and preached in their own idiom and subject to their own interpretation) had become a source of revitalization."[58]

The Black churches, which usually included both free and enslaved Blacks, were frequently under suspicion because "an independent Black church with its own system of biblical interpretation was the single greatest threat to White authority because of the degree to which it upheld a vision of Black autonomy, solidarity, and mission." Whites often feared and distrusted Black churches, which were harassed by legal restrictions and sometimes "attacked by angry mobs which disbanded many of the most promising black institutions and forced black leaders to flee from the South." Nor was this suspicion always unfounded; "in northeast North Carolina in early 1802, where revival activity was particularly intense, Blacks were clearly using religious gatherings to plan for revolt." In fact, "Blacks became the unintended and dangerous beneficiaries of Protestant America's remarkably successful combination of democratic ideology with evangelicalism's emphasis on liberty and equality before God." For Blacks, especially in the South, "evangelical gatherings supplied both the ideological foundation and the forums for communication and the experience of solidarity."[59]

There was also a certain amount of schooling provided by self-help associations of free Blacks, like the Brown Fellowship Society organized in Charleston in 1790, with one of its purposes being to open and maintain schools for Black youth. "The Society's membership was limited specifically to free brown (light-color) men only, and the school enrolled free youth. Gender and color status were the basis for the organization, and possibly for the school. Along with this school, the Society provided insurance benefits for the survivors of members who had died, purchased a cemetery for members, and contributed to the support of orphans. Although the organization was predicated on distinctions of gender, color, and status, the Society did subsidize the Minor's Moralist Society, lasting from 1803 to 1847, which schooled indigent free African-Americans."[60]

Of the areas where slavery continued to be established by law, the 1850 federal census found 217 free Blacks attending school in North Carolina, 467 in the District of Columbia, 1,616 in Maryland, and (as noted previously) 1,219 in Louisiana.[61] All of these schools were "private," mostly of a religious character, and none received any public funding that we are aware of.

In the North

Slavery existed in much of the North during the colonial period, when Black slaves made-up between 6 and 9 percent of the population of Rhode Island, New Jersey, and Pennsylvania after 1700, and by some estimates up to 25 percent of the population of New York City and vicinity,[62] but the nature of the northern economy and political culture was more hospitable to free labor and slavery was gradually abolished, state by state, in the first years of independence. By 1784 Vermont, Pennsylvania, and other northeastern states had abolished slavery, and it was excluded in 1787 from the Northwest Territory that became Ohio and states to the west. As a result, for a few years there was a sort of anticipation of the "underground railroad" in reverse, with Blacks enslaved in Canada slipping across the border into the United States. It was not until 1834 that slavery was officially abolished in all parts of British North America, though it had been so severely limited by the 1820s by provincial legislative and judicial action in Canada that there were only a few dozen slaves left at the point of final emancipation.[63]

Subsequent to the legal abolition of slavery (often phased in over a number of years), northern free Black population was concentrated largely in Philadelphia, New York City, and to a lesser extent in other cities, often working at the docks or in the service trades. Several states considered (Massachusetts in 1822) or actually adopted legislation barring Blacks from living in the state; in 1851, Indiana prohibited Blacks from entering the state, as did Illinois in 1853.

> The white working man disliked the thought of having to share his rising place in the world with the African-American... in many [northern] states the adoption of white manhood suffrage led directly to the political disenfranchisement of the black man. New states admitted to the Union after 1819 restricted suffrage to white males. Most northern states also limited or barred black immigration and qualified black participation in the courts. City codes separated blacks from whites in public transportation, accommodations, entertainment, schools, and churches. Public opinion and direct action by violent mobs enforced these practices.[64]

Blacks in Illinois could not vote or hold public office or attend public schools in the antebellum period, and similar exclusions existed in other states.[65] Tocqueville observed, in the 1830s, that those "states in which slavery has been abolished ordinarily apply themselves to rendering the stay in their territory unpleasant to free Negroes; and as a sort of emulation is established on this point among the different states, the unfortunate Negroes can only choose among evils."[66]

Among abolitionists in the 1830s and after, a common complaint about slavery was that it left slaves in ignorance, and thus prevented them from becoming fully human as New Englanders understood what that required. Poet John Greenleaf Whittier, in a pamphlet self-published in 1833 (and subsequently widely distributed throughout the North), called for the "establishment of schools for the instruction of the slave children, a general diffusion of the lights of Christianity, and the introduction of a sacred respect for the social obligations of marriage and for the relations between parents and children, among our black population," thus countering the degrading effects of bondage. This, he assured his readers, "would render emancipation not only completely safe, but also of the highest advantage to the country."[67] This was entirely consistent with the contemporary ferment over social reform centered upon education in many forms, of which the "common school" promoted by Horace Mann as an almost universal panacea was the most prominent.[68]

This was a period when, apart from New England and areas of the upper Midwest settled by New Englanders, the provision of schooling still rested largely with churches and voluntary associations, encouraged sporadically by state government exhortation and occasional meager funding. It was entirely natural, then, that free Blacks looked to their own efforts and to those of their White allies rather than to government to provide schooling for their children. The opening editorial of the first newspaper published by African-Americans, *Freedom's Journal* (March 1827), promised "to urge upon our brethren the necessity and expediency of training their children, while young, to habits of industry, and thus forming them for becoming useful members of society. It is surely time that we should wake from this lethargy of years, and make a concentrated effort for the education of our youth." A social organization founded by Blacks in New York City, in 1833, set as one of its tasks "to help to clothe poor children of color, if they will attend school—the clothes to be loaned, and to be taken away from them if they neglect their schools, and to impress on the parents the importance of having the children punctual and regular in their attendance at school." Nor was primary schooling enough; the organization pledged also "to seek out young men of talents and good moral character, that they may be assisted to obtain a liberal education."[69]

The annual meeting of the Ohio Anti-Slavery Society in 1837 was attended, according to one of the participants in a letter to her cousins, by "a hundred young women...who have been teaching coloured schools in different parts of the state...most of them have gone a great distance from home and have undergone a great many trials and have barely received enough to buy them provisions...there are but a few of them that could get boarding in white families some have boarded with coloured people."[70] Thirty years later, other young women from Ohio and New England would be undertaking a similar mission in the South and encountering similar difficulties.

In some cases, Black children were admitted to the existing schools, but more often they were excluded because of opposition by White parents. Novelist and abolitionist Lydia Maria Child of Boston, noted in 1833, that "our prejudice against colored people is even more inveterate than it is at the South." Similarly, Black minister and abolitionist Theodore Wright in New York City complained, in 1837, that despite the legal status of freemen, "still we are slaves—everywhere we feel the chain galling us" as a result of White prejudice. "This spirit is withering all our hopes, and ofttimes causes the colored parent as he looks upon his child, to wish he had never been born."[71]

Such prejudice against Blacks was evident in Canada as well. When, in 1853, a debating society took as its question, "Whether have the Indian or the Negro suffered most from the aggression of the white man?" it is reported that "all assembled agreed that Negroes were thieves." As in the United States, school authorities warned that if racial integration was imposed on schools, White parents will withdraw their children; indeed, the White school trustees in one Ontario community informed provincial authorities, in 1846, that rather than send their children "to school with niggers they will cut their children's heads off and throw them into the road side ditch"; the Black parents were forced to establish a private school for their children. Provincial law, in 1850, provided for racially segregated schools; while they were already segregated informally, this action formalized second-class status. Any group of five Black families could ask local school authorities to create a separate school for their children, and the law was used by local authorities even when no such request had been made.[72]

It is interesting to note that Ontario superintendent of education Egerton Ryerson, often described as the "Horace Mann of Canada," was no more willing than his counterpart in Massachusetts to confront White prejudice and call for racially integrated schools. His deference to local decisions in this sphere (though he was an energetic reformer in other ways) resulted in situations where, lacking funds for separate schools, local authorities required Black pupils to sit on separate benches in the common school. In one community the White voters decided that a separate school for Blacks should be built next to the

White school and the single teacher would serve both by moving back and forth during the school day![73]

Similarly, laws in New York, Pennsylvania, and Ohio explicitly permitted separate public schooling for Black pupils and, as we will see, this became a legal and political issue in Massachusetts, where initially Blacks had sought separate schools. As early as 1787, free Blacks in Boston complained to the state legislature—unsuccessfully—that their children "now receive no benefit from the free schools in the town of Boston, which we think is a great grievance, as by woeful experience we now feel the want of a common education. We, therefore, much fear for our rising offspring to see them in ignorance in a land of gospel light when there is provision made for them as well as others and yet [they] can't enjoy them, and for not other reason can be given this they are Black."[74] The same year, Jupiter Hammon, in his "Address to the Negroes in the State of New York," called upon them to "let all the time you can get be spent in trying to learn to read."[75]

As in the South, Anglicans and Quakers provided schooling for northern Blacks—some of them slaves—during the eighteenth century. The former established a school for Blacks in Newport, Rhode Island in 1763, and it was later reestablished and supported by the Black community.[76] There were similar efforts for Canada's small Black population: St. Andrew's Presbyterian Church in Niagara had its own schoolhouse in 1817, while in its upstairs room "a black teacher conducted a school especially for the black children of the area. Separate missionary schools also existed for native children."[77] An Anglican organization, The Associates of the Late Dr. Bray, established a school for free Blacks in 1758 in Philadelphia, and in the 1780s, they gave financial support to several small schools for Blacks in Nova Scotia, subsidizing teachers and schoolbooks but requiring that the local Black community provide the buildings. "Although most teachers originally were white, they were replaced in time by Negroes, giving rise to new sources of leadership within the isolated black communities." Nor were Anglicans the only supporters of such schools; in Philadelphia the Quaker Monthly Meeting, in 1770, started a class for the slaves of Quakers who were being prepared for manumission and for free Blacks[78] and, urged on by Anthony Benezet, opened a school for Black children in 1774, with free tuition. By 1797, they were helping to support seven such schools,[79] several of them operated by Black churches and organizations.

Apparently this provision remained unsatisfactory in quality, since a self-help organization was formed by Black leaders in Philadelphia in 1818 "for the education of people of colour." Its constitution stated that "it is to the prominently defective system of instruction, as it now exists among us, that we must in great measure attribute the contemptible and degraded situation which we occupy in society, and most of the disadvantages under which we suffer." The members pledged themselves "to use the best energies of our minds and of our hearts, in devising and adapting the most effectual means to procure for our children a more extensive and useful education than we have heretofore had in our power to effect," including "all the useful and scientific branches of education."[80] Noble as these intentions were, they reflect an early instance of the illusion that education could serve as a sort of magic wand to conjure away every form of social and economic disadvantage suffered by Black Americans.

Pennsylvania state laws in 1802, 1804, and 1809 required that poor children be taught free, but it was not until 1818 that five public schools were established for poor White children in Philadelphia, and there were none for Black children until 1822, "when the abolitionists donated a building to the state authorities upon hearing their excuse that they could not build a colored school because no funds were available."[81]

In New York City, funds appropriated by the state for the schooling of poor children, under laws enacted in 1795 and 1813, were granted directly to private and church-run charity schools. This included the African Free School,[82] founded in 1787 by private efforts for Black pupils. In 1832, six such schools with 1,400 pupils were taken over by the (private) Public School Society, though they continued to be operated as "colored schools"; "this consolidation resulted at first in reduced attendance by Negro children because of the insensitivity of the Public School Society."[83] It was only after 1873, when a state law directed that all public schools be open to all "without distinction of color," that New York City began to desegregate its schools. There were still several "colored" schools in the 1880s; however, and Brooklyn "abandoned its policy of segregated schools in 1890. After the metropolitan city was consolidated in 1898, the borough of Queens had the city's only colored schools," and the courts supported the authority of school officials to assign Black children to them. "As a result, Governor Theodore Roosevelt had the legislature pass a law abolishing colored schools in the state."[84]

Most of the schools attended by Black children, before the Civil War, were supported by Black communities and their White friends. In 1860, Philadelphia—the center of Black population in the North—had fifty-six private schools for Black pupils, only twelve of which under White management. Almost without exception, the surviving resolutions by the associations and churches organized by free Blacks in the North, and especially the Negro Convention Movement that began in 1830, emphasize their commitment to improving the education available to their children, as part of a broader strategy of improving their situation. Thus, at the first annual convention, bringing together fifteen delegates from New York, Pennsylvania, Delaware, Maryland, and Virginia, four "rallying points" were chosen: Education, Temperance, Economy, and Universal Liberty. As a concrete measure to promote the first of these themes, the convention endorsed a plan to establish "a College for the instruction of young men of colour, on the manual labour system [i.e., sustained in part by the work of the students], by which the children of the poor may receive a regular classical education...and the charge will be so regulated as to put it within the reach of all."[85] The result of the uneven and inadequate provision of schooling opportunities for the children of free Black families was that "only four Negroes had graduated from an American college by 1830."[86]

Such efforts were sometimes opposed by local citizens who did not want Black families to be attracted to their communities by the existence of schools for their children. The most notorious incident occurred in Canterbury, Connecticut, where a young woman named Prudence Crandall had responded to the invitation of local citizens to establish a day and boarding school for girls in 1831. Her own Quaker education and her reading of William Lloyd Garrison's *Liberator* (founded the same year as her school) predisposed her to accept "a colored girl of respectability" who asked to study at her school in order "to get a little more learning, enough if possible to teach colored children." Although Sarah Harris boarded separately "at her own father's house at some little distance from the village," Crandall was warned that she was likely to lose all her White students. Refusing to be cowed, "she proceeded to convert the Canterbury Female Boarding School into an institution for the training of Negro girls who should themselves become teachers for the children of their race."

The local community was outraged, and a committee met with her to warn "that by putting her design into execution she would bring disgrace upon them all." The committee "professed to feel a real regard for the colored people, and were perfectly willing they should be educated, provided it could be effected in some *other* place." Despite the support of Garrison's paper and of Samuel May, a local minister who would later be one of Horace Mann's allies in the creation of the first state teacher-training institutions, Crandall's school was forced to close, and she moved to the West with her new husband.[87] Several years later her brother, Dr. Reuben Crandall, was jailed in the District of Columbia for distributing abolitionist publications, suggesting that zeal for the cause ran in her family. He was prosecuted by District Attorney Francis Scott Key (of *Star Spangled Banner* fame), who said he deserved to be hanged, and imprisoned for eight months; though acquitted, his health was ruined, and he soon died.[88]

The proposal, in 1831, for a college for Black students in New Haven was successfully blocked by the mayor and others who charged that it would damage the interests of Yale and of the city.[89] The organizers, a group of Black and White abolitionists, had aimed to help students to "cultivate habits of personal industry and obtain a useful mechanical or agricultural occupation, while pursuing classical studies," and they hoped to attract them from all parts of the North and from the British West Indies, "whose 'respectable' free colored families might be persuaded to choose the school for their sons." The townspeople of New Haven, reacting in part to the news of the Nat Turner slave rebellion in Virginia, voted 700 to 4 to resist the proposed college "by every legal means" and, not content with such means, some formed a mob and attacked New Haven's colored neighborhood for two nights of rioting and vandalism.[90]

Despite this disappointment, the second annual National Negro Convention, in 1831, while deploring "the proceedings of the citizens of New Haven [which]... were a disgrace to themselves, and cast a stigma on the reputed fame of New England," reaffirmed their determination to establish colleges and high schools "on the Manual Labor system, where our youth may be instructed in all the arts of civilized life." After all, they pointed out,

> If we ever expect to see the influence of prejudice decrease, and ourselves respected, it must be by the blessings of an enlightened education. It must be by being in possession of that classical knowledge which promotes genius, and causes man to soar up to those high intellectual enjoyments and acquirements, which places him in a situation, to shed upon a country and a people, that scientific grandeur which is imperishable by time, and drowns in oblivion's cup their moral degradation. Those who think that out primary schools are capable of effecting this, are a century behind the age.[91]

We find expressed here, more than half a century before the controversy between Du Bois and Washington, the conviction on the part of Black leaders that their sons required the same liberal education that was standard for the children of the White elite.

While Black abolitionists were understandably most concerned about practical issues affecting themselves and their families, including in the North where all of them lived, White abolitionists were commonly motivated by religious convictions about the evils of human bondage and its dehumanizing effects upon those enslaved. For many of them, antislavery was just one of a cluster of reforms that included supporting foreign missions, evangelizing the western frontier, promoting temperance, and encouraging family devotions, all energized by the religious revivals that flourished in the 1830s as they had before and would again. It was these religious motivations that would ensure that a strong minority of evangelicals in the North continued to give generously to educational and religious missions to the South after emancipation, and to send their daughters and sons to teach the children of freedmen. Sometimes, it must be admitted, this involved overlooking the educational needs of Black children in the North.

For Blacks in the North, by contrast, that was a central concern. In Boston, David Walker and his associates "believed that the key to the uplift of the race was a zealous commitment to the tenets of individual moral improvement: education, temperance, Protestant religious practice, regular work habits, and self-regulation."[92] "Philadelphia in the mid-thirties had ten self-supporting colored schools. Cincinnati in 1838 had two Negro schools 'deriving no aid from their White neighbors.' In 1857 Wilmington, Delaware, had two schools supported by Negroes. For six years, 1854 to 1860, San Francisco Negroes supported a one-teacher school, touching a total of some two hundred and fifty students. Baltimore, which outstripped any other city in free Negro population, had fifteen colored schools in 1859, every one of them self-sustaining."[93]

It was above all Black churches that supported education, as when the African Methodist Episcopal Church, in 1840, called upon all its preachers "to enjoin undeviating attention to its promotion" and urged "all our people to neglect no opportunity of advancing it."[94]

CHAPTER 3

Equipping the Freedman

The confidence, so often expressed in the North during the three decades before the Civil War, that properly organized education would bring about a profound regeneration of society was quite naturally applied to the rebel South. "The North, a missionary spokesman wrote in the Atlanta *Christian Index* in 1866, 'should teach the South...by military garrisons, by [Freedmen's] Bureau courts, by Congregational churches, by Northern settlers, by constitutional amendments, by christian missionaries, by free schools, lectures, newspapers and reading rooms, what be the first principles of social order, political eminence, moral worth and industrial success.' "[1] On the eve of the war, in the preface for the latest of his widely read accounts of tours of inquiry through the South, Frederick Law Olmstead had suggested that both Blacks and Whites in the South would have to be educated before emancipation could be a success:

> Popular prejudice, if not popular instinct, points to a separation of black from white as a condition of the abolition of slavery.... I think a happy and peaceful association of a large negro, with a large white population, can not at present be calculated on as a permanent thing. I think that the emancipation from slavery of such part of the existing actual negro population as shall remain in the country until the white population is sufficiently christianized and civilized, and properly educated to understand that its interests are identical with its duty, will take place gradually, and only after an intermediate period of systematic pupilage, restraint, and encouragement.[2]

The White leadership of the South, even in the immediate aftermath of defeat, had no intention of being "christianized and civilized" to northern standards and showed no inclination to reconsider the status of the now-emancipated Blacks. As W. J. Cash wrote, "If the war had smashed the Southern world, it had left the essential [White] Southern mind and will—the mind and will arising from, corresponding to, and requiring this world—entirely unshaken."[3] There were to be no second thoughts about White supremacy or the necessary subordination of Blacks.

The new governor of Mississippi, in his inaugural address, asserted that "ours is and it shall ever be, a government of white men," while a Democratic convention in Louisiana insisted that "the people of African descent cannot be considered as citizens of the United States." "Black Codes" were enacted to keep the freedmen in a serf-like attachment to the soil and in economic, social, and political subordination, including prohibition against serving on juries or testifying against Whites. (It should be noted that these prohibitions were common in the North, apart from Massachusetts, before and in some cases after the Civil War.[4]) As the editor of the South Carolina Black Code wrote in 1866, "To institute...between the Anglo-Saxon, the high-minded, virtuous, intelligent, patriotic Southerner and the freedman a social or political approximation more intimate—to mingle the social or political existence of the two classes more closely—would surely be one of the highest exhibitions of treason to the [White] race."[5]

Several southern states, during the period of "Presidential Reconstruction" when there were few limits on such efforts, took steps to establish for the first time systems of universal schooling...for White children only.[6] It may be that they were motivated, as were the Austrians in the same years and the French a few years later, by a belief that it was the superior educational provisions of their late enemy that had led to their defeat. Blaming the Prussian schoolmaster or the Yankee schoolma'am was perhaps more acceptable than acknowledging a failure of military valor or skill.

It was in reaction to the defiance of Union victory through new measures to keep emancipated Blacks in semi-slavery that Radical Republicans in Congress instituted "Congressional Reconstruction" under military control. This, in turn, led to the conviction that persisted for a century among White Southerners that, as Republican Thaddeus Stevens accurately predicted, the northern radicals "would thrust the negro into your parlors, your bedrooms, and the bosoms of your wives and daughters."[7] Despite the later assurances by Booker T. Washington, White Southerners could never quite believe that their social system could be preserved without systematically subordinating Blacks in economic and political domains.

While zeal for a reform of consciousness and thus of social relations was directed toward the whole population of the South, northerners recognized a special obligation toward its Black population. "Where southern whites generally were perfectly content to allow the blacks to stew in their own cultural juices, the northerners pined to wipe them clean and participate as midwives at a rebirth...it was necessary for 'Civilization' to triumph over 'Barbarism' so that the 'power that had its germ in the Mayflower' could create 'one common civilization' throughout the nation."[8]

Even before the war was over, as the efforts of the national government to bring the South under its control led to the occupation, by the Union army, of portions of the rebellious states, the military authorities were faced with the challenge of what to do with the slaves whose masters had fled. As early as February 1862, one Union general called for assistance from "a highly favored and philanthropic people" to meet the needs of the Blacks under his authority. "To relieve the government of a burden that may hereafter become unsupportable, and to enable the Blacks to support and govern themselves in the absence of their disloyal guardians, a suitable system of cultivation and instruction must be combined with one providing for physical wants."[9]

There was significant support in the North for providing the education that, it was believed, would enable freed slaves, or at least their children, to rise out of the degradation that slavery had imposed. As the U.S. Commissioner of Education would recall in 1871, "the sentiment of the country adopted the ex-slaves as the nation's wards."[10] Certainly there was a great deal to do with respect to schooling: In 1865, only 1.7 percent of Blacks of school age attended school, and only 5 percent could read. Nor was illiteracy the only problem; northern abolitionists and evangelical reformers headed South "to establish beachheads of Christian piety and Yankee know-how in the moral wilderness of the defeated Confederacy, dispelling the darkness which two centuries of human slavery had cast over the region [and]...make a New England of the whole South."[11] As the National Freedman's Relief Association put it in 1866, "We want, not schools merely, but Northern schools, Northern men and women, down south, teaching, mingling with the people, and instituting the North there among the old populations. In this way we civilize all at once, by communicating simultaneously all the chief intellectual elements of civilization."[12] That is, northern "civilization."

One of the most eloquent summaries of this mission and how it was perceived by White Southerners was that of Black historian Horace Mann Bond; it deserves quotation at length:

> The Northern missionary teachers who came to the South to educate Negroes in the period after the Civil War are remembered as having been

among the vilest of all mankind.... They found the Negro an oppressed economic class; their education sought to teach him thrift, independence of his former masters, good work habits as a free citizen, sobriety, and honesty. All of these virtues they saw as necessary to the end of creating Negroes able to survive in a competitive laissez-faire system. The Negro was, furthermore, a subordinate social caste; by example and by precept they sought to raise him to a plane where the only differences between men would be those of economic status. They established colleges and universities for Negroes, and for this J. L. M. Curry, himself a member of the old Southern elite and a friend to the education of Negroes, called them "misguided fanatics." The missionaries, said Curry, laid especial stress on classics and liberal culture, "to bring the race *per saltum* [in a single leap] to the same plane with their former masters, and to realize the theory of social and political equality." This was a precise appraisal of the objectives of the Northerners. This system of education, offering to ex-slaves the forbidden fruits of a "gentleman's education," was bound to "make all possible mischief" for a social order founded on the dominance of a plantation aristocracy within a framework of racial caste.[13]

Bishop Daniel Payne, returning to his native Charleston after an exile of thirty years, wept "tears of gratitude," convinced "that New England ideas, sentiments, and principles will ultimately rule the entire South."[14] Similarly, Lyman Abbott, general secretary of the American Freedman's Union Commission, predicted in 1864 that "we have not only to conquer the South—we have to convert it. We have not only to occupy it by bayonets and bullets—but also by ideas and institutions."[15]

In retrospect, following through on the offer of "forty acres and a mule" for freed slaves might have provided a more stable basis for Black progress in the South. This economic foundation had been offered by General Sherman in consultation with Secretary of War Stanton, in the famous Special Field Order #15 (January 16, 1865), setting aside extensive tracts of South Carolina and Florida for settlement exclusively by Blacks, and the Freedman's Bureau, established two months later, was intended in part to help this settlement. In February 1866, however, that power was removed from the Bureau, and President Johnson soon ordered all the land returned to its White former owners. As a result of an unwillingness to interfere with the rights of private property, "the Republican Party solution to African-American postwar poverty became mass education and not land reform."[16]

Efforts were made by ex-slaves as well as by Blacks who had been free before emancipation to meet the need for schooling. As early as September 1861, Mrs. Mary Peake, a Black woman who had been teaching a clandestine school for "men and women, children and adults, free and enslaved, in her house, most likely in small groups as large congregations would have been likely to draw attention (and repression by whites)" since 1851, began to be subsidized by the American Missionary Association (AMA) to teach Black refugees from slavery—"freedmen"—who had taken shelter under protection of the Union Army in Hampton, Virginia. "Religion played an important part in how Mary Peake approached her teaching. Christianity seems to have been both her reason for teaching and the way in which she made sense of her work. Peake is reported to have considered her day school primarily as a way to help prepare her pupils for Sunday services."[17]

This was soon followed by other AMA-funded schools in nearby areas under the control of Union troops. Other schools were started on the initiative of free Negroes in the South; indeed, reported John W. Alford, general superintendent of schools for the Freedman's Bureau, "Throughout the entire South an effort is being made by the colored people to educate themselves. In absence of other teaching they are determined to be self-taught; and everywhere some elementary textbook, or the fragment of one may be seen in the hands of negroes."[18] Nor was all instruction so informal: "South Carolina had an ample source of competent native teachers...a predictably large number emanated from Charleston's ante-bellum free-Negro population."[19]

Several Negro conventions held in 1865 petitioned their state governments to provide them with schools.[20] For example, fifty-six Black men met in Mobile, Alabama in November 1865 and passed a resolution "that we regard the education of our children and youth as vital to the preservation of our liberties...and shall use our utmost endeavors to promote these blessings in our common country." So eager were the freed slaves for schooling for themselves and their children—often in the naive belief that this would instantly open to them all the advantages that had been enjoyed by their White masters—that in some cases plantation owners established schools to keep their workers from leaving.[21] A similar gathering in South Carolina the same month adopted an address to the White people of their state, asking "that schools be established for the education of *colored children* as well as *White*, and that the advantages of both colors shall, in this respect, be *equal*."[22] The National Colored Labor Union adopted a platform, in 1869, proclaiming that education was "one of the strongest safeguards of the Republican Party, the bulwark of American citizens, and a defense against the invasion of the rights of man."[23]

It has been estimated that there were, by 1866, at least five-hundred elementary schools "founded and maintained exclusively by ex-slaves." The following year, "there were sixty-five private schools in New Orleans enrolling 2,967 [Black] pupils; the [federal Freedmen's Bureau] maintained fifty-six schools with 2,527 pupils.... In Savannah... there were 28 schools in 1866, and 16 of them... were 'under the control of an Educational Board of Colored Men, taught by colored teachers, and sustained by the freed people.'" In Kentucky, it was reported, "the places of worship owned by the colored people are almost the only available school houses in the State." Black Protestant denominations also moved to fill the gap: "In 1868 the African Methodist Episcopal Church (AME)... enrolled 40,000 pupils in its Sabbath schools. By 1885, the AME church reported having '200,000 children in Sunday schools' for 'intellectual and moral' instruction."[24] In Louisiana, Tennessee, and Virginia, by 1867, Blacks "had sustained forty-six schools entirely, contributed to the support of forty-two others, and had purchased thirty-three buildings—all through their own resources."[25]

Black historian Carter Woodson noted how many of the teachers of Black children, in West Virginia at least, were northern Blacks from Ohio who came, not as missionaries, but looking for satisfying work. Woodson pointed out that "although the Negroes were early permitted to attend school in Ohio, race prejudice had not sufficiently diminished to permit them to instruct white persons in public schools. Looking out for a new field, their eyes quickly fell on the waiting harvest across the Ohio in West Virginia. Some of these workers from adjacent States, moreover, served the people not only as teachers but also as ministers of the gospel. They were largely instrumental in establishing practically all of the Methodist and Baptist churches in the State, and while they taught school during the week, they inspired and edified their congregations on Sunday."[26] Throughout the South, this combination of teaching during the week and preaching on Sunday became a common pattern in the Black community.

Other Blacks educated in the North began teaching in the schools established by missionary groups in Union-occupied Virginia as early as 1862. That year Clement Robinson, a graduate of Lincoln University, established Virginia's first "normal school" to train Black teachers. "No sooner was Savannah liberated than blacks formed the Savannah Education Association, which swiftly raised eight hundred dollars and founded several schools. 'It is wholly their own,' noted Rev. John W. Alvord. 'The officers of the Assoc. are all colored men. The teachers are all colored.' In the rural areas, black people organized 'freedmen's schools' and 'Sunday schools,' acting independently of northern whites. Black teachers outnumbered white ones very soon after the Civil War."[27] Within two years, it is reported, the Savannah association had organized 120 schools serving many of Georgia's counties.[28]

These initiatives by the Black community had a lasting impact, even after northern interest faded. In Atlanta, White children had had only a few private schools and one free "pauper" school before Reconstruction, when the support of Black voters led to the establishment of a public-school system in 1872. Before there were public schools for White pupils, the efforts of former slaves and of northern missionaries had created a number of schools for Blacks. In 1871, the Republican-dominated city council offered to provide teachers for the schools established by Black community initiative if the buildings were put at the disposal of the public authorities; but the next year, the Democrats were again in control and the newly established school system did not initially provide schooling for Black children, and it had to be continued under private auspices. Eventually, however, the Board of Education took over two Black elementary schools, while Whites had two high schools as well as five elementary schools.[29] "By the end of 1883, there were three Black grammar schools, only one more than had existed when the school system had begun, the combined capacity of the three schools was woefully inadequate."[30]

Much of the schooling available to Blacks in the South during Reconstruction and after, however, was provided by White teachers from the North who saw themselves as engaged in a missionary enterprise, and who were often supported as such by northern churches. Historians have noted that these educational efforts were carried out primarily by the evangelical wing of the abolitionist movement, which did not see its task accomplished with the formal emancipation of enslaved Blacks, rather than by its more secular wing identified with William Lloyd Garrison. Garrison himself, while acknowledging that there was "a mighty work of enlightenment and regeneration yet to be accomplished at the South," suspended publication of the *Liberator* in 1865, after thirty-five years of struggle against slavery.[31] For many evangelicals, by contrast, the job had just begun.

The Black journalist (and cofounder of the NAACP in 1909) Ida B. Wells, born in Mississippi in 1862, recalled, "all my teachers had been the consecrated White men and women from the North who came into the South to teach immediately after the end of the war. It was they who brought us the light of knowledge and their splendid example of Christian courage."[32] "Of 1,013 Northern teachers in the 1860s whose homes have been located, 520 came from New England ... at a time when

17 percent of the *northern* population lived in New England...that section furnished 51 percent of the northern teachers."[33] W. E. B. Du Bois wrote, in *The Souls of Black Folk* (1903), about "the crusade of the New England schoolma'am."

> The annals of this Ninth Crusade are yet to be written,—the tale of a mission that seemed to our age far more quixotic than the quest of St. Louis seemed to his. Behind the mists of ruin and rapine waved the calico dresses of women who dared, and after the hoarse mouthings of the field guns rang the rhythm of the alphabet. Rich and poor they were, serious and curious. Bereaved now of a father, now of a brother, now of more than these, they came seeking a life work in planting New England schoolhouses among the White and Black of the South. They did their work well. In that first year they taught one hundred thousand souls, and more.[34]

The effort had started even before the war ended. It has been estimated that two hundred thousand women were mobilized in scores of societies established throughout the North, mostly on a denominational or interdenominational basis, to send books, clothing, and food to former slaves,[35] and before the fighting stopped there were some seven hundred and fifty northern teachers instructing Black children in areas occupied by the Union Army. The amount raised and spent by churches and benevolent societies to educate freedmen exceeded that spent by the government's Freedmen's Bureau, and altogether the societies sent about eight thousand teachers who instructed some one hundred and fifty thousand Blacks in three or four thousand schools.[36]

> The New York [Freedmen's Aid] Society quadrupled the number of teachers it was supporting in the South during the year after the war, maintaining 206 teachers by the spring of 1866. The New England Freedmen's Aid Society...did proportionally well and sent 180 teachers in the spring of 1866. The Philadelphia society was supporting 60 teachers. Vigorous new societies had grown up in Cincinnati and Chicago, supporting 130 teachers in the year after the war, and Baltimore's new society financed approximately 50. The American Missionary Association, stronger than any individual society, but not so strong as the combined force of all of them, was maintaining, during the winter after the war, not less than 327 Northern schoolteachers.[37]

Of those teaching in schools staffed by the northern missionary organizations, by 1868 the majority (4,213 of 8,004) were Black, some from the North and others recruited in the South.[38]

In Savannah, Montgomery, and other southern cities, the northern missionaries staffed schools that had been established before they arrived by local Black communities, sometimes displacing what they considered less-qualified Black teachers. In some cases, according to the AMA), this caused problems; in St. Louis, in 1863, its agent reported that "in order to avoid bruising sensitive feelings, 'superior' White AMA teachers were forced to teach primary pupils while Blacks instructed advanced classes." Similarly, in Savannah "Blacks hoped to operate schools 'by their own wit & will' and, in the AMA's view, admit 'their White friends only to inferior places & as assistants in carrying out their duties & wishes.' The AMA was to provide the funds." These tensions may have been inevitable; after all its schools were—along with its churches, with which they were commonly associated—the only institutions that the newly emancipated Black community could call their own, and their symbolic importance was very great. On the other hand, "the AMA's perception of the seriousness of the task to be done and its views of efficiency prevented it, with rare exceptions, from financially supporting Black-administered and Black-taught schools."[39]

Nevertheless, as Reconstruction went on, "from all parts of the South came complaints that representatives of 'colored churches' were attempting to draw students away from schools maintained by the freedmen's aid societies.... Black churches became increasingly involved in establishing their own schools, a development that profoundly disturbed many White educators."[40] From our perspective, it is easy to understand how important it must have been to many Black communities to demonstrate to themselves and to others that they could, as a later generation would say, "take care of business," even if it meant spurning well-meaning assistance from the North.

Despite the tensions, northern observers admired the initiative that these Black community schools represented. When, in what has been called a "rehearsal for Reconstruction," a group of volunteers from New England arrived in the Sea Islands of Georgia, already under Union control in 1862, "they found two schools already in operation, one of them taught by a Black cabinetmaker who for years had conducted secret night classes for slaves.... By the end of April 1865, less than a month after Union troops occupied the city, over 1,000 Black children and seventy-five adults attended schools established by Richmond's Black churches and the American Missionary Society.... Freedmen's Bureau officials repeatedly expressed surprise at discovering classes organized by Blacks already meeting in churches." However, "poverty undercut Black educational efforts, forcing many schools to turn to the

Freedmen's Bureau and Northern societies for aid.... By 1866, unable to finance its schools, the Savannah Educational Association had no alternative but to turn them over to the AMA, which replaced the Black teachers with its own employees, retaining a few of the Blacks as assistants."[41]

Much of the extension of schooling to Blacks in the South was the result of a collaboration between the AMA and other religious organizations, the federal Freedmen's Bureau, with some state support, although the states played very much the junior role. In Alabama, for example, the Board of Education created by the Reconstruction Constitution of 1868 enacted an arrangement under which it promised to pay the salaries of teachers recruited by the voluntary societies, in schoolhouses provided by the Freedmen's Bureau, but "this system seldom worked very well." In particular, many Alabama Whites "protested vigorously against Northern teachers in Black Southern schools." Racially separate schools were required unless the parents of children in a school gave unanimous consent to integration, and Black schools were given two-thirds the funding provided to White schools... an arrangement, ironically, recommended to the Alabama Board by the Rev. Barnas Sears, the agent of the Peabody Fund, a major source of private funding from the North to spread schooling throughout the South.[42]

Under Sears's leadership, the Peabody Fund directed most of its efforts to creating public common-school systems for White pupils, it refused to provide funding for racially mixed schools—even in Louisiana, where these were for a time required by law—on the grounds that their effect would be to destroy the support of White Southerners for public schooling altogether.[43] A White visitor from Georgia received assurances from Sears that the fund would "'in no wise conflict with any sentiment, institution, or custom peculiar to us.' Sears's position was that the mixing or separation of the races in school was a matter for the people to decide themselves. The Peabody Fund would be happy to cooperate either with a system that separated the races, or a system that put the races together, provided that the schools were supported by the people and were, in fact, generally attended by the children."[44] Between 1867 and the death of Barnas Sears in 1880, the fund provided about $1,200,000 for education in the South, of which only 6.5 percent, or $75,750 was given to Black schools. White schools with the required minimum of one hundred pupils would receive $300, and more for a larger enrollment, while Black schools of the minimum size received only $200 because "it costs less to maintain schools for the colored children than for the white."[45]

Sears was extremely concerned to use the resources of the fund in ways that would not offend White sensibilities. It has been suggested that this reflected his experience as successor to Horace Mann's often stormy tenure as secretary of education in Massachusetts:

> True social progress, [Sears] felt, came not by legislation imposed upon people, but by "the spirit of a whole people feeling out its path, and manifesting itself in different degrees in many minds." Unless legislation followed rather than led public sentiment, the result would often be rash experiments that by causing negative public reaction would hinder educational progress even more than ignorance itself. Sears felt that Mr. Mann had erred in precisely this regard. Thus, when Mann resigned, he left several substantial segments of people in the state alienated from the school system. Sears saw his work as Mann's successor more that of developing greater confidence in the system among the people than "perfecting the system theoretically."[46]

The Peabody Fund was unusual among northern benevolent initiatives in that it provided funding focused on the development of public schools through local government and had no explicitly religious mission; more common were the many efforts to serve Black children directly, usually in schools under private or semipublic sponsorship. By 1869, there were almost eighty northern aid organizations supporting schooling for southern Blacks, most with a distinctly evangelical character, with the exception of the Quakers, who continued their long tradition of concern in this area. Initial support by Unitarian and secular organizations faded more quickly than did that associated with evangelical churches; it seems that the former, with their more optimistic view of human nature, assumed that abolition of slavery would enable the former slaves to immediately begin behaving like New Englanders, while the evangelicals had a more realistic view of how long it would take to learn new attitudes and habits. "The anticlericalism of Garrisonian abolitionists has obscured the importance of evangelical Protestantism in the antislavery movement. The revivals of the Second Great Awakening left in their wake an army of reformers on the march against sin, especially the sin of slavery.... Seven-eighths of the members of antislavery societies were members of Protestant churches at a time when fewer than one in four adult Americans belonged to any church."[47]

Selleck notes that "the preaching evangelicals...espoused the more radical program for Black reconstruction over the cautious Unitarians," while "reliance on education as being the only needed ingredient to full citizenship betrayed the blind spot of many Quakers. Friends did not always readily identify the other basic conditions necessary for complete African American liberation."[48]

The most important of the voluntary organizations with a religious character was the AMA, which had grown out of the Amistad Committee, created in 1839 to defend a group of slaves accused of piracy and murder. A group of northern Black clergymen established the Union Missionary Society in 1841 to continue this work, and five years later this was subsumed into the AMA under the leadership of businessman Lewis Tappan and other White evangelicals who had grown frustrated with the refusal of the American Board of Commissioners for Foreign Missions (ABCFM) to take an antislavery position for fear of alienating the slave-owning Cherokee among whom it worked. The AMA had worked among freed slaves in Jamaica and among the fugitive Blacks in Canada, and had made some effort in the South in the face of growing hostility toward northern do-gooders, especially after the John Brown raid at Harper's Ferry.[49]

The AMA was explicitly evangelical, with Congregationalist roots, though initially also involving the Wesleyan Methodists and the Free Will Baptists; "immediately after the war, at least twelve other denominations expressed support for the AMA," which made it easier for the Freedmen's Bureau to regard it as nonsectarian and thus an appropriate collaborator.[50] A number of secular or non-evangelical organizations affiliated into the American Freedmen's Union Commission (AFUC); Methodists, Presbyterians, and Northern Baptists formed their own organizations.

The AFUC was critical of the AMA for giving its schools a religious character, but in fact this seemed to give the AMA an advantage in gaining the confidence of Black parents. "As one teacher said, the surest way to Black 'affection and confidence' was 'through their religious feelings. In fact, they distrust no one so soon as he who *depreciates religion.*'" The AMA also had the advantage that its church connections ensured a more steady source of income, while the AFUC faded away with declining northern enthusiasm for educating freedmen, and it closed in 1869.[51] While its officers claimed that there was no longer a need for northern efforts for schooling of Blacks in the South, "honesty should have compelled [them] to admit that the organized churches had triumphed and that nearly all the would be done in the future by the North for Negro education would come through the American Missionary Association and other denominational groups."[52]

The AMA and other denominational groups were able to continue and even expand their work over the next half-century "because they were firmly rooted in the institutional structure of American Protestantism.

Northern churches took up collections for the freedmen just as they did for other missions, and they did so on the basis of a specific theological expectation (based on Colossians 3:11) that, as expressed by the AMA in 1872, 'the Christ-like mission of the teachers and ministers, instructing the emancipated slaves' was only preparation for the day when "the Pentecostal baptism [of the Holy Spirit] shall fall upon teachers, missionaries, and people...giving them a power...that shall break down all walls of caste prejudice, so that there shall be no Blacks and no Whites, no North and no South, but when all shall be one in Christ Jesus."[53]

Most of the hundreds of White women and men who went South to teach freed slaves "shared roots in the missionary culture of evangelical reform, and in its rhetoric conflating moral and social uplift." Their efforts were only the latest wave of decades of reform through voluntary efforts, whether addressing alcohol abuse or insanity or ignorance of the Gospel on the frontier and in foreign lands. Coming from a religious tradition that placed great stress on the distorting effects of human sinfulness and the possibility of redemption from those effects, "missionary philanthropists held that slavery had generated pathological religious and cultural practices in the Black community. Slavery, not race, kept Blacks from acquiring the moral and social values of thrift, industry, frugality, and sobriety, all of which were necessary to live a sustained Christian life. In turn, these missing morals and values prevented the development of a stable family life among Afro-Americans.... Without education, they concluded, Blacks would rapidly degenerate and become a national menace to American civilization."[54] Their optimism about what could be accomplished through voluntary action "was deemed by Black elites a significant advance over the view that Blacks were biologically inferior and unassimilable."[55] Northern teachers would bring about "the 'regeneration' of the South, transplanting there, as Frederick Douglass put it, 'the higher civilization of the North' ";[56] it was thus

> strongly motivated people who composed the active teams of the benevolent and religious groups of the North. They were by more orientation and training peculiarly prepared to shoulder the responsibility. They were in the main devout Christians. The spiritual aspirations that fed their missionary zeal also kept alive their antislavery belief that teaching the Negro to read and understand the Bible was absolutely essential to his religious and moral development. They...were probably some of the best prepared of the nation's small supply of common school teachers.... Tradition had set no sharp and unfavorable image of the Negro in their minds.[57]

These missionaries from the North were by no means welcomed by White Southerners, one of whom, even decades later, "could not suppress her indignation at the Yankee schoolmarms who 'overran the country' with their 'holier than thou' expressions and who, she said, were bent upon instructing native Whites in what they ought to be doing as much as upon 'teaching the negroes to struggle indecorously for the semblance of a non-existent equality.'" In *The Mind of the South* (1941), Cash expressed a retrospective southern White opinion of

> the Yankee schoolma'am who, in such numbers, moved down upon the unfortunate South in the train of the army of occupation, to "educate" the Black man for his new place in the sun and to furnish an example of Christian love and philanthropy to the benighted native whites. Generally horsefaced, bespectacled, and spare of frame, she was, of course, no proper intellectual, but at best a comic character, at worst a dangerous fool, playing with explosive forces which she did not understand. She had no little part in developing Southern [White] bitterness.[58]

A Virginia newspaper editor charged, in 1866, that the northern "schoolmarms" had done "incalculable mischief."[59]

This bitterness often took physical form. White teachers, even many born in the South, were warned by the Klan not to teach Blacks. "From every part of the South came the report that no white family dared provide board and room for a northern teacher.... The state superintendent in Texas said that few teachers had the hardihood to endure the insults, social ostracism, annoyances, and threats to which they were constantly subjected."[60] The remarkable fact is that many hundreds did so. John Alvord noted, in 1866, that the Freedman's Bureau educational work in Maryland "has had much opposition, such as stoning children and teachers at Easton, rough handling and blackening the teacher at Cambridge," a community that again became notorious for violence directed against the Freedom Movement in the 1960s. Alvord reported that "colored churches have been burned in Cecil, Queen Ann, and Somerset counties, to prevent schools being opened in them, all showing that [anti-]negro hate is not by any means confined to the low south."[61]

In contrast with the stereotype of a naive do-gooder, a study of the careers of these northern teachers reveals that some had worked for years—even for decades—in the education of Black pupils in the North, the West Indies, and even in Africa, and that many more had worked among immigrants, Indians on the frontier, or in schools in

New England or the Midwest, and went on to significant careers after their services to freedmen's education. Others were still working in Black schools in the South after thirty or even forty years. The AFUC required that its recruits have "high moral character, purity of heart and mind, self-control, firmness, command of temper, the soldier's spirit of obedience, without its uncomprehending slavishness, frank and honest deportment, self-respect, and dignified propriety of manner," while the AMA insisted that no teachers would be sent who were not "prepared to ensure hardness as a good soldier of Jesus Christ" or who sought "the poetry or the pay" of service among the freedmen. Men or women who had failed in their careers in the North should not seek new opportunities as teachers of Blacks in the South.[62] A sample application letter for a teaching position, in the AMA's widely circulated magazine in 1864, made clear that it was seeking young women who possessed "missionary spirit," "lack of romantic or mercenary motives," health, physical energy, "cultural and common sense," "benevolence, gravity, and earnestness," teaching experience, and an evangelical background.[63]

Though its schools were almost exclusively segregated because of the strong White opposition to integrated education, the AMA "'did quietly witness against caste in America.' ... Living among the people they taught, the missionaries and their families (at work, play, or worship) gave daily witness to their belief in the basic equality and essential human dignity of Blacks."[64] In a few cases, they found White families—generally from the poor who had no access to the private schools that served the White elite—willing to have their children attend school with Black children; the Freedman's Bureau reported 470 White and 78,000 Black pupils in its schools in thirteen states.[65]

A glimpse of the spirit of these northern teachers, and of the climate of suspicion in which they were forced to live and work, is found in an exchange in 1867 featuring Anna Gardner, a teacher from Nantucket Island working with Black pupils in Virginia. The editor of the Charlottesville newspaper wrote Miss Gardner that the impression existed among Whites that "your instruction of the colored people who attend your school contemplates something more than the communication of ordinary knowledge.... The idea prevails that you instruct them in politics and sociology, that you come among us not merely as an ordinary school teacher, but as a political missionary; that you communicate to the colored people ideas of social equality with the Whites... [thus] tending to disturb the good feeling between the races." She replied, "I teach in school and out, so far as my influence extends, the fundamental principles of 'politics' and 'sociology,' viz.: 'Whatsoever ye would that men should do to you, do ye even so unto them.' Yours on behalf of peace and justice."⁶⁶

Whatever was the reality of Miss Gardner's instruction, there were a number of schools for Blacks that made no apologies for introducing northern attitudes into the South. One of the outstanding private elementary and secondary schools for Blacks was the Lincoln Normal School in Marion, Alabama, closely associated with Oberlin College in Ohio and sponsored by the AMA.

> Academic as well as moral and social discipline in the school was exact. Northern text-books were used, principally supplied by mission agencies; the School teachers, all of them imports from the North, until a small corps of Negro teachers developed principally by the school, and usually assigned to the lower grades, began to make their appearance. The Northern textbooks, including "Union" songs and anti-slavery poems, and readings and declamations extolling the heroes of the anti-slavery movement, did not endear the institution to the local Whites, who accused the mission schools of teaching politics to the children, and "poisoning" their minds against their former masters.⁶⁷

Blacks were not necessarily prepared to accept the whole package of New England behaviors and attitudes that the northern teachers sought to develop in their pupils—"piety, self-control, industriousness, and individualism. Blacks, on the other hand, had created their own system of emotional support through the extended family and friends... [and they] seized upon emancipation as an opportunity to consolidate their customs and institutions and secure them from outside interference"⁶⁸— even from sympathetic White allies.

After all, "Black southerners entered emancipation with an alternative culture, a history they could draw upon, one that contained enduring beliefs in learning and self-improvement."⁶⁹ Bostonian Thomas Wentworth Higginson, who had served as commander of a Black regiment during the war, wrote that "we abolitionists had underrated the suffering produced by slavery among the negroes, but had overrated the demoralization. Or rather, we did not know how the religious temperament of the negroes had checked the demoralization."⁷⁰

As a result, there was a "continued increase of schools under the sole financial and operational care of Blacks, and of their churches. In a section of Georgia where Boston teachers had been welcomed in 1866, five teachers sent from New England in the fall of 1868 could not find a home among the Blacks, nor a school in which to teach"⁷¹ because of the existing self-help efforts. Such situations, however, were exceptional; the need for teachers was in fact far greater than the voluntary associations could hope to fill, and the AMA and other organizations successfully increased the proportion of their teachers who were Black, including both northerners and former slaves.[72]

In the 1870s, the AMA concluded that its revenues were insufficient to continue to provide common schools taught by Whites from the North and should instead be committed to secondary-level normal schools to prepare Black teachers. Black parents often opposed the transfer of the common schools to public authorities. "One AMA secretary wrote that his 'most painful experiences have been connected with such occasions.' He believed that 'the way the mission school operated' made the difference between AMA schools and the typical public schools which replaced them. The AMA began schools 'as an act of love' and continued them 'on the basis of the actual human oneness of the workers with their pupils and the parents. In the process, the latter came to believe that there were White people who would treat them as equals.'"[73]

The third force for the education of freed slaves, only slightly later in the field than the Black community itself and the northern evangelicals, was an agency of the federal government, the Freedmen's Bureau, officially, "The Bureau of Refugees, Freedmen, and Abandoned Lands," established by Congress in March 1865 after "more than three years of lobbying by abolitionists and others who believed the government had a responsibility to help the former slaves until they were able to take care of themselves."[74] Much of the bureau's work in education was carried out through the northern organizations, and it had no hesitation in providing practical assistance to the AMA and others with a religious character. Commissioner O. O. Howard responded frostily to an effort, by the AFUC, to suggest that the AMA should be disqualified because the education that it provided included religious elements.

> Howard testily denied that he was "disposed" to grant public funds for sectarian purposes and added that in his view "the so called liberal Christians," meaning the AFUC, were as sectarian as Episcopalians. "It does seem to me," he continued, "that some of our friends take too much pains to search out and worry themselves about the forces that separate the different lots, instead of... caring for the sheep in the lot."[75]

The bureau supported the efforts of the various voluntary associations through turning over to their use confiscated buildings, paying for the travel of their teachers from the North, providing salaries to some of their supervisory staff, and in a variety of other ways. Congress appropriated funds in 1866 to pay the salaries of superintendents of schooling of freedmen and for "repairs and rent of schoolhouses."[76] This support was even more crucial as the AMA shifted its concern to secondary and higher education, in order to train Black teachers for the public elementary schools that were beginning to be established. "Almost every association college, normal, and secondary school was partially built with Bureau funds."[77]

By 1870, when the Freedmen's Bureau wound up its work, it was helping to sponsor 4,239 schools, employing 9,300 teachers to teach more than 247,000 pupils. While expressing satisfaction that "the whole race is recovering from the effects of slavery; in all industrial pursuits, in moral status, and intellectual development even the adult population is rapidly 'marching on,'" the bureau's final report noted that "the masses of the people are, after all, still ignorant. Nearly a million and a half of their children have never as yet been under any instruction." Thus, fewer than one in ten of the children of the formerly enslaved had enjoyed any schooling at all, despite the unprecedented flood of volunteer northern teachers. What was worse, the prospects were not encouraging in the absence of continuing federal support. "With sorrow we anticipate... the closing of hundreds of our school buildings, sending thousands of children who beg for continued instruction to the streets, or what is far worse to squalid, degraded homes to grow up not as props and pillars of society, but its pests."[78]

The effect of the termination of the Freedmen's Bureau was felt immediately by the voluntary associations as well; in 1870 the AMA had 461 teachers serving in the South, but the following year the number dropped to 309.[79] Northern support had been falling off as well:

> as early as 1867 most societies dependent on private contributions were already feeling the effects of waning interest in Northern-based reform efforts. The April 1867 of the *American Freedman* observed that "the enthusiasm which accompanies a new movement, one especially which appealed so strongly to philanthropic and humane considerations as did this during the desolations of war, has somewhat passed away and left as its supporters only those who are attached to it by cardinal and well-considered principles."[80]

Efforts were made to replace these temporary and voluntary supports for schooling in the South with a more systematic approach. A Massachusetts congressman introduced, in 1870, a bill "to compel by national authority the establishment of a thorough and efficient system of public instruction throughout the whole country." The purpose of this measure, he stressed, "is not to supersede, but to stimulate, compel, and supplement action by the States," but the proposal met strong opposition in the North as well as the South. Pennsylvania's superintendent of schools, James P. Wickersham, attacked the idea at the National Education Association convention, insisting that Republican principles required keeping the oversight of schooling in local hands.[81]

Equally in vain, a Virginia congressman, in 1876, called for a program of federal aid to education targeted upon the southern states where, despite "efforts to clothe the freedmen with rights he could not understand and load him responsibilities which he was unable to comprehend," there had been no provision "for his education and elevation even to a partial comprehension of the duties and responsibilities which these rights impose." As a result, "although the negro was emancipated from physical slavery, he was left bound in the more terrible chains of universal ignorance" and lacked any "knowledge of the high duties and responsibilities which that citizenship imposes." While it was not his intention to recommend "a governmental system of education except by the States," he urged that funding for schools be provided through sale of public lands in the West.[82]

Whether provided by Black community and church initiatives, northern missionary societies, or the federal government's Freedman's Bureau, there is extensive evidence that the Black population welcomed schooling—and to a greater degree than did working-class Whites.[83] Black communities often bought the land and built the schoolhouses, sometimes with outside financial assistance from the Freedmen's Bureau and, later, from northern philanthropies, "then held benefits to sustain the school, augment the extremely low state salary of the teacher, or extend the school term beyond the two to three months provided many county schools by the state."[84] One northern observer reported, in 1866, that

> There is, I think, a more earnest desire to learn, and a more general opinion that it is a great favor to have the opportunity. There is less destruction of books, less whittling of school furniture, less disposition to set up petty revolts against the teacher's authority. The progress in learning to read is exceptionally rapid. I do not believe that in the best schools at the North they learn the alphabet and First Reader quicker than do the average of these slave children. The negroes are not quicker-witted, but they are more anxious to learn.[85]

Reports from the first group of northern teachers working among the newly freed Blacks off the Georgia coast noted that their pupils did very well in the first stages of schooling, with its strong stress upon rote learning, perhaps because of "a long heritage of oral communication of folk customs, songs, and stories," but "predicted trouble in the more advanced levels of study, where reason and application were more directly involved." They were, however, "optimistic about the ultimate achievements to be made by Negroes. The institution of slavery had retarded the development of the colored people, and it was now the responsibility of Christianity to assist them to further progress. At this early stage these thoughtful people were relatively free of contemporary notions about *inherent* superiority and inferiority of races."[86] A decade later, a northern teacher in Memphis wrote that "eight years of culture has made its impress upon the people here so plainly that one can read at a glance the change in the countenances of those who have been under the influence of the mission work."[87]

Booker T. Washington, in his autobiographical *Up from Slavery*, described his early schooling in rural West Virginia.

> In the midst of the discussion about a teacher, another young coloured man from Ohio, who had been a soldier, found his way into town. It was soon learned that he possessed considerable education, and he was engaged by the coloured people to teach their first school. As yet no free schools had been started for coloured people in that section, hence each family agreed to pay a certain amount per month.... This experience of a whole race beginning to go to school for the first time presents one of the most interesting studies that has ever occurred in connection with the development of any race. Few people who were not right in the midst of the scenes can form any exact idea of the intense desire which the people of my race showed for an education...it was a whole race trying to go to school. Few were too young, and none too old, to make the attempt to learn.... The great ambition of the older people was to try to learn to read the Bible before they died.[88]

Black historian Carter Woodson gave, in 1922, more details of this school attended by Washington, and it will serve as an example of the almost haphazard way in which schooling developed in thousands of communities across the South:

> the people of Malden, under the wise guidance of Lewis Rice, a beloved pioneer minister, better known among the early Negroes of the State as Father Rice because of his persistent efforts in behalf of religion and

education, had decided to establish a school for the education of their children. Mr. William Davis thereupon abandoned his work on the boat and became the teacher of this private school, established at Malden in the home of Father Rice, in 1865. As the school had to be conducted in the very bed-room of this philanthropist, it was necessary for him to take down his bed in the morning and bring in the benches, which would be replaced in the evening by the bed in its turn. The school was next held in the same church thereafter constructed, and finally in the schoolroom provided at public expense, as one of the schools of the county.[89]

This enthusiasm about learning was observed in southern cities as well; "in 1867 there is evidence that all of the classes in Savannah that were opened to educate the former slaves were filled to capacity despite the absence of a correlation between literacy and employment—given the devastated conditions of the southern economy after the Civil War."[90]

Although the mass enthusiasm among freedmen for schooling seems to have faded somewhat as it became evident that it would have little payoff in improved opportunities for most, it left at least one lasting imprint in state legislation that (though implemented in a way that discriminated against Blacks) put the South on the way to creating systems of public schooling. Reconstruction state legislatures established state boards of education, provided (however inadequately) for schools for Black and White children, though in almost all cases these were separate even before the period of reaction at the end of Reconstruction, established statewide property and poll taxes to support schools, and promoted the training of teachers through teacher institutes and normal schools, those also segregated.[91]

"There is no doubt," Du Bois wrote in 1910, "but that the thirst of the Black man for knowledge—a thirst which has been too persistent and durable to be a mere curiosity or whim—gave birth to the public free school system of the South. It was the question upon which Black voters and legislators insisted more than anything else."[92] Or again, in 1941, "the public school system of the whole South is the gift of Black folk."[93]

Among the delegates to the South Carolina Constitutional Convention of 1868 there were thirteen Black teachers, who included nearly half of the members of the committee on education, which "developed and pushed through an educational plan stipulating that:

1. It would be the duty of the legislature, once public schools had been 'thoroughly' organized, to provide for the compulsory

attendance in public or private schools of children between six and sixteen for at least twenty-four months.
2. All public schools, colleges, and universities supported wholly or in part by public funds 'shall be free and open to all children of this state, without regard to race or color.' "[94]

It should be noted that at this point most states in the North did not have compulsory school attendance. While not implemented effectively, this insistence upon universal schooling had the effect that, while "in 1870 there were 30,448 children in South Carolina's 769 schools[,] six years later there were 123,035 students attending 2,776 schools. Similar increases were to be found in other states and included Negro as well as White students."[95] In the decades after emancipation, "far from indicating apathy toward education, enrollment [of Black children] mounted rapidly: 91,000 in 1866; 150,000 in 1870; 572,000 in 1877; 785,000 in 1880; and slightly more than a million by 1884.... In some instances, Black enrollment rates were actually higher than for Whites in the same area."[96]

The Freedmen's Bureau's final report pointed out, however, that southern state and local governments were not prepared to pick up where the bureau's efforts were leaving off. "No one of them is fully prepared with funds, buildings, teachers, and actual organizations to sustain these schools."[97] Unfortunately, this was true. Schooling for Blacks was by no means welcomed by the White majority; thirty-seven schools were burned down in Tennessee in 1869 alone.[98] In Mississippi, in 1871, it was officially reported that thirty buildings used as schools had been destroyed by mobs or burned by arsonists, and that "there was fierce opposition to paying taxes for schools that would demoralize the Negro."[99] The editor of the *Charleston Daily Courier* insisted, in 1865, that " 'the sole aim should be to educate every White child in the Commonwealth.' A member of the Louisiana legislature said he was 'not in favor of positively imposing upon any legislature the unqualified and imperative duty of educating any but the superior race of man—the White race.' "[100] As the initial efforts by northern voluntary associations and by the national government flagged, it became evident that nothing like universal schooling would be achieved. "In 1880, 70 percent of the Black population [of the South] remained illiterate."[101]

During the short period of "Radical Reconstruction," "Republicans had established, for the first time in southern history, the principle of state responsibility for public education," but "schooling was a major casualty of Democratic rule." During the last decades of the nineteenth century, "some states all but dismantled the education systems established during Reconstruction. Texas began charging fees in its schools... Louisiana spent so little on education that it became the only state in the Union in which the percentage of native Whites unable to read or write actually rose between 1880 and 1900,"[102] while "between 1880 and 1900, the number of Black children of school age increased 25 percent, but the proportion attending public school fell."[103]

White elites in the South insisted that they would substitute paternalistic benevolence toward Blacks for the vote and other rights that—so they argued—had been misused. Unfortunately, "despite the fact that several hundred thousand freedmen were taught in the freedmen's schools, private and public alike, and though dozens of colleges were founded (some eighty by 1895), the hostility of White Southerners toward the civilizing mission never eased."[104] A prominent Alabama minister had been quoted, in 1866, as arguing that "if we do not mean to suffer the distinction of races to be destroyed, and permit equality in every respect, we must keep these [northern teachers] from among us. We can keep them out only by ourselves giving these people the instruction they need,"[105] and this attitude persisted until well into the twentieth century. Education of the right sort (the industrial training provided by Hampton and Tuskegee) would fit Blacks for a subordinate but secure place in society. Liberal arts education of the sort that had been supported by northern missionary efforts would simply encourage Blacks to think themselves superior to their fated station in life. This paternalistic model, however, implied continued economic and political dominance by elites that were already being challenged by poorer Whites.

While the northern societies and the southern Black churches focused initially upon primary schooling to teach basic literacy, they insisted that this task should be carried out through a universal system of public schools. Their priority shifted, after several years, to creating colleges that would develop leaders for the Black community. "Although the AMA advocated equality, most of its officers believed that Blacks were 'an absolutely undeveloped race with a long heredity of ignorance, superstition and degradation' that would require generations to erase. Their 'civilizing mission' demanded permanent institutions where exceptional Black youth could be educated to uplift their brethren.... Their elementary work was to be pursued only until it could be turned over to the states.... Black colleges, on the other hand, were to be permanent."[106] Wilberforce University in Ohio had already been founded in 1856 by the African Methodist Episcopal Church through the initiative of

Bishop Daniel Payne, the former teacher from Charleston, but the great flourishing of these institutions was in response to the need described by Du Bois:

> no adequate common schools could be founded until there were teachers to teach them. Southern Whites would not teach them; northern Whites in sufficient numbers could not be had. If the Negro was to learn, he must teach himself, and the most effective help that could be given him was the establishment of schools to train Negro teachers. This conclusion was slowly but surely reached by every student of the situation until simultaneously, in widely separated regions, without consultation or systematic plan, there arose a series of institutions designed to furnish teachers for the untaught. Above the sneers of critics at the obvious defects of this procedure must ever stand its one crushing rejoinder: in a single generation they put thirty thousand Black teachers in the South; they wiped out the illiteracy of the majority of the Black people of the land, and they made Tuskegee possible.[107]

The Freedmen's Bureau and northern missionary societies collaborated with Black churches in establishing a number of Black colleges, including Fisk in 1866 and Atlanta, Morehouse, and Howard in 1867. By 1871 there were eleven colleges and sixty-one normal schools serving Black students.[108] Launching colleges was by no means an unusual activity for denominational groups; "of the 207 American colleges existing in 1860, 180 had been established by churches."[109] Although these new Black colleges sought to prepare men and women for a variety of roles, a high proportion found the only opportunities not involving manual labor to be in the ministry or in teaching: "approximately 84 percent of the 723 graduates from Hampton's first twenty classes became teachers."[110] As a result of these efforts, "by 1869, among the approximately 3,000 freedmen's teachers in the South, Blacks for the first time outnumbered Whites...the number of Black educators in South Carolina rose from fifty in 1869 to over 1,000 six years later."[111]

The story of each of these institutions is one of constant struggle, and some failed to survive. Even prior to the cessation of Freedmen's Bureau assistance in 1870, northern philanthropy had declined precipitately. A few years later the panic of 1873 curtailed the income and operations of the schools even further. Meanwhile, beginning in the late 1860s, the violence, including murder and arson, perpetuated by southern Whites against the northern schoolteachers and their institutions, forced a number to close their doors. Moreover, fewer Whites felt a commitment to work among the freedmen.... In the 1880s and 1890s the millionaire philanthropists began to turn their attention to Black schools, but even then the assistance was directed more toward providing industrial training than college graduates.[112]

It is true, as Du Bois pointed out in 1903, that "the Negro colleges, hurriedly founded, were inadequately equipped, illogically distributed, and of varying efficiency and grade; the normal and high schools were doing little more than common-school work, and the common schools were training but a third of the children who ought to be in them, and training these too often poorly."[113] Twenty years later, a study of the 52 "major" Black colleges found that, of more than a thousand men preparing for the ministry, only 34 had graduated from a college program, and 214 from high school; they "graduated in two or three years even though most had entered the theological course after a mere fifth- or sixth-grade education."[114] Despite these evident weaknesses, the largely spontaneous effort by tens of thousands of former slaves and Black men and women who had already been free before the war, and by thousands of self-sacrificing northern women and men, represents one of the great epics in the history of education. Private initiatives by Black churches and individuals and by their northern allies, only very imperfectly supplemented by government, made it possible for a Black middle class to begin to develop. Until the First World War "virtually all the Black college students in the southern states were enrolled in privately owned colleges."[115]

It should be noted that it was similarly common in the years after the Civil War for colleges serving White students in the North to enroll a high proportion of them in preparatory divisions because of the inadequacies of secondary education; one study found that "in Illinois's private colleges and seminaries 2,441 students pursued a full course of study and 1,618 a partial course, and 3,299 pupils attended the preparatory departments... for every five legitimate college students on Illinois campuses there were four pupils who might have been better served in a public high school."[116] In the South, Black colleges, mostly church-sponsored, proliferated "recklessly,"[117] far beyond the supply of Black high schools that could prepare for college work, with the inevitable result that much of their instruction was in fact at the secondary level or even below.

Of the nondenominational private schools and colleges serving Black students in the South, most stressed "industrial" training, but those established and supported by the White and Black churches sought to provide a liberal education. In Alabama, the only Black institution providing a traditional collegiate curriculum was Talladega, associated with the AMA), which developed this instructional program carefully over more than ten years to ensure that the first graduates, in 1895, had received an education equivalent in expectations to those in northern colleges. Talladega thus exemplified the alternative to the "industrial" education provided to Alabama Blacks at Tuskegee. "The AMA schools, therefore, offered Alabama's Blacks the fullest opportunity to develop the intellectual, elite leaders denied Blacks by the public school system." Similarly, the Freedmen's Aid Society, established by the Methodist Church (North) "decided to organize its schools like New England schools, following the classical, liberal arts curriculum." A leading Black denomination, the African Methodist Episcopal Church, founded Payne Institute in Selma, Alabama in 1889; it "offered College, Normal, and Academic courses of study. There is no evidence that the school ever offered industrial training."[118]

While most of the practical work of educating the freedmen was carried out by northern teachers and—increasingly—by a new generation of Black teachers and other leaders, Congress debated how to ensure that the interests of southern Blacks would be protected after the restoration of political control to southern state governments. As a Republican senator from Michigan put it in the debates over the Fourteenth Amendment in 1866, "the colored race are destined to remain among us...the destiny of the colored race in this country is wrapped up with our own." For the southern states, in particular, it was important that the freed slaves be educated and admitted to share in the processes of government; "they should not retain in their midst a race of pariahs, so circumstanced as to be obliged to bear the burdens of Government and to obey its laws without any participation in the enactment of the laws." Other northerners disagreed, however. A Democratic senator from Indiana asked whether "the inhabitants of the United States who were descended from the great races of peoples who inhabit the countries of Europe" would be content to "carry the title and enjoy [the] advantages" of citizenship "in common with the negroes, the coolies, and the Indians." "I will support," he promised, "all measures necessary and proper for the protection and elevation of the colored race; measures safe and just to both races; but I do not believe that it is for the good of either race that they should be brought into close social and political relations."[119]

Meanwhile, in June 1866, the Joint Committee on Reconstruction of the Congress reported that

> the Freedmen's Bureau...is almost universally opposed by the mass of the [White] population, and exists in an efficient condition only under

military protection...without the protection of United States troops, [pro-]Union men, whether of northern or southern origin, would be obliged to abandon their homes. The feeling in many portions of the country towards emancipated slaves...is one of vindictive and malicious hatred. This deep-seated prejudice against color is assiduously cultivated by the public journals, and leads to acts of cruelty, oppression, and murder, which the local authorities are at no pains to prevent or punish. There is no general disposition to place the colored race, constituting at least two-fifths of the population, upon terms even of civil equality.[120]

Eventually, and with the final withdrawal of federal troops fast approaching, Congress debated what was "the most important of the post–Civil War statutes designed to ensure equal rights for the Negro," the Civil Rights Act of 1875; there would not be another significant law with this goal until the 1960s. The Act was adopted as a last gasp of Republican dominance of Congress; more than half of the Republican members of the House had been defeated in 1874, in part as a reaction against the perception that they were intent upon promoting social equality for Blacks through school integration, and thus ninety of the one hundred and sixty Republicans who voted for it were about to leave office. In fact, the effect of the legislation would be largely symbolic, and its reach was decisively limited by the Supreme Court in 1883. Nevertheless, the debate that accompanied its passage is highly instructive.

One of the most controversial aspects of the proposed legislation was its prohibition of discrimination in public education. Senator Frelinghuysen, Republican of New Jersey (and nephew of the senator of the same name who had opposed the "removal" of the Indians from the Southeast), in introducing the bill, stated that it expressed a single idea: "the equality of races before the law," a phrase upon which Charles Sumner had built his argument for school integration in the *Roberts* case in Boston. "The language of this bill," Frelinghuysen went on, "secures full and equal privileges in the schools...the bill does not permit the exclusion of one from a public school on account of his nationality alone." On the other hand, he was careful to point out, "when in a school district there are two schools, and the White children choose to go to one and the colored to the other, there is nothing in this bill that prevents their doing so"; in fact, he suggested, "this voluntary division into separate schools would often be the solution of difficulty." In other words, what we have come to call de facto segregation would not be forbidden, but de jure segregation by official action would not be allowed. After all, "we know that if we establish separate schools for colored people, those schools will be inferior to those for the Whites."[121]

There is considerable evidence, in fact, that southern Blacks were not especially concerned to have their children attend schools with White children, but that they were opposed to a legal requirement that schools be segregated. "In 1867–1868, Black delegates in the Southern state constitutional conventions succeeded in preventing such provisions from being adopted." Their primary concern was that schools enrolling Black children receive a fair share of public funding; "this could only be ensured in a public-education system in which schools were open to all, irrespective of race. South Carolina wrote such a provision into its new state constitution, while in practice this system came to be operated on a segregated basis." On the other hand, the "hostility of Blacks to constitutionally mandated segregated schools was interpreted by most Southern Whites as revealing a Black desire to associate with Whites in 'mixed schools.' This was feared as a first step toward racial amalgamation"[122] through intermarriage.

The one southern state in which a measure of school integration existed for a time was Louisiana, whose Reconstruction-era Constitution provided that "all children of this state . . . shall be admitted to the public schools or other institutions of learning sustained or established by the State in common, without distinction of race, color, or previous condition. There shall be no separate schools or institutions of learning established for any race by the State of Louisiana."[123]

In a debate at the South Carolina constitutional convention, Black delegates argued that integrated schools were important to teach about the new order in the South; a White delegate warned, however, that integration would simply prevent White children from attending school and they would "continue ignorant and degraded and prejudiced."[124] Barnas Sears of the Peabody Fund fully agreed with this argument and went to Washington to lobby against the provision in the draft Civil Rights Act providing for integrated schools. In a widely noted *Atlantic Monthly* article, Sears claimed that his extensive travels on behalf of schooling in the South had convinced him that about one-third of the (White) public was opposed to public schools, one-third favorable, and one-third undecided. "If racially mixed schools were to be forced, he was certain that it would swing the balance away from public education and the region would revert to its traditional private school system. . . . To those whose principal concern was the welfare of the Negro, Sears argued that to require mixed schools would only harm [them]. Adequate education for Negroes required state supported systems of education. If zeal for the freedman's needs caused the South to revert to private schools, it would be the Negro and the poor white that would suffer."[125]

Opponents of the provision for school integration in the Civil Rights Act warned that it could lead to the destruction of public education altogether. "The result," a Democratic senator from Ohio warned, "will be that schools will not be established; the taxes will not be paid; the laws for the common-school system will be repealed or rendered nugatory; and the consequence will be that both the negro children and the poor White children too will go without education." The warning was echoed by a Democratic senator from New Jersey, who predicted that the bill would "break up the whole common-school system in this country; it will leave uneducated the colored people.... It will leave them no free schools." In addition, "the poor German and Irishman... is to be deprived of his liberties and privileges... and he is to see his children turned out of the school-houses because he does not wish them to associate with the colored people."[126]

A Connecticut-born Republican senator from Mississippi—previously superintendent of education of Louisiana while that state was under military rule, superintendent of education of freedmen in Mississippi in 1867, and elected superintendent of education of that state in 1869—retorted that "equal advantages in separate schools" were not sufficient. "Whenever a State shall legislate that the races shall be separated,... it is a distinction the intent of which is to foster a concomitant of slavery and to degrade [former slaves].... There is no equality in that." His fellow-Republican from Mississippi, Congressman John Lynch (a slave until age 17), insisted that "it is not social rights that we desire.... What we ask is protection in the enjoyment of public rights." In communities where there were substantial numbers of each race, he predicted, "separate institutions of learning will continue to exist, for a number of years at least." The important consideration, for Blacks, was that "the separation is their own voluntary act and not legislative compulsion." A harder line was taken by another Black Republican, Joseph Rainey of South Carolina, who warned that

> the time is at hand when you must cease to take us for cringing slaves.... We do not intend to be driven to the frontier as you have driven the Indian. Our purpose is to remain in your midst as integral part of the body-politic. We are training our children to take our places when we are gone. We desire this bill that we may train them intelligently and respectably, that they may thus be qualified to be useful citizens in their day and time.[127]

Supporters of racially mixed schools argued that they would "end the midnight targeting of Black schools by arsonists. If schoolhouses continued to burn after integration, White children would suffer equally with Blacks. Classroom competition with Whites... would also stimulate African-American ambition and self-respect and 'add dignity to their character.'"[128]

But the real intention behind the provision for school integration, a Democratic senator from Delaware insisted, was "to enforce association and companionship between the races in this country." It was a terrible mistake, he charged, "to bring forward a proposition so revolting to the sense and so injurious to the interests of the American people." And he reiterated the prediction that "the public judgment of the people of the States will compel their Legislatures to abolish the school system" altogether; indeed, he warned his fellow-senators, "sooner than see mixed schools in the State of Delaware, I would be glad to see the Legislature destroy the common-school system in the State."[129] After all, most northern states allowed local school authorities to provide segregated schools—or no schools at all—for Black pupils, and the proposed law would forbid such arrangements. Such warnings were sufficiently convincing that, although the school provision was adopted by the Senate, in large part as a tribute to the dying exhortation of Senator Charles Sumner of Massachusetts, it was eliminated by the House and did not appear in the final version of the 1875 Civil Rights Act.

It has been suggested that Sumner's insistence on school integration had a decisive effect on the failure of Reconstruction and "inaugurated the long period of reaction that followed," alienating much of northern public opinion as well as galvanizing White southern opposition. Sumner's Black allies complained that "our tender children... are taught by separate schools that they are not as good as other children. White children are taught by White schools that colored children are inferior, and are to be despised. Such are the debasing results of the separate school system." White popular opinion was not ready to heed such concerns, though, nor would it be for a hundred years; more characteristic was the warning of a Memphis newspaper about "lovely children with pure Caucasian blood throbbing through their pure White veins" being forced to associate in school "with dirty, lousy pickaninnies," and the warning of a Missouri Democratic senator that school integration would lead to "'moral debauch' and 'saturnalian revel' and 'pander to all the baser passions of our nature,'" since Blacks had "coarse animal natures."

In the congressional elections of 1874, "White Northerners identified with the 'moral' outrage of Southerners over forcing racial intimacy in the public schools. Before 1874, White racism often appeared as the dying ideology of slavery. During and after 1874, it was recast as the bulwark of civilization itself."[130] For the resurgent Democratic Party, the issue of racially mixed schools provided a splendid opportunity to present itself as the instrument of White solidarity against the threat of degradation through association with Blacks. The Republican Party received a rude shock, losing heavily in the North as well as in the South; it was in an effort to regain the political initiative that it made anti-Catholicism rather than racial justice its primary focus for the next election cycles.[131]

Even famous author Harriet Beecher Stowe, providing a little school on her Florida property, explained that it had to be segregated by a partition down the middle of the room, since the White parents "would greatly prefer that [their children] should grow up without any education at all" than that they be with Blacks.[132]

In the case of Louisiana, where the state constitution's prohibition of segregated schools was reinforced by a school law providing fines and even jail for any public-school teacher who excluded children entitled to attend the school, it is estimated that about a third of the pupils in New Orleans were in integrated schools between 1868 and 1877. There was "sustained and bitter opposition" to integrated schooling; however, and in 1874 White men "stormed an interracial girls high school and removed all girls who were identifiably black."[133] Integration was also undermined by the Peabody Fund, which abandoned its usual policy of supporting only public schools in order to fund a system of private schools for White pupils.[134]

Although the educational efforts of Reconstruction seem deeply disappointing, it did lay the basis for the gradual development of tax-funded schooling for both White and Black children who, before the Civil War, would have had no such provision. Strange as it may now seem, until recent decades it was common to deny any such positive outcomes of Reconstruction, described by respectable historians as an almost unmitigated disaster "established by the bayonet policies of the North." Woodrow Wilson referred in 1880 to "the damnable cruelty and folly of reconstruction." Thus we are told, in a book first published in 1937 and highly commended by Arthur Schlesinger, Sr., that "the leading authority on education in the South, is unwilling to admit that the section owed much to the carpetbag governments. He...saw in the efforts to force Northern conceptions upon the South without sufficient allowance for local differences an influence which alienated Southern opinion on schools in general."[135]

It is worth recalling at some length, in this context, the words of Black social scientist and historian Horace Mann Bond about the same time, while Reconstruction was still generally denounced in the North as well as in the South. The premise of Reconstruction, Bond wrote, was that

> the Negro was a man and a brother; to be uplifted by educational missionaries, saved from sin by religious efforts, brought to economic equality by the twin agents of an "education" and political measures. The first efforts, in the South, to educate Negroes were carried on largely by missionary teachers from New England, equalitarians all, disciples of Calvin on the one hand and Horace Mann on the other. To a strict insistence on the severest standards of a puritanical moral code they added the faith in the common man implicit in the New England common-school revival. It was all to be very simple: spelling books, temperance lectures, the ballot; and the brother in black would emerge, no longer a chattel or a serf, but a man, a brother, a citizen. To give all credit to the host of New England schoolmarms..., the great majority of them soon realized the terrific nature of the uplift in which they were engaged, but stuck doggedly to their simple rules, in the midst of tremendous discouragements, for the rest of their active lives. To their credit be it said also that they did perform miracles. In each place, they touched both the children of disorganized ex-slaves and of free people of color, and under this almost magic touch of the schoolmarm..., there did emerge from chattels and serfs men and women. Viewed in perspective, the failure of these missionary teachers to achieve the goals set was due to three difficulties. In the first place, they were spread too thinly through the South. Of a population of almost two million educables of school age at the end of the Civil War, not to mention the equally numerous illiterate adults, the mission schools could touch but a few thousand. In the second place, the decline of war hysteria and of humanitarianism in the North meant that replacements and support were scanty. And, finally, they ran head on in the postreconstruction South into a nationwide revival of racial dogma that was to persist for a generation, unequaled anywhere else in the world until the resurgence of race hatred in Nazi, Jew-hating Germany.... Whatever the reason, the schoolmarm fought in a lost cause: lost for bitter antagonism toward the uplift of the Negro, lost for desperate financial destitution that made impossible the provision of adequate funds for the education even of white children. And yet, as suggested above, the cause was not entirely lost; for in the little academies and grammar schools, where interrupted promise lent

mockery to the pretentious names of "college" and "university," men and women were being educated to do, in their generation, what the missionaries had been unable to do—staff little schools for little children through the length and breadth of the land.

And Bond concluded with an exhortation to take the mission up again:

> To teach children to read, when their parents are illiterate, and the culture too destitute to provide material for them to read. To teach children to be clean, when the housing afforded by the economic system, the type of labor engaged in, the pitiful clothing they have money to buy make cleanliness, neatness, order a task for Hercules. To teach children to have self-respect, when the structure, we are told, negates self-respect, because it negates racial respect. To teach children respect for life, when the high homicide rate of their parents, we are told, derives from the pattern of violence woven by the superior caste to keep the lower caste subordinated. Yes—each is to be done. The schoolmarms did it, and so must we.[136]

CHAPTER 4

Jim Crow South

The period after the end of Reconstruction (conventionally dated from the political compromise of 1877, though in fact it occurred over a number of years) is often called that of "Jim Crow," after a nineteenth-century black-face vaudeville character: it is marked by the systematic exclusion of Blacks from the political and much of the economic gains that they had made in the previous decade. For our purposes, it includes most notably the formal exclusion of Black children, by law and public policy, from the schools attended by White children. Of course, they had already been excluded from those schools by common practice, but legally imposed segregation had a different moral significance. As the Supreme Court, in *Brown v. Board of Education* (1954), would point out in quoting approvingly the finding of a lower court in the same case, "Segregation of white and colored children in public schools has a detrimental effect upon the colored children. The impact is greater when it has the sanction of the law; for the policy of separating the races is usually interpreted as denoting the inferiority of the negro group." This chapter and the next are concerned with how the matter-of-fact separate schooling of Black pupils that had developed became translated into official policies that they should and must be schooled apart.

Although much of this discussion will focus on the limitations of the schooling provided to Blacks, it is well to remember that—often more as a result of the efforts of Black adults and White philanthropists than because of government support—the literacy rate among Black adults in the United States increased from about 7 percent at emancipation in 1863 to an estimated 20 percent in 1870, 44 percent in 1890, 56 percent in 1900, 70 percent in 1910, 84 percent in 1930, and 90 percent in 1950. Mere literacy, of course, is not an indication of an adequate education, but we can see that real progress was being made. Surely the success of the "Second Reconstruction" in the 1950s and 1960s, North as well as South, owed not a little to the rising education level among Blacks, despite all the degrading circumstances associated with their schooling, over several generations.

It was a long and painful way from the 1870s, when "it was clear that despite losing the war, the South had won the peace,"[1] to the 1950s. Already in 1874, celebrating the strong showing of the Democrats in the national congressional election, the governor of Georgia announced that Congress would no longer be able to interfere with how the South treated its Black population, saying "we intend to control the poor creatures ourselves."[2] The South, as a sympathetic historian pointed out, "maintained that the problem was a domestic one in which it alone should participate.... The South believed that its social stability required a discipline over the inferior race."[3]

Under slavery, segregation would have been inconvenient to Whites, both to the large plantation owners who relied on Black servants and to the small farmers with two or three slaves with whom they often lived on terms of some intimacy. It would also have worked against the close control of Blacks upon which the system depended. Physical separation of the races did not reach full development in the South until the early twentieth century, and it came in a sense as an import from the North where it had long been established. On the other hand, and significantly, strict segregation of schooling was a feature of the southern states (apart from New Orleans, for a time) even during decades when it had not yet been imposed upon public transportation and other institutions. This, surely, reflects the tremendous symbolic significance of schooling. Just as powerful and enduring as what I have called "the myth of the common school"[4] for White pupils is the antithetical "myth" that Black pupils should be kept separate.

Determined to keep Blacks subordinated—or to return them to that condition—southern state legislatures passed laws undermining gains under Reconstruction, and the number of annual recorded lynchings of Blacks rose to 160 by 1892. When South Carolina held a Constitutional Convention in 1895, the presiding officer told the delegates that the state's constitution of 1868 "was made by aliens [i.e., citizens from other American states], negroes and natives without character, all the enemies of South Carolina, and was designed to degrade our State, insult our people and overturn our civilization."[5]

The last decades of the nineteenth century and the first of the twentieth were a period when Blacks in the South were systematically deprived of every measure of political rights and personal dignity that they had acquired under Reconstruction and subjected to increasingly rigid segregation in every aspect of social and economic life, while some quietly continued to make progress through the limited opportunities available to them within the Black community. Schooling for Blacks was a particular target for those who agreed, as future Mississippi governor James K. Vardaman said in 1896, campaigning for a reduction in the state funds thus "wasted," that schooling was a "positive unkindness" to Blacks, since it made them "unfit for the work which the white man has prescribed, and which he will be forced to perform." Vardaman objected, also, to the support coming from northern philanthropies, which he described as "not money but dynamite," since "this education is ruining our Negroes. They're demanding equality."[6]

Until the 1950s, this period of "rectification" of race relations was looked upon favorably by much enlightened opinion in the North as well as the South, confident that it had represented an appropriate and lasting arrangement given the relative capacity of Black and White individuals. As a well-regarded study of the period, originally published in 1937, asserted confidently, the "discipline" of second-class status for Blacks and of the color bar necessary to an "orderly society"

> possessed advantages which far outweighed its evils. The South lived no longer in the fear of "Negro domination." The centrifugal force engendered by the doctrinaire theories of Reconstruction was definitely blocked. The new order gave a sense of security, a feeling of permanence and stability, upon which the basis of a better understanding between the races could be soundly erected. The clearly expressed superiority of the white race carried with it implications of responsibility. Throughout the South forward-looking men began advocating improved opportunities and improved training for the Negro. Best of all, the discipline prevented the Negro from slipping into semi-barbarism, gave him a job and a permanent place in Southern life, and permitted a slow but definite progress for the race as a whole.[7]

From this upbeat perspective, "segregation did not proceed from or necessarily imply race antagonism. It was in harmony with a basic Southern assumption that 'there is an instinct, ineradicable and positive, that will keep the races apart.'"[8] Certainly it was based, as well, on a determination to keep Black men and women "in their place," and that place at the bottom of the social and economic system. This required undoing many of the accomplishments achieved with great hope and great sacrifices during Reconstruction. Not that all the progress that had been made was reversed:

> A false impression exists that the missionary educators began to "melt away" as Reconstruction collapsed. If this were true, one might wonder how the 39 missionary colleges and secondary schools founded before 1880 had multiplied threefold by 1915, how the number of institutions offering college-level courses had grown from 9 in 1880 to 27 by 1915, or how the combined budgets of the four major freedmen's education societies had gone from $315,000 in 1878 to $1,360,000 forty years later, with the latter figure not including a half-dozen important schools that had become independent of the societies' support in the interval.[9]

On the other hand, the shift of emphasis, on the part of these northern societies, to secondary and higher education left the elementary schools that served the vast majority of those Blacks able to attend school at all at the mercy of southern Whites who were determined to put Blacks back into the subordinate position that, at least to some extent, they had escaped during Reconstruction. Many Whites warned against the schooling of Black children; for example, "the *Southern Planter and Farmer* in 1875 condemned the education of freedmen, calling them 'sweating animals' suitable only for the fields."[10]

Even when schooling was provided for Black children, it was almost always—Louisiana was, briefly, an exception—both segregated and inferior in resources to schools for White children. Not that the latter was anything to boast about. "By 1914 every state had some sort of uniform school system.... The standard, to be sure, was still pathetically low. The rural school was ordinarily a one-room shack and ran only three to five months in the year. And the teachers, grotesquely ill paid, were literate only by the most elementary measure." Note that what is described here is the schooling provided to *White* pupils.

The growing influence of theories of racial differences that claimed the authority of science "thwarted advances toward Black citizenship and provided the justification for social separation in all areas of life."[11] State education laws enacted during Reconstruction were amended to require racial segregation of schools; Tennessee and Arkansas imposed legal segregation of schools in 1867, Alabama in 1868, Virginia and Georgia in 1870, Texas in 1876, and Mississippi in 1878.[12] Virginia's school chief warned, in 1874, "that racial integration would destroy the South's public schools. The war had ended slavery, but not the 'social inequality' upon which it rested. Pointing to the widespread segregation of free Northern Blacks, Ruffner urged readers not to confuse Yankee war propaganda with reality' "; only communists and anarchists favored racial integration.[13] Typically, South Carolina ordered in 1895 that "no child of either race shall ever be permitted to attend a school provided for children of the other race."[14]

Writing in 1935, Horace Mann Bond reported that "by the law of nineteen states and the District of Columbia, school authorities are required to maintain separate schools for white and Negro pupils. In three other states, school authorities are vested with the discretionary power to establish separate schools for the races." On the other hand, there were twelve states whose constitutions or laws prohibited racial segregation of schools, and fourteen in which the law was silent on the matter.[15]

In addition to southern White resistance, the influence of the northern secular philanthropies that had a powerful influence on the development of schooling in the South after Reconstruction was often thrown behind segregation. Barnas Sears directed the Peabody Fund's grants to support segregated teacher training, arguing that "mixed schools would destroy the public school systems in the South," and as we have seen he lobbied against efforts in Congress to incorporate into the Civil Rights bill a provision against school segregation.[16]

North Carolina, which has long been the most active of the southern states with respect to schooling, required that its schools be segregated in 1876, and ten years later the Black teachers' association in that state conceded that "to have separate schools seems to be a part of the political organism of the South; and we would not have it otherwise, but there should not be any wide disparagement in favor of or against either race." They called upon the state government to "make reasonable and just provisions for the training of the colored teachers of the State and for the high school training of the colored youth."[17] Later in the century, the "progressives" who worked to transform the economy of North Carolina through the development of industry, for which they saw popular schooling as essential, were also convinced that separation of the races and a subordinate position for Blacks was not only essential but also the essence of kindness. "Public-spirited professional people of a humanitarian bent who gathered at periodic conferences to discuss the race problem took a deeply pessimistic or despairing view of the Negro.... They were convinced that the race was rapidly deteriorating in morals and manners, in health and efficiency, and losing out in the struggle for survival."[18]

Sometimes this separation went to absurd lengths; "North Carolina and Florida required that textbooks used by the public school children of one race be kept separate from those used by the other, and the Florida law specified separation even while the books were in storage. South Carolina for a time segregated a third caste by establishing separate schools for mulatto as well as for White and Negro children."[19]

There were some voices, even among the White elite, raised against this segregation. Lewis Harvie Blair, a Confederate veteran and wealthy businessman, published in 1889 *The Prosperity of the South Dependent upon the Elevation of the Negro*, calling for an end to segregated schools because they placed "the stigma of degradation" on Black children and taught them "feelings of abasement and of servile fear."[20]

Such voices were exceptional; other southern White leaders considered "progressive" because of their concern to improve the economic and social condition of the region

> framed a diagnosis of the South's racial ills which was grounded in the theories of scientific racism that had gained credence during the 1880s and 1890s. The reformers started from an assumption that "the negro [was] a child-race...grown up in body and physical passions, weak in judgment, foresight, self-control and character." They argued that slavery had tempered those traits and advanced Blacks rapidly toward civilization, thanks largely to harsh lessons in the "discipline of work."...Reformers described slavery as "the first [and] most fruitful chapter in the history of negro education"

that had rescued Blacks from African backwardness and prepared them, in the only way possible, for life in a civilized nation. Nor was this interpretation of the effects of slavery limited to White southerners; in April 1861, just as the Civil War was breaking out, Lutheran theologian Philip Schaff of Pennsylvania, one of the leading American intellectuals of his generation, published an article arguing that the "wholesome discipline of slavery" would "no doubt prove an immense blessing to the whole race of Ham."[21]

From this perspective, "southern prosperity, as well as the very survival of the Negro race, demanded that the old 'tutelage of slavery' should not be rejected but instead should be adapted to the new circumstances of freedom."[22] There were many Whites in the North as well as the South who feared that the "thin veneer of civilization, the result of a few generations of slavery, proved ineffectual against a more deeply implanted call of the wild. Religious, moral, and industrial retrogression commenced immediately, and ceasing largely from work, Negroes began to revert to savagery."[23] Or so it seemed to their fevered imaginations.

This made it urgent that the right sort of schooling be provided to replace the disciplines of slavery. Progressive White opinion in the South, as described by Cash in 1941, held "that the instructed Black man can be trusted never to commit rape, and that taught the elementals and perhaps some mechanics (we shall rigidly veto the idea of academic schools for him), he will be distinctly more useful, both to himself and to us. And...since it is going to be done anyhow—since the Yankee is plainly determined on it—since Yankee money and Yankee teachers are pouring down—it would be better if we beat him to the draw and did it ourselves.... It will enable us to make sure that he acquires no dangerous notions, to control what he is taught, to make sure that he is educated to fit into, and to stay in, his place."[24]

Opinion in the North did not necessarily disagree; school segregation came to be considered, by many "progressives," to be in the interest of Black pupils. It was important, they insisted, very much in the spirit of Progressive Education's focus on the child, that "the Negro's education must suit his racial peculiarities and capabilities. It must differ fundamentally both in quality and content from that of the Caucasian."[25] An article published by the National Education Association in 1890 stated, as a matter beyond debate, that "the intelligent Southern negroes do not think that social equality with the Whites is either practicable or desirable... they would be unwilling to have their offspring to undergo the unavoidable embarrassments that would surely attend the presence of their children among those of the White race."[26]

After emancipation, much of northern opinion had taken for granted that freed slaves would "find their natural level" in a subordinate position, and opposed special efforts to raise them to equality with Whites. This was based upon the best scientific opinion of the time, that different races were fitted for different climates and sorts of work, and that it was useless to interfere with the majestic process of natural selection. Toward the end of the century, however, oppression of Blacks in the South became more systematic, and the role of schools was seen as a form of social control. Some proposed that Black teachers in Black schools should be replaced by White teachers, to ensure that the message given to children reinforced racial subordination;[27] the schools that had been operated by northern missionaries had been suspected, as we have seen, of giving their pupils dangerous ideas.

A classic study of race relations published in 1908 found that White southerners were willing to accept the inefficiency of much Black labor as the price of keeping Blacks in their place. "Such methods mean, of course, the lowest possible efficiency of labour—ignorant, hopeless, shiftless. The harsh planter naturally opposes Negro education in the bitterest terms and prevents it wherever possible; for education means the doom of the system by which he thrives." One of the most notorious race-baiting politicians, Senator Tillman, warned that "with Negroes constantly going to school, the increasing number of people who can read and write among the coloured race...will in time encroach upon our White men."[28]

This pattern continued for nearly a hundred years; Swedish observer Gunnar Myrdal noted, in his 1944 report on race in America, that

> Negro teachers on all levels are dependent on the White community leaders. This dependence is particularly strong in the case of elementary school teachers in rural districts. Their salaries are low, and their security as to tenure almost nothing. They can be used as disseminators of the Whites' expectations and demands on the Negro community. But the extreme dependence and poverty of rural Negro school teachers...practically excluded them from having any status of leadership in the Negro community.[29]

"The supremacy of individual Whites," Myrdal pointed out, "is bound up with Negro ignorance. If the Negro stays in the only 'place' where he should be, then he does not need any education."[30]

Although the church-related colleges continued to insist upon offering a liberal arts education for Black youth, northern philanthropists came increasingly to support the "industrial education" model exemplified by Hampton Institute, founded by General Samuel Armstrong (a commander of Black troops during the war) with support from the American Missionary Association in 1868. In discussing how he had arrived at the approach he took at Hampton, Armstrong described his experience with two contrasting schools for Hawaiian natives: "The Lahainaluna [government] Seminary for young men, where, with manual labor, mathematics and other higher branches were taught; and the Hilo Boarding and Manual Labor [missionary] School for boys, on a simpler basis.... As a rule, the former turned out more brilliant, the latter, less advanced but more solid, men. In making the plan of the Hampton Institute, that of the Hilo School seemed the best to follow."[31]

Armstrong, like many of his contemporaries, was convinced that former slaves needed (in modern terms) to be rehabilitated from the "deficient character" of those emerging from slavery with insufficient preparation through disciplined work within the context of a semi-academic program.

> The thing to be done is clear: to train selected Negro youth who should go out to teach and lead their people, first by example by getting land and homes; to give them not a dollar that they could not earn for themselves; to teach respect for labor; to replace stupid drudgery with skilled hands; and to these ends to build up an industrial system, for the sake not only of self-support and intelligent labor, but also for the sake of character.[32]

In furtherance of this emphasis, he required testimonials of good character rather than academic performance for admission, and a commitment to remain for three years—unless, as happened frequently, the student was expelled.[33]

Armstrong established Hampton Institute "as a counterweight to what he viewed as the overly politicized education offered to ex-slaves by northern church workers and the freedmen's own subscription schools," to teach "the virtues of order, fidelity, temperance, and obedience" through domestic science, agriculture, and the building trades.[34] At Hampton, "the primary aim was to work the prospective teachers long and hard so that they would embody, accept, and preach an ethic of hard toil or the 'dignity of labor.'... Most of Hampton's beginning students arrived with a less than adequate elementary school education and successfully completed the normal school program with an education equivalent in quality to that of a fair tenth grade program."[35]

The Hampton model would attract favorable attention nationwide among educators concerned to adapt the educational system to the needs of a developing economy and the increasing proportion of youth who continued in school beyond their ABCs. An article in the *Review of Reviews* in 1900, for example, noted that Hampton provided "the right kind of instruction" for youth who "needed to be taught and trained in good conduct, the rudiments of book knowledge, and the plain tasks that go with farming, the ordinary handcrafts, and the duties of home and family." The author noted approvingly that the instruction "never for one minute loses sight of the general conditions under which these children have been born and the range of social and industrial possibilities that the future has in store for them." The clear implication was that those possibilities were very limited indeed. Hampton Institute sought to address "all phases of that most practical of questions—namely, how plain boys and girls and men and women under conditions now existing in our country can make their lives useful and successful." As a result, he concluded, "by all odds the finest, soundest, and most effective educational methods in use in the United States are to be found in certain schools for Negroes and Indians, and in others for young criminals in reformatory prisons." Apparently, the author did not see any irony in this parallel! For several decades, indeed, the Hampton model was influential among those promoting a system of vocational education for White youth as well as Black; for example, a 1908 textbook on *The Administration of Public Education in the United States* gave Hampton and Tuskegee as examples of the sort "integral education" that should be promoted.[36]

The "industrial education" provided by Hampton and other schools and colleges in the South was not oriented toward manufacturing but toward "industry" as a synonym for hard work. Hampton provided hands-on instruction in agriculture and handicrafts, as well as domestic occupations for women, through the work that the students did to support themselves and support the cost of their education. As Booker T. Washington would later describe his education at Hampton Institute between 1872 and 1875, there were no specifically vocational courses but rather an "English" as contrasted with the usual secondary curriculum including the study of Latin; he nowhere mentions having studied any specific industry and his primary work was as a janitor, though he did learn "a valuable lesson at Hampton by coming into contact with the best breeds of live stock and fowl." When he adapted the Hampton model to the new state-funded normal school for Black teachers at Tuskegee, Alabama, it was to provide a program, as Horace Mann Bond would describe it, "derived from a glorified common sense, amounting in this case to genius.... The students were raw, uncultivated, undisciplined country youth; Washington started to induct them into the American culture through a discipline based on the fundamentals which they lacked. That was the process which had touched him, when, as a ragged, hungry boy, he had applied for admission to Hampton Institute, and had been asked to sweep a room as his entrance examination."[37]

This was not a new prescription adopted just for Blacks; indeed, manual training schools—ultimately derived from Swiss reformer Johann Heinrich Pestalozzi (1746–1827)—had been advocated by William Ellery Channing, Orestes Brownson, and other reformers for decades, as a means to make secondary schooling available to poor children while also dignifying labor.[38] The Oneida Manual Labor Academy in New York State was founded in 1827 "to educate young men who have ultimately in view the gospel ministry.... The students were to support themselves and the school and benefit their health by three to four hours of mechanical or agricultural labor daily."[39] Oneida was celebrated as a seedbed of reformers of all sorts, attracting a diverse collection of idealistic students for whom the spartan program was among its greatest appeals. Its schedule in the 1830s began with prayers at four, classes until breakfast at six, and then alternating sessions of farmwork and classroom instruction all day.[40] In 1831, several White antislavery leaders had proposed establishment of a manual-labor college "for the education of Young Men of Colour," where they could "cultivate habits of industry and obtain a useful mechanical or agricultural profession, while pursuing classical studies," and two years later abolitionist William Lloyd Garrison announced that he would be visiting England to raise funds to establish a "manual labor school ... [for] colored youth," and appealed to free people of color for the necessary travel funds. His trip overlapped with that of Black activist Nathaniel Paul, who was seeking support for a manual labor school for Blacks in Lower Canada, what is now Quebec.[41] Such institutions were subsequently established in New York, Ohio, Indiana, and Pennsylvania.[42]

Thus one should not think of the Hampton/Tuskegee model as necessarily based upon a racist underestimation of what Blacks were capable of (though that was certainly widespread); it was an established and recommended approach to what we might now call a "holistic" education and attribute to John Dewey. Through including disciplined manual labor along with academic study, it was widely believed among reformers, students would develop the characteristics necessary for free men and which slavery, with its invitation to malingering, had failed to develop. As Armstrong would tell a conference of northerners interested in the education of southern Blacks, in 1890, their moral uplift could be achieved through labor.[43]

Hampton was intended, first and foremost, to train leaders for the uplift of freed slaves. "Let us make the teachers and we will make the people," Armstrong and his allies promised. It would be a simple matter to mold these teachers and, through them, the freedmen in general because they were "in the early stages of civilization." "Our students," he stated, "are docile, impressible, imitative and earnest, and they come to us as a *tabula rasa* so far as real culture is concerned." By making Hampton a boarding institution, the teachers could "control the entire twenty-four hours of each day—only thus can old ideas and ways be pushed out and new ones take their place.... When the whole routine of life is controlled," Armstrong believed, "the Negro pupil is like clay in the potter's hands." There was no patience for those who were not willing to accept the discipline of the school and its alternation of manual labor and academic study. "In the nineteenth century, Hampton graduated only one-fifth of its students, and many of those expelled were disqualified because of bad work habits and 'weakness of character'."[44]

Along with habits of laborious attention to duty, it has been charged that Hampton sought to teach Black students "that the position of their race in the South was not the result of oppression but of the natural process of cultural evolution."[45] Armstrong would tell the National Education Association, in 1872, that the Negro was "capable of acquiring knowledge to any degree, and, to a certain age, at least, with about the same facility as White children; but lacks the power to assimilate and digest it. The Negro matures sooner than the White, but does not have his steady development of mental strength up to advanced years. He is a child of the tropics, and the differentiation of races lies deeper than the skin."[46]

It should be noted that not all contemporary educators agreed with Armstrong that industrial education was sufficient for the Negro. At the same conference in 1890 at which Armstrong argued that moral uplift must be accomplished through labor, William Torrey Harris (philosopher, former superintendent of schools in St. Louis, and now U.S. Commissioner of Education) insisted that "education, intellectual and moral, is the only means yet discovered that is always sure to help people to help themselves." Nothing, he said a few years later to Black students in Atlanta, is more "practical" that an acquaintance with the achievements of Western civilization.[47]

Better known today than Armstrong is his disciple, the former slave Booker T. Washington, who established Tuskegee Normal and Industrial Institute in 1881, after receiving his own education and then working on staff at Hampton Institute. Washington insisted on the industrial education model (which, as we have seen, was not the same thing as specialized vocational training) even for those preparing to be teachers. Though this approach was later much criticized by Du Bois and others, including such recent judgments as that "the 'Hampton-Tuskegee Idea' represented the ideological antithesis of the educational and social movement begun by ex-slaves,"[48] it was in fact not a fundamental departure from a continuing theme among Black leaders. The national Black conventions of 1831, 1836, 1847, and 1853 had called for industrial education as most suitable for most Blacks, and the "leading spokesman of the race, Frederick Douglass, had even defended, in his paper *The North Star*, the solicitation of funds in England by Harriet Beecher Stowe for the industrial training institute proposed by the last convention."[49]

Such training in habits of hard work, with rudimentary knowledge of a variety of trades useful in a rural setting, was practical given the limited opportunities available to most of the graduates of Tuskegee; emphasis (rather exaggerated) on the humble nature of the education provided was also politically prudent. Washington wrote, in 1884, that "any movement for the elevation of the Southern negro, in order to be successful, must have to a certain extent the co-operation of the Southern Whites.... Brains, property, and character for the Negro will settle the question of civil right.... Good school teachers and plenty of money to pay them will be more potent in settling the race question than many civil rights bills and investigating committees.... Harmony will come in proportion as the Black man gets something that the White man wants, whether it be of brains or of material."[50] Nor was Washington devoid of long-term goals for Blacks.

> If, on the one hand, Tuskegee encouraged individual goals of education, "to have a bank account, get a home and own property," it was more adamant in encouraging its students to improve their communal life by returning to their communities to work and live. Their diplomas were not "evidence of individual superiority" but opportunities to do "something constructive and life-giving" in their respective communities. Black education must meet the needs of the black masses by putting "brains and skills" into common occupations—those jobs by which 90 percent of humanity earned its living. Education was worthless unless it was used; the previous emphasis on "literary" education had made blacks into an unskilled labor force. Whites, trained in state schools, were replacing black workers in the trades.[51]

Washington's great opportunity to promote his vision of progress for Blacks and to gain White support, both South and North, came when he was invited to speak at the Atlanta Exposition in 1895, an event organized by White southern leadership to reassure northern investors and businessmen that the populist agitation in the South (which included strongly anti-Black rhetoric) did not threaten economic stability. The New York Chamber of Commerce was assured that "one of the good effects of our Exposition will be to dissipate the political usefulness of the color-line bugaboo and set our white people free to form and act upon their best judgment as to governmental policies, uncontrolled by prejudices engendered by issues that are now happily of the past." The board of directors was "made up of fifty men, who are the best of our city-bank presidents, wholesale dealers, manufacturers and retired capitalists." All was well in the South, while the "colored labor in our section is the best, safest and most conservative in the world. Inviting a Black educator as one of the speakers was somewhat risky, but in Booker T. Washington they had picked the right man."[52]

Washington reported in his autobiography how, on the way to Atlanta to give the speech, he felt as "a man feels when he is on his way to the gallows," and afterwards he came under a great deal of criticism from Black church leaders for seeming to surrender the claim to equal dignity. This criticism he indignantly rejected and he claimed that it was gradually withdrawn.[53] With the White audience, however, the speech was a great success; and, in Horace Mann Bond's words, "the effect of the speech was as dramatic as the circumstances surrounding its delivery. Clark Howell wired the New York *World* that 'the whole speech is a platform upon which blacks and whites can stand with full justice to each other.' [President] Grover Cleveland thought that the speech justified holding the exposition. It made Washington the arbiter of matters affecting the Negro, not only in education, but in social, economic, and political affairs as well. It also gave him an opportunity to reach more persons of wealth in the country, and so obtain more money for Tuskegee Institute."[54]

In what became known as his "Atlanta Compromise" speech, Washington pointed out that "we [Blacks] shall prosper in proportion as we learn to dignify and glorify common labor and put brains and skill into the common occupations of life." He went on to assert that "the wisest among my race understand that the agitation of questions of social equality is the extremest folly, and that progress in the enjoyment of all the privileges *that will come to us* must be the result of severe and constant struggle, rather than of artificial forcing. No race that has anything to contribute to the markets of the world is long in any degree ostracized. It is important and right that all privileges of the law be ours, but it is vastly more important that we be prepared for the exercises of these privileges."[55] Note that, despite accusations to the contrary, Washington was not accepting a permanently inferior status, but merely recognizing—as did many during the Freedom Movement seven decades later—that the enjoyment of the benefits of freedom depend upon one's own actions. The tragedy, of course, is that the White South was not prepared to allow Blacks the opportunity to prove their worth. As Du Bois would ask, "is it possible, and probable, that nine millions of men can make effective progress in economic lines if they are deprived of political rights, made a servile caste, and allowed only the most meagre chance for developing their exceptional men?"[56]

Washington criticized the emphasis of the colleges founded by church efforts, complaining that "boys have been taken from the farms and educated in law, theology, Hebrew and Greek,—educated in everything else except the very subject that they should know most about. I question whether among all the educated coloured people in the United States you can find six, if we exclude those from [Hampton and Tuskegee], who have received anything like a thorough training in agriculture.... We had scores of young men learned in Greek, but few in carpentry or mechanical or architectural drawing. We had trained many in Latin, but almost none as engineers, bridge-builders, and machinists."[57] A historian of Black education in Alabama notes that Washington "seemed totally oblivious to the importance of abstraction, reasoning, and any ideas or study that could not be immediately and directly related to the students' everyday experiences or to a specific trade. This philosophy was Tuskegee's strength and its weakness." While the American Missionary Association and Black and White church leaders believed that "industrial education," though valuable, should build upon a students prior acquisition of a general education, Tuskegee "began this training too early in a student's course of study. Introducing industries into the grade school interfered with students acquiring a full, basic education."[58]

Washington responded to such criticisms, in 1903, by stating his conviction that "no race can be lifted up until its mind is awakened and strengthened. By the side of industrial training should always go mental and moral training," then completing his sentence with "but the pushing of mere abstract knowledge into the head means little." In this emphasis upon concrete tasks rather than abstract learning he was expressing a view of education that was in important ways consistent with the contemporary thinking of John Dewey and other pioneers of Progressive Education; Washington went on to stress that "the education of the people of my race should be so directed that the greatest proportion of the mental strength of the masses will be brought to bear upon the every-day practical things of life, upon something that is needed to be done." His concern was not exclusively with teaching useful skills that Blacks would "be permitted to do in the community in which they reside"; he was convinced that vocational training was educational in a broader sense for those whose attitude toward work had been shaped by enslavement: "As a slave the Negro was worked, and...as a freeman he must learn to work," and he stressed that "I plead for industrial education and development for the Negro not because I want to cramp him, but because I want to free him."[59]

Similarly, in 1905, Washington insisted that "there should be no limit placed upon the development of any individual because of color, and let it be understood that no one kind of training can safely be prescribed for any entire race."⁶⁰ As Horace Mann Bond would write in 1937, Washington "was a ceaseless educational propagandist. On the platform, through periodicals and in the white and Negro press, he lost no opportunity to plead for the education of Negroes. In a series of annual letters, published in white and Negro newspapers in the South, and widely circulated, he gave advice to the Negroes as to the possibility of improving their schools. Where the Negroes were being discriminated against in the distribution of the school fund, they were advised to 'bear in mind that we are citizens,' [and] to make 'a direct appeal to the public school authorities for a more just distribution of the public school fund.' If the authorities did not immediately give the Negroes a fair share of the fund, they should ask for it until they did receive it."⁶¹

Despite his advocacy of the whole range of education (apart from Latin and Greek) for Blacks, Washington came to be widely associated with the idea that "industrial training" was especially suitable for Blacks, and that even after receiving a Hampton or Tuskegee education, Blacks should be content to work within the limits imposed by what was becoming an increasingly oppressive society. Nevertheless, in the context of extreme hostility, among leading southern politicians and the White public, to all measures to "uplift" the minds and status of Blacks, Washington's strategy deserves more sympathy than it has commonly received.

> While accommodating to the outward forms of white supremacy, [Black] teachers engaged in institution building, professional organization, and social activism to promote democracy and equal opportunity. Viewed in this light, the accommodationist strategy of Washington and his followers takes on a different meaning. As a method of raising the status of black education, it was a qualified success. Through skillful racial diplomacy, Washington fended off the threat that disfranchisement might cause the destruction of black public schools altogether. His advocacy of industrial education also helped to untie the purse strings of both northern philanthropists and southern white taxpayers. Washington's gradualist policies struck many black southerners as a sensible, pragmatic strategy for securing and strengthening black schools.... For all his economic and political conservatism, Washington stoutly defended black humanity and never renounced the ultimate goal of equality.... The Tuskegee ethic of hard work, self-improvement, and Christian virtue was apolitical and individualistic. Yet that ethic, Washington insisted, would "give the lie to the assertion of his enemies North and South that the Negro is the inferior of the white man." Such statements explain why many white southerners never abandoned their suspicion of Washington.⁶²

Virtually all of those involved with the education of Blacks in the South would have agreed with Armstrong and Washington that the cultivation of character and virtuous habits was essential. Of course, this was also a constant theme at the time in schools serving White children in the North, but it seemed to have a special urgency in the case of those who had grown up under slavery, and their children. This theme comes across clearly in the report, in 1895, of the Slater Fund, a northern philanthropy that, since 1881, had funded the development of Black industrial education.[63] Among its conclusions were that "in addition to thorough and intelligent training in the discipline of character and virtue, there should be given rigorous and continuous attention to domestic and social life."[64]

In fact, despite recent assertions that the partial collapse of family structures in urban Black communities is a heritage of slavery, there is evidence that this is a recent development, related at least in part to the incentives built into social policies in the 1960s: post-slavery Blacks placed a high value on establishing the family patterns that had often been denied to them. "Emancipation allowed Blacks to reaffirm and solidify their family connections.... By 1870, a large majority of Blacks lived in two-parent family households.... Many contemporaries, who viewed White women who remained at home as paragons of the domestic ideal, saw their Black counterparts as lazy and slightly ludicrous" because they sought to "make a home" rather than go out and labor for pay. In addition, "White employers resented their inability to force Black children to labor in the fields, especially after the spread of schools in rural areas."[65]

The Reconstruction period also allowed some Blacks—whether former slaves or born free—to occupy political roles from which, when supervision by the national government ended, they were quickly ejected. Two served as U.S. senators, fourteen as congressmen, and more than six hundred in state legislatures. All of these positions were forfeited in the decades after Reconstruction. This makes a further recommendation by the Slater Fund in 1895 seem particularly out of touch with reality: "The race should be trained to acquire habits of thrift, of saving earnings, or avoiding waste, of accumulating property, of having a stake in good government, in progressive civilization."[66] As though a people most of whom lived in the most grinding poverty and unavoidable debt under the sharecropping system could save earnings or accumulate property, or a people denied the right to vote could have any effective stake in government! What "progressive civilization" meant under those circumstances is difficult to decipher.

On the other hand, the "industrial education" model followed by Hampton and then Tuskegee, to the extent that it sought to train skilled craftsmen to continue to fill many of the roles that slaves and free Blacks had filled before the Civil War, was ultimately unsuccessful. The "Black Codes" adopted by White-dominated state legislatures and increasingly discriminatory practices, often demanded by White workers, excluded Blacks from many of the skilled occupations that they had exercised prior to emancipation.

> Hordes of blacks had poured into all the towns from the first.... But most of them had gone into domestic service or other menial callings despised by the whites. Only relatively small numbers of them even attempted to enter the mechanical trades. And, when competition in a trade did develop, as when white men began to move into the barber shops, once almost exclusively manned by Negroes, the latter were routed so quickly and thoroughly that there was no time for trouble to develop.[67]

In addition, the growth of industry—especially the processing of cotton—was eliminating much of the small-scale artisanship that had employed free and enslaved Blacks before the Civil War, and Blacks were employed in factories only as sweepers and in other menial roles. As an economist wrote in 1905,

> There is no line of expansion in the south more important than the growth of cotton mills.... The number of spindles in the four cotton manufacturing States—North Carolina, South Carolina, Georgia, and Alabama—more than trebled in [1890–1900]. But this invasion of the negroes' home by cotton manufacturing has furnished little occupation to the negro. In 1900 the number of cotton-mill operatives reported in the country was 246,000, about one-third of them in the cotton mills of the south; but only a paltry 1,400 were negroes. Cotton manufacturing is far the most important industry in Georgia.... There are more than 1,000,000 negroes in Georgia, yet only 417 are reported as cotton-mill operatives.[68]

The new trade unions (though slow to develop in the South) commonly excluded Blacks and thus shut them out of skilled employment. "In industry it became a principle that all skilled jobs should be reserved for Whites."[69] "By 1890, Blacks were virtually excluded from industrial jobs in the South. Eighty-six percent of Black workers toiled on farms or as domestic servants,"[70] not in the roles for which industrial education had prepared some.

As a result, "approximately 84 percent of the 723 graduates from Hampton's first twenty classes became teachers."[71] By 1900, 1,883 Blacks had graduated from the 30 Negro colleges in the South; of these, 37.2 percent were then working as teachers, 11.3 percent as clergymen,

4 percent as doctors, and 3.3 percent as lawyers. Only 1.4 percent were farmers.[72]

There was, as Kelly Miller pointed out in 1914, a fundamental disagreement about what meaning to attach to industrial education. "In the mind of one man it meant that the negro should be taught only to know the relative distance between two rows of cotton or corn, or how to deport himself with becoming behavior behind the chair while his White lord and master sits at meat; while in the mind of another it stood for the awakening of the best powers and possibilities.... However variant may have been the interpretations of the meaning of industrial education, there was a general agreement to discredit the higher culture of the race."[73] William Sinclair, a Black physician, had pointed out in *The Aftermath of Slavery* (1905) that

> If they had yielded to a "craze" for industrial education... the colored race could not have gained in a hundred years the great advance in civilization and the splendid achievements which not... [stood] to its credit after only a single generation of endeavor. For emphasis on industrial education would have circumscribed the mental vision, limited the aspiration, narrowed the ambitions, stunted all higher and broader growth, and held the race close down to the lines of hewers of wood and drawers of water.[74]

The alternative to the industrial education model was the sort of secondary and tertiary education supported by the missionary societies and the institutions created by Black churches, which sought to echo the curriculum of "liberal studies" provided by northern academies and colleges. In contrast, industrial education—which received much more support from northern philanthropists, sought "to adjust the Black population to its subordinate position in the emergent New South." To this end, the institutions modeled on Hampton "would make no attempt to insert 'into the mind of the negro, as [if] by a surgical operation, the culture... which the Anglo-Saxon race had [acquired] through long centuries' of development. Instead, Blacks would be trained to work out their own salvation through an education adapted to 'their lives' and 'present needs'."[75]

This was not sufficient, insisted Du Bois and some of his allies, including President Charles W. Eliot of Harvard, who pointed out in 1896 that

> the teachers, preachers, physicians, lawyers, engineers, and superior mechanics, the leaders of industry, throughout the Negro communities of the South, should be trained in superior institutions. If any expect that

the Negro teachers of the South can be adequately educated in primary schools or grammar schools or industrial schools pure and simple, I can only say that that is more than we can do at the North with the White race. The only way to have good primary schools in Massachusetts is to have high and normal schools and colleges, in which the higher teachers are trained. It must be so throughout the South: the Negro race need absolutely these higher facilities of education.[76]

The independent church-related Black colleges and normal schools (which—like the Hampton model—primarily provided secondary- and even elementary-level instruction to their poorly prepared students) received little support from outside the Black community, but they sprang up all over the South; in North Carolina alone there may have been sixty of them in operation by 1914. The level of instruction was rarely that of White colleges (though even that was greatly varied at the time, and it was common for colleges in the North to provide secondary-level instruction for their poorly prepared students) because so few Black students had received a thorough secondary-level education. On the other hand, these institutions played an important role in developing Black leadership. "The independent schools operated outside the bounds of state supervision, and for that reason they could not be counted on to promote the 'harmony' and 'kindly feeling' that Whites considered so essential." In fact, they helped to incubate the cautiously independent thinking among a Black elite of ministers and teachers that would lead eventually to the Freedom Movement of the 1960s. "In a world deprived of politics, Black North Carolinians found in the classroom both a refuge and a place to test and renegotiate the limits of White supremacy."[77]

Such independent educational developments, with their touching belief in the value of "higher culture" in developing Black leadership, was out of step not only with those determined to keep Blacks in an uneducated and subordinate position but also with much of Progressive thought at the time. White Progressives who sought to narrow the gap in economic development between the South and the rest of the nation found one voice in the Southern Educational Association's resolutions (1907):

1. We endorse the accepted policy of the states of the South in providing educational facilities for the youth of the Negro race, believing that, whatever the ultimate solution of this grievous problem may be, education must be an important factor in that solution.
2. We believe that the education of the Negro in the elementary branches of education should be made thorough, and should include specific instruction in hygiene and home sanitation, for the better protection of both races.

3. We believe that in the secondary education of Negro youth emphasis should be placed upon agriculture and the industrial occupations, including nurse training, domestic science, and home economics.
4. We believe that for practical, economical and psychological reasons Negro teachers should be provided for Negro schools.
5. We advise instruction in normal schools and normal institutions by White teachers, wherever possible, and closer supervision... by the State Department of Education.
6. We recommend that in urban and rural Negro schools there should be closer and more thorough supervision...
7. [Need for adequate buildings.]
8. We deplore the isolation of many Negro schools, established through motives of philanthropy, from the life and sympathies of the communities in which they are located. We recommend the supervision of all such schools by the state, and urge that their work and their methods be adjusted to the civilization in which they exist, in order that the maximum good of the race and of the community be thereby attained.
9. On account of economic and psychological differences in the two races, we believe that there should be a difference in courses of study and methods of teaching, and that there should be such an adjustment of school curricula as shall meet the evident needs of Negro youth.
10. We insist upon such an equitable distribution of the school funds that all the youth of the Negro race shall have at least an opportunity to receive the elementary education provided by the state...[78]

The significance of most of these recommendations—and what they reveal about existing conditions—should be clear enough, but attention is called to the implied concern about dangerous ideas that might be propagated through Black normal schools and through insufficiently supervised Black teachers. The concern in #8 is with the institutions supported by Black churches and northern philanthropies, which might be out of line with the "sympathies of the communities in which they are located"—that is, the local White leadership. The Southern Educational Association was recommending that these private schools and colleges be brought under state supervision to ensure their compliance with the prevailing racial ideology of the White South.

Exhortation, and concrete political action, were undoubtedly needed to stimulate southern communities into providing adequate schooling for Whites and even more for Blacks. "Georgia did not pass its compulsory school attendance bill until 1916, and it still allowed local school boards to exempt Black children from the law.... The disparity in per capita expenditures between Blacks and Whites in the public schools was greater in 1910 than in 1900 and greater in 1900 than earlier, in every southern state.... The percentage of Black children five to eighteen years old enrolled in the public schools of the South decreased during the first decades of the twentieth century."[79]

There is ample evidence that White southerners, like those interviewed by Baker early in the twentieth century, regarded this situation as perfectly natural and appropriate. "When North Carolina's commissioner of labor polled White farmers in 1905 about a proposal for a compulsory school attendance law, nine out of ten respondents said that the requirement would be all right for White children but not for Blacks, because 'educated' Negroes, in nearly all cases, become valueless as farm laborers."[80]

White leaders intent on creating the "New South" saw Black schooling as a way to ensure "permanent White supremacy" through teaching habits of obedience and deference. They saw the period of slavery as having "advanced Blacks rapidly toward civilization," but deplored the "false" ideas of equality that had been promoted by Reconstruction. Failing to educate Blacks at all, they argued, would lead to their sinking back into a state of savagery.[81] On the other hand, the schooling provided should be appropriate to the subordinate position of Blacks, then and in the future. The governor of Georgia is reported to have said: "We can attend to the education of the darkey in the South without the aid of these Yankees and give them the education that they most need. I do not believe in higher education of the darkey. He must be taught the trades. When he is taught the fine arts, he is educated above his caste, and it makes him unhappy."[82]

As a result of such assumptions, there were only forty-six public schools offering high school courses for Blacks in 1900; five states provided none at all. There were 6,443 southern Blacks in public high schools in 1909, compared with 142,837 Whites.[83] W. E. B. Du Bois concluded, in 1911, "that the Negro common [public elementary] schools are worse off than they were twenty years ago."[84] In 1917, about half of all Black secondary students attended private schools funded by either northern foundations or religious organizations. There were 1,238 public high schools in the South for White children, but only sixty-four for Black students.[85] Across the South, Blacks remained concentrated in rural areas, in part because they had been squeezed out of trade and industrial work in cities. A study for the Rosenwald Fund's school-building program in 1925–1926 found that 93.4 percent of the 24,079 schools enrolling Blacks in fourteen southern states were rural, 63.8 percent of them with a single teacher, and 18.8 percent with two.

On the eve of the Second World War, 52.8 percent of the Black schools in the South were still single-teacher, while 26.9 percent had two teachers. Obviously, the widespread "school consolidation and pupil transportation movements of the 1920s and 1930s largely ignored black schools."[86]

Many of these little public schools were accommodated in private property, typically in Black churches, as the federal Bureau of Education reported in 1919 in a study of education in Alabama: "The fact that such a large percentage of Negro school buildings are privately owned [65.1 percent, as opposed to 22.2 percent of the White schools] explains in part the poor condition of many of the buildings and their unsuitableness for school purposes."[87]

Nor were the qualifications of the teachers of Black children much more adequate than the facilities in which they were constrained to work. Horace Mann Bond administered the Stanford Achievement Test to 306 Black public-school teachers in Alabama in 1931; their scores averaged below national norms for ninth graders.[88] "Caliver's 1933 report, *Education of Negro Teachers*, the benchmark study on this topic, found that although the modal length of training for most elementary teachers of both races fell within the broad range of six weeks to two years of college (approximately 55.7 percent of the black teachers and 66.7 percent of the white teachers met this standard), 22.5 percent of the African American elementary teachers, as compared to 5.7 percent of the white elementary teachers, had not gone beyond high school."[89] Whatever the limitations of the education provided in a Hampton or Tuskegee, it is evident that many Black teachers had not even progressed that far in their preparation to teach.

Apart from the limitation of the schooling of the great majority of Black children to the elementary level, voters (all White since the systematic disenfranchisement of Black voters) were not prepared to support adequate expenditures for this schooling. "With the passage of legislation giving each [Alabama] county some option in the allocation of funds to the schools of each group, for each dollar spent on Black children the discrepancy moved from $1.18 for each White in 1890 to $5.83 per White child in 1909."[90] In Georgia, the average annual salary for White teachers in 1905 was $214, for Black teachers $124. Three years later, Blacks lost the right to vote in Democratic primaries (where elections were in fact decided), and three years after that White teachers were averaging $319, Black teachers $119. These racial disparities were compounded by stark regional differences: In 1900, Massachusetts spent $37.36 per pupil, while North Carolina spent only $4.34 for White and

Black pupils combined. Since the great majority of Blacks still lived in the South, they suffered with education systems that were inadequate even for White pupils, and much more so for Black.[91]

Much of the development of schooling in the South, for White pupils as well as Black, was the result of initiatives and incentive grants by northern philanthropies like the Rosenwald Fund that, between 1913 and 1932, helped to build 5,357 public schools and other educational facilities in fifteen southern states. Of the cost of these facilities, only 16.5 percent was covered by the fund, but this was matched by a 19 percent contribution from Blacks (often at great effort), a 4.5 percent contribution from southern Whites, and 60 percent from southern county and state governments. Similarly, the Slater Fund established 384 country training schools providing a high school education in thirteen states between 1914 and 1930.[92]

During this period, "enormous amounts of northern money poured into the South from a number of new philanthropic foundations. School attendance increased rapidly from around 30 percent of Negro children (age five to nineteen) in 1910 to 60 percent by 1930; literacy (age ten and over) moved up from around 19 percent in 1870 to 84 percent in 1930; and an educated Black leadership was being trained in the segregated Negro colleges."[93] In Atlanta, which prided itself as being the center of Southern Progress, there had been public high schools for White boys and girls since 1872, but the first public high school for Blacks did not open until 1924. "Pupil/teacher ratios were commonly twice as large in the black schools as in the white. Per-pupil expenditure levels revealed an even greater disparity; as late as 1945, $139 was spent on the education of each white child, while only $58 was spent on each black child."[94]

Despite such obvious disparities, the northern industrialists and merchants who gave millions to promote schooling in the South were content to accept the lead of White Southerners on racial matters, unlike the northern church men and women who, after emancipation, had sought to ensure that Blacks were treated equally and educated liberally.[95] Increasingly, White opinion across the country grew sympathetic with the southern White belief that, as expressed by George W. Cable in 1885, the "man of African tincture was, by nature and unalterably, an alien." Cash, no friend of Reconstruction, points out that "in 1903 the reigning hit upon Broadway would be *The Leopard's Spots*, by Thomas Dixon, Jr., of North Carolina: a picture of Reconstruction from the most rabid Southern viewpoint, and a bitter attack on the Negro."[96] Dixon's novel *The Clansman*, made into the first "Hollywood blockbuster" *The Birth of a Nation* (1915) would be even more widely popular among Whites nationwide.

On the other hand, many White Southerners who had opposed the schooling of Blacks began to concede that there it was in fact advisable to train them at least for their "place in the lower sphere of life."[97] In Atlanta, for example, the Board of Education decided, in 1913, "that manual training and domestic science be added to the curricula of the seventh and eighth grades in Black schools. The recommendation was justified by the need for 'more industrially trained workers and fewer professionals among the Negro population.' "[98]

There was also considerable discouragement among northern supporters of education for southern Blacks. As early as 1870 "the *American Missionary* printed a letter from a Northern teacher who admitted 'we have not accomplished all we anticipated, for we were unreasonable in our expectations. We underestimated the benumbing, degrading effects of centuries of slavery.' "[99] Three decades later, the author of an American Missionary Society pamphlet wrote of "disappointment that after the expenditure of millions and millions of dollars and hundreds of devoted lives, the typical negro is still lazy and shiftless." Too much, many believed, had been expected of Blacks, who were still in the childhood of civilization.[100]

Similarly, the muckraking northern journalist Ray Stannard Baker, in a highly influential series of articles, while expressing considerable sympathy with the situation of Blacks in both South and North, concludes, "the Negro had indeed suffered—suffered on his way upward; but the White man, with his higher cultivation, his keener sensibilities, his memories of a departed glory, has suffered far more."[101]

The situation for Blacks improved somewhat during the First World War, when the slowing of European immigration led northern industrialists to seek to recruit Black labor in the South, and forced White leadership in the South to become somewhat more supportive of schooling for Black children, seen as one of the major reasons why families were moving North. There had been "scarcely any change in the geographical distribution of the Negro population...between 1860 and 1910,"[102] but suddenly it was a people on the move to better jobs and less oppressive social conditions. This movement would continue over the next half-century, though it slowed somewhat during the Depression, only to pick up in even greater volume during and after the Second World War; "Mississippi experienced a net loss of more than 68,000 Blacks between 1930 and 1940. During the 1920s the loss was 83,000, and during the 1940s the number totaled nearly 315,000 persons."[103]

Booker T. Washington had sought to discourage the idea that Blacks could improve their situation by moving to the North; in 1913 he declared that he had "never seen any part of the world where it seemed to me the masses of the Negro people would be better off than right here in these southern states."[104] By 1917, however, the annual conference of Black leaders at Tuskegee argued that "the disposition of so many thousands of our people to leave is not because they do not love the Southland, but because they believe that in the North, they will have, not only an opportunity to make more money than they are making here, but also that they will there get better treatment, better protection under the law and better school facilities for their children." The same year, a group of Black men called upon the Atlanta Board of Education to

> discharge your public function honestly and conscientiously to the Black boys and girls by providing them with the same adequate ample and efficient facilities in the grades, in industries, in preparation for a high school—and a high school.... Much of the unrest in the South to-day which prompts migration North...because public officials charged with the responsibility of public trust, fail to make ample and adequate protection for the education of Negro children. When you fail to provide a Negro with a place to educate his children...he has a tendency to hunt a country where he can serve God, educate his children and enjoy life and property in common with all men. Migration to the North can be stopped; unrest among the working Blacks can be dispelled if you will give us ample educational facilities and make safe our lives.[105]

Despite such appeals, improvements were slow in coming. As a result of this frustration, some half-million Blacks moved North between 1914 and 1920, and nearly a million did so during the 1920s. Many must have agreed with the recording by Charles "Cow Cow" Davenport of Alabama, who sang,

> I'm tired of this Jim Crow,
> Gonna leave this Jim Crow town,
> Doggone my Black soul,
> I'm sweet Chicago bound,
> Yes, I'm leavin' here,
> From this ole Jim Crow town.[106]

It is sadly ironical that, as we will see, the response of the Chicago Public Schools to this Black migration was to install its own version of "Jim Crow."

A Black woman in Macon, Georgia, writing to a friend or relative in the North in 1917, reported that

> There were more people left last week than ever. 2 hundred left at once. the whites an colored people had a meeting Thursday an Friday telling the people if they stay here they will treat them better an pay better.... The colored people say they or too late now.... May it is lonesome it fills my heart with sadness to write to my friend that gone... if I don't come to Chgo I will go to Detroit I don't think we will be so far apart an we will get chance to see each other agin.... May now is the time to leave here...[107]

In North Carolina, "eighty-seven of the state's one hundred counties reported severe labor shortages by 1916."[108] *Negro Schools in the Southern States* (1928) described "events in a Mississippi county, where a few years ago migration to the North was producing a serious shortage of labour. Consultation between White employers and Negro leaders brought to light the fact that the prospect of securing better homes and facilities for education accounted in part for the exodus. As a result of the conference the leaders of both races agreed to cooperate in a programme of school improvement and the country now possesses a system of Negro schools judged by competent observers to be one of the best organized in the Southern States. The exodus, for the time being, has been arrested." More generally, however, the picture provided was grim, as was pointed out in 1928:

> a great part of the rural South presents a depressing picture of small schools, housed in dilapidated and insanitary wooden buildings, often in churches or the lodge-halls of friendly societies, irregularly attended by boys and girls of all ages who come from distances of from two to seven miles, and stay away whenever the work of home or field appears to require their help, or the weather is at all inclement. Such schools are rarely open for half the year, are often devoid of any furniture but rough plank benches, while the teacher, usually a woman, and little better educated in any real sense than those whom she teaches, endeavours to impart the rudiments of reading, writing and arithmetic with the help of a few ragged and incomplete books, the veriest scraps of paper, and no apparatus what her ingenuity may devise or she may prevail upon the

community to buy. The picture is not overdrawn, but fortunately there are many brighter spots, and the movement for better schools is making progress. For this forward movement [northern philanthropies] are in a large measure responsible.[109]

Despite these efforts, by 1940 the average Negro over twenty-five had had only 5.7 years of schooling.

The education of rural-farm Negroes (practically all Southern) has been least complete: 15 percent have had no formal education at all, and almost 60 percent never reached the fifth grade. Only 5.5 percent of rural-farm Negroes (compared to 28.1 percent of rural-farm native Whites) have received any high school training whatsoever. In the country as a whole only 1.2 percent of adult Negroes are college graduates (compared with 5.4 percent of native Whites) and only 7.1 percent can claim to be high school graduates (compared to 28.6 percent of the native Whites).[110]

Nor was the education provided the same. Myrdal noted that "where White students are taught the Constitution and the structure of governments, Negroes are given courses in 'character building,' by which is meant courtesy, humility, self-control, satisfaction with the poorer things of life, and all the traits that mark a 'good nigger' in the eyes of the Southern Whites. The content of the courses for Negroes throughout the South, except at the colleges with a tradition dating back to the 'classical' influence of the New England 'carpetbagger,' is molded by the caste system at every turn.... The whole Southern Negro educational structure is in a pathological state. Lack of support, low standards, and extreme dependence on the Whites make Negro education inadequate to meet the aims of citizenship, character or vocational preparation."[111]

The many studies of the causes of rural poverty conducted during the Depression raised disturbing questions about whether formal education, as provided to Blacks in the South, actually contributed to their well-being or progress. "Surveys compiled a grim picture of schools being held in decrepit structures—run-down churches and ramshackle Masonic halls—that lacked adequate lighting, heating, toilets, and washing facilities and even such basic items as desks and tables. In such places a lone teacher, usually a young woman with less than half a year's training past high school, struggled with classes of as many as seventy-five children spread over eight grades (the average class size in 1928–1929 was forty-seven). By Washington's death in 1915 it was painfully clear that the appeasement of southern whites had done little to soften racial discrimination."[112]

School segregation remained a massive reality nearly a century after emancipation; in 1951, twenty-one states and the District of Columbia still either required or permitted by law the separate education of Black and White pupils. Racial segregation in schooling—and the illusion that, in a Jim Crow society, separate schools could ever be truly equal—was finally condemned by the Supreme Court in 1954, and began to be dismantled effectively in the South in the 1960s.

Segregation's rationale was still defended in 1956; however, by most southern congressmen (including Senators Fulbright, Russell, Erwin, Thurmond, Byrd, and others of national influence) in "The Southern Manifesto," charging that the separate but equal doctrine "became a part of the life of the people of many of the States and confirmed their habits, customs, traditions, and way of life. It is founded on elemental humanity and common sense, for parents should not be deprived by Government of the right to direct the lives and education of their own children." The *Brown v. Board of Education* decision, they insisted, "is destroying the amicable relations between the White and Negro races that have been created through 90 years of patient effort by the good people of both races. It has planted hatred and suspicion where there has been heretofore friendship and understanding."[113]

Hypocrisy? Self-deception? One hesitates to say. Certainly such views reflect a massive and deliberate refusal to face the realities of southern life and race relations. But the situation was only relatively better in the North.

CHAPTER 5

Jim Crow North

When post-Reconstruction White leaders in the South set out to undo the previous efforts to provide basic rights to Blacks, they were confident that they could do so because "the racial attitudes of the great majority of Northerners were not much different from their own."[1] In fact, racial segregation of schools is an invention of the North and of Canada, not of the South, and one of long standing. In colonial Philadelphia, in 1740, "a Mr. Bolton was arraigned...for teaching blacks in his private-venture school," though he was able to defend this practice in court.[2]

In the early national period, a few northern Blacks attended White schools; there was an integrated school on Long Island and another near Springfield, Massachusetts. The New Jersey Abolition Society pointed out in 1804, however, that it was difficult for Black children to obtain admission to schools, and suggested that a better solution would be Black schools with Black teachers.[3] In Boston,

> a few Negro children did attend the public schools with Whites at the end of the eighteenth century but most withdrew because of ridicule and mistreatment. In 1798 some Black parents, supported by White friends, opened a private school in Prince Hall's home. Seven years later the institution moved to the African Meeting House. Not until 1820, however, was a Black public school opened, and within a short time Negroes lost their right to use the White schools.[4]

As we have seen, a number of private schools for Blacks across the North were founded and sustained by Quaker, Anglican, and other benevolent groups, as well as by Black churches.

Racial segregation of schools was the norm in Canada and in the North of the United States, where New York State gave school boards the option of establishing segregated schools for Blacks, and Pennsylvania and Ohio required separate schools wherever the number of Black pupils exceeded twenty. "In certain cities, like Rochester and Hartford, where Negro children were insulted in the mixed public schools, Black citizens successfully appealed for separate schools during the 1830's."[5] In New Haven, in 1821, there were eleven schools for (White) children under eight, four for (White) girls over eight, and two for "colored" children. When reformer Henry Barnard was appointed Secretary of the new Board of Commissioners of the Common Schools for Connecticut, in 1838, he proposed a structure of schooling including separate "departments for 'colored' children."[6] Philadelphia was operating eight "colored public schools" by 1850.[7]

In Nova Scotia, where there was a significant Black population deriving from slaves who took refuge with the British forces during the American Revolution and from subsequent migrations, a school law in 1811 provided for government aid to communities that established schools at their own expense, but none of the Black communities could afford to do so. Two Black schools were specifically authorized in 1816, but neither was opened. Occasional small grants were made to Black schools established by local communities over the next decades, and in 1836 the Board of School Commissioners was authorized to open schools for Blacks. Such measures "had the effect of putting schools legally but not actually within the reach of black initiative and of segregating black from white children." Monitorial schools for Blacks were established by Anglican missions in New Brunswick, and Canada West (later Ontario), like Nova Scotia, "established separate schools so that they might preserve the assumption of equality of opportunity while slowing cultural assimilation."[8]

The thousands (estimates vary widely) of Blacks who made their way to Canada to escape from slavery or from discrimination in the northern states often "encountered race and color prejudice not unlike that they found in Massachusetts or Ohio. Free they were but equal they were not." Many failed to make a successful adjustment to Canadian society or to find a place in the economy; in fact, in the argument against abolition of slavery in the United States, the "deterioration of the Negroes in Canada and the West Indies after emancipation was [cited as] an indication of the unpleasant fate that might befall the slave were he deprived of the shelter of beneficent bondage."[9] William King, a White former slave owner from Louisiana, set up a community for Blacks at Elgin in Ontario in 1849, pointing out that the hopes of those who had fled from slavery and discrimination in the United States had been disappointed since, while the Canadian "law is good, owing to the prejudice which exists against coloured persons they do not enjoy its benefits." At the heart of this community would be schools created by the benevolent sponsors of the project.[10] The schools of this communitarian experiment for Blacks "were recognized as superior to the nearby public institutions"; as a result, some White parents enrolled their children, "providing a salutary if brief period of interracial education." In general, however, those who sought to provide schooling for Blacks came reluctantly to the conclusion that separate schools were required because of White opposition.[11]

After the Civil War, as many as two-thirds of the Blacks who had fled to Canada returned to the United States to try their chances there, some of them as teachers of freedmen in the South. They had not been able to establish the hoped-for "Canadian Canaan" because of an unshakeable prejudice against them on the part of White Canadians.[12]

Racial segregation was challenged in Boston in the 1840s, when several other Massachusetts cities (Cambridge, New Bedford, Worcester, Lowell) already had integrated their schools. Blacks in Boston, in the 1787 and again in 1798 requested public funding for separate schools because of the prejudice that their children experienced in town schools, but were forced to start a privately funded school with help from White supporters; in 1812 the public authorities began to provide a subsidy for this separate school.[13] Black citizens petitioned the Boston School Committee, in 1844, "respectfully praying for the abolition of the separate schools for colored children and asking for ... the right to send our children to the schools established in the respective districts in which we reside." Justifying the practice of separate schools, the Boston School Committee, in 1846, insisted that it was based upon a "distinction ... which the Almighty has seen fit to establish, and it is founded deep in the physical, mental, and moral natures of the two races."[14] Rejecting this response, the Black citizens petitioned again in 1845, 1846, and 1849. "It was Negroes who led this petition movement, though the opposition often charged that white abolitionists were behind them." The 1846 petition insisted that "all experience teaches that where a small and despised class are ... confined to separate schools, few or none interest themselves about the schools—neglect ensues, abuses creep in, the standard of scholarship degenerates." Separate schools were "insulting."[15]

In fact, Boston's Black community was divided, since some "colored men, exposed alike to oppression and prejudice," continued to believe "colored schools to be institutions, when properly conducted, of great advantage to the colored people."[16] Frederick Douglass argued, in 1848, "Let colored children be educated and grow up side by side with White children, come up friends from unsophisticated and generous childhood together, and it will require a powerful agent to convert them into enemies, and lead them to prey upon each other's rights and liberties."[17] It was reported that a number of leading Black families had moved out of Boston to communities with integrated schools, while many families for whom that was not possible boycotted the schools.

Turning to the courts, Benjamin Roberts sued to force the Boston Primary School Committee to admit his daughter Sarah to a White school nearer their home than the "colored" Smith School. Despite eloquent advocacy by Charles Sumner, the suit failed. Sumner argued that the Massachusetts Constitution of 1780 made the natural inequalities among men

> disappear. He is not poor, weak, humble, or black; nor is he Caucasian, Jew, Indian, or Ethiopian; nor is he French, German, English, or Irish; he is a MAN, the equal of all his fellow-men. He is one of the children of the State, which, like an impartial parent, regards all its offspring with an equal care.... There is but one Public School in Massachusetts. This is the Common School, equally free to all the inhabitants. There is nothing establishing an exclusive or separate school for any particular class, rich or poor, Catholic or Protestant, white or black.[18]

The Boston School Committee had no right to "brand a whole race with the stigma of inferiority and degradation, constituting them a Caste." What the Committee was doing, Sumner charged, was to "assume *a priori*, and without individual examination, that all of an *entire race* are so deficient in proper moral and intellectual qualifications as to justify their universal degradation to a class by themselves."[19]

Anticipating the argument that the Supreme Court would make in *Brown v. Board of Education* in 1954, Sumner pointed out that, even if the matters taught were the same, "a school exclusively devoted to one class must differ essentially in spirit and character from the Common School...where all classes meet together in Equality.... This compulsory segregation from the mass of citizens is of itself an *inequality* which we condemn. It is a vestige of ancient intolerance directed against a despised people." And in fact White children were also harmed by the separation, since "they are taught to regard a portion of the human family, children of God, created in his image...as a separate and degraded class." For Black children, already a "despised class, blasted by prejudice and shut out from various opportunities," separate schooling "adds to their discouragements. It widens their separation from the rest of the community and postpones that great day of reconciliation which is sure to come."[20]

The Massachusetts Supreme Judicial Court found that the Boston School Committee, "apparently upon great deliberation, have come to the conclusion, that the good of both classes of schools will be best promoted, by maintaining the separate primary schools for colored and for white children and we can perceive no ground to doubt, that this is the honest result of their experience and judgment." Since making such decisions was within the committee's authority, the justices rejected the arguments advanced by Sumner.[21] Roberts lost his suit, but a few years later the state legislature—under the temporary control of the "Know-Nothing" party—would adopt the country's first antidiscrimination law. This was achieved in part through a petition campaign that struck a positive chord in the popular reaction against the Fugitive Slave Law. The legislature approved a bill prohibiting all distinctions of color and religion in admitting children to Massachusetts public schools with little opposition and it was signed into law on April 28, 1855.[22]

It seems likely that this antidiscrimination law—which was not emulated elsewhere in the North for a decade and more—responded in part to nativist resistance to the growing demand, on the part of Catholics, for public funding for Catholic schools. How better to counter such demands than to reaffirm the undivided and indivisible "common school" by insisting that it was intended to serve *all* pupils... including Blacks? And there may have been other, related motivations:

> For the mildly [this is too kind] anti-immigration Know-Nothings, their natural enemies were the unwashed, Catholic, pro-slavery Irish, who in turn were the natural enemies of the Negroes who competed with them for menial jobs. A Catholic weekly, the *Boston Pilot*, said that the Know-Nothings "in their ignorance" probably intended the desegregation law "as an insult" to the large number of Catholics in the public schools. In the debate in the legislature before the desegregation bill passed, a Boston representative who supported the bill hinted how anti-Irish prejudice affected the issue for him when he said that Negroes living on the outskirts of Boston were forced to go a long distance to Smith School, passing other schools on the way, while white children, including the "dirtiest Irish," were allowed to step from their houses into the nearest school.[23]

And of course it was true that the schools to which Black children would now be admitted were those in which the children of Irish immigrants—and not of most nativists, who did not live in the same urban neighborhoods—were enrolled.

It is interesting to note that Horace Mann, the state's chief education official from 1837 to 1848, "withheld his own support for desegregation of the Boston schools for fear it might damage the common-school cause. His doctrine of neutrality beyond the realm of commonly approved opinions, while seductive and politically apt, would prove a dubious legacy for future leaders, while his version of civic morality contributed to turning the common school into a place where teachers preached virtues that few adults cared to practice."[24] Abolitionist Wendell Phillips charged Mann, in 1846, with "timid silence" on the segregation controversy in Boston, and repeated the charge the following year, suggesting that Mann was "sacrificing despised Negroes for the sake of obtaining well-ventilated school rooms, new books, 'physiological seats,' and 'broad playgrounds.'"[25] Neither on this nor on other occasions did Mann, in his official capacity, urge that schooling be provided to Black children, and after resigning as Secretary of the Massachusetts Board of Education, he said in a speech that "in intellect, the Blacks are inferior to the Whites, while in sentiment and affections, the Whites are inferior to the Blacks."[26] It seems likely that Mann's views on Black capacities were influenced by his admiration for the phrenological theories of his Scottish friend George Combe, which postulated a determinism unresponsive to education based upon the shape of the brain, and attributed to the brains of Blacks "small organs of 'Conscientiousness' or 'Justice.'"[27]

Elsewhere in the North there was less willingness to accept racial integration; Boston remained "the only major city with desegregated schools."[28] In many parts of the North there was a growing hostility toward Blacks, in part because of the growing immigrant population that found itself in competition with Black workers, and in part also because of anger at agitation by abolitionists, as when the house of White businessman and abolitionist leader Lewis Tappan was wrecked by a mob in New York City in 1834.[29] The worst outbreak was the Cincinnati race riot of 1829 in which armed mobs reduced homes and churches to rubble and killed several Blacks. In addition, local authorities applied various restrictions upon the free Black population, which had grown to nearly three thousand. More than six-hundred African-Americans fled from the city, some moving permanently to Canada.[30]

There were anti-Black riots in other northern cities, and state legislatures enacted laws that restricted the rights of Blacks and blocked their access to the ballot box. "Newspapers, barrooms, and theaters suddenly teemed with racist cartoons and slurs, a trend in popular culture that closely mirrored the dominant ideology of the nation's emergent two-party political system as it courted a much expanded white, male electorate."[31] An editorial in the *New York Herald* claimed that the Massachusetts law forbidding school segregation pretended that "now the niggers are really just as good as White folks. The North is to be Africanized. Amalgamation has commenced. New England heads the column. God save the Commonwealth of Massachusetts."[32]

In 1857, the New York Society for the Promotion of Education Among Colored Children made a careful study of the schools provided for them, concluding that they were grossly inadequate. While citing the example of Massachusetts to argue that "there is no sound reason why colored children should be excluded from any of the common schools," the report confined itself to recommending—with some success—specific improvements in facilities.[33]

Although the Midwest had been strongly opposed to slavery before the Civil War, it was almost equally opposed to the presence of Blacks fleeing the slave states; indeed, one of the arguments used by the Western Reserve Anti-Slavery Convention, in 1842, for abolition of slavery was that otherwise the North would continue to be flooded with Black fugitives. Only emancipation "could relieve them of the presence of a class whose contiguity was so offensive."[34] In this spirit, when the Ohio legislature, in 1853, enacted a comprehensive law requiring free schooling paid for by local taxes, clarifying the authority of town and district committees and prescribing county examinations of teacher competence, it also provided for segregated schools for Blacks.[35]

Some Blacks continued to favor separate schools, where they would be "cheered on by the unanimous shout of encouragement of all [their] fellows with no jeers or unkindness to make heavy [their] heart,"[36] and which provided a major source of jobs for educated Black men and women, but gradually a near-consensus developed that public authorities would always neglect such schools, and that a better strategy was to press for integration.

Even as the North fought to end slavery in the South, and began to send teachers to instruct freed slaves, racial segregation continued in most of its schools and other institutions.

> On the home front, most of the severe legal disabilities that fostered segregation went untouched.... Michigan, Ohio, Illinois, and Indiana retained their bans on interracial marriages. Colored children were still excluded from the public schools of Indiana, were not provided for in the

education laws of Illinois, and were segregated into separate schools by statute in most parts of Ohio.... Dubuque, Detroit, St. Paul, and other cities and towns, by local action, shunted Negro pupils into separate schools.[37]

Chicago's city charter, adopted in 1837, restricted public-school attendance to White children, echoing an Illinois state law. This had little effect, since most White school-aged children were not in school, and there were few Blacks in the city at the time. In response to abolitionist sentiment, however, ordinances adopted in 1849 and 1851 allowed Black children to attend the public schools.[38] In 1863, however, the city council adopted an ordinance requiring that Black children attend separate schools; this was repealed in 1865 after Black parents refused to remove their children from White schools. For some years, in the rapidly growing city, public schools were integrated, in part because the Black numbers were too small and too dispersed to produce patterns of racial concentration. This situation did not last, as Democrats won state and municipal elections "by assailing abolition and warning of the 'Africanization' of Illinois."

The emancipation of enslaved Blacks and the short-lived efforts of "Radical Reconstruction" in the defeated South did not do much to create a more favorable situation for Blacks in the North. In a reaction against what was perceived by many northern Whites as excessive concern on the part of Republicans in Congress for the interest of Blacks, the Democrats began to develop momentum again in the North after their wartime identification with disloyalty. When they took control of the New York State legislature, they repealed the state's earlier ratification of the Fifteenth Amendment that had been enacted to protect the voting rights of Blacks; that had no legal effect, but it showed which way the wind was blowing. *Harper's Weekly* responded that "the Democratic party went out of power in this State trying to make the Negro a slave. It returns to power trying to prevent his becoming an equal citizen."[39]

In 1874, the Illinois legislature finally enacted a law forbidding school segregation,[40] but in Chicago as also elsewhere school authorities would commonly redraw school attendance districts to reflect changing racial residential patterns, or allowed White pupils resident in racially transitional areas to transfer out to schools with a higher White proportion,[41] practices that would be the basis for findings of unconstitutional de jure segregation in the 1970s. Occasional efforts by school officials to transfer pupils or to redraw attendance zones to promote or stabilize racial integration met strong resistance from Whites, including immigrants.

There was a sharp increase of Black population in Chicago and other Midwestern cities as European immigration was interrupted by the First World War and industry—responding to wartime demands—required more workers. Black migrants from Mississippi and Alabama—about 190,000 arrived between 1915 and 1940—were concentrated into residential ghettos (restrictive covenants closed up to half of Chicago's South Side to Black residents), and this in turn led to increased segregation of schools. But the concentration of most Black pupils in schools with 90 to 100 percent Black enrolment was also fostered by school-system policies: In the 1920s, Black leaders complained that attendance boundaries were being drawn to separate the races, and when "district lines did not produce racial separation, whites could desert neighborhood schools by obtaining transfer permits.... Efforts to close the transfer loophole failed because parents throughout the city demanded the special privilege. Politicians also liked the permit system, since it provided an opportunity to perform favors for constituents."[42]

While there were regular protests at a leadership level about this pattern of racial segregation in the schools, by the 1920s "integration had become an abstract or theoretical matter for the great majority of black residents.... The black population was so large and housing so rigidly segregated that racially mixed classes were no longer possible on a wide scale.... Integration had become a symbolic issue, requiring an assertion of principle but having little relation to the experience of most black Chicagoans."[43]

As late as 1864, New York State enacted a law providing that local-school authorities "may, when they shall deem it expedient, establish a separate school or separate schools for the instruction of children and youth of African descent"; this was not repealed until 1900, when a new law mandated that "no person shall be refused admission or be excluded from any public school in the state of New York on account of race or color."[44]

In Ohio, in 1874, fewer than six thousand of the state's 23,000 Black children attended school at all.[45]

A separate public school for Black children was established in San Francisco in 1855, and in 1860 California enacted a law requiring that "Negroes, Mongolians, and Indians shall not be admitted into the public schools," but allowing local authorities to create separate schools for these pupils; legislation to the same effect was enacted in 1864, 1870, 1874, and the state's requirements were not changed until 1880.

The California Supreme Court ruled, in 1874, that this exclusion was permissible only "where separate schools are actually maintained for the education of colored children," but that racial segregation did not deprive Black children of their constitutional rights.[46]

It was not only Whites who insisted on segregating Black pupils: this was also the official policy of the Cherokee Nation when it reestablished its public schools after the Civil War and was forced to accommodate the children of its former slaves. In 1870, the Cherokee had fifty-four schools, including two for Black pupils, and by 1885 there were one hundred Cherokee schools, fourteen for Blacks. Black orphans were not admitted to the orphan asylum established for those whose fathers had been killed during the Civil War.[47]

Although the primary impetus behind the passage of the Civil Rights Act of 1875 was the continuing discrimination against Blacks in the South, at least some members of Congress saw the problems as extending to the North as well. A Black congressman from South Carolina, for example, told his fellow-legislators that

> the report of the commissioner of education of California shows that, under the operation of law and of prejudice, the colored children of that State are practically excluded from schooling. Here is a case where a large class if children are growing up in our midst in a state of ignorance and semi-barbarism.... [In Indiana] the prejudice is so great that it debars the colored children from enjoying all the rights that they ought to enjoy under the law. In Illinois, too, the superintendent of education makes this statement: that, while the law guarantees education to every child, yet such are the operations among the school trustees that they almost ignore, in some places, the education of colored children.... I do not ask any legislation for the colored people of this country that is not applied to the White people. All that we ask is equal laws, equal legislation, and equal rights throughout the length and breadth of this land.[48]

But there were few ready to respond to this appeal. The Illinois school superintendent addressed the question of separate schools for Black pupils in his biennial report in 1870, stating that "it is one of those matters which involve no principle worth striving about, and which are best left to regulate themselves." Many of the "leading minds" among "our colored citizens" had assured him "that they preferred separate schools; that they did not desire, and indeed would not permit their children to go where they were not wanted, and where they would be exposed to unfeeling taunts and insults."[49]

On the other hand, a Black-published newspaper in California in 1872 rejected this argument, pointing out sarcastically that "so great has been the solicitude of some for the welfare of our children that they would sooner deprive them of all means of education than subject them to insult from White children, by admitting them to the same schools. This we have always denied, and have said the antagonism would soon wear away by the irresistible power of attraction, and recent events have proven that our opinion was correct." The following year, a National Civil Rights Convention insisted that "the common school, paid for and owned by all citizens in common, shall not be made to serve in the degradation and humiliation of any class thereof.... Citizens are to be educated with the idea that we are a nation, one of many, with a common identity and interest; that all are equal before the law;... the States must not foster distinctions based on race or color."[50]

Horace Mann Bond would comment, in 1935, on the logic behind the continuing pattern of school segregation, official or unofficial, throughout the North as well as the South. "Separate but equal," he suggested, had never worked in practice.

> As in Boston, equality was maintained for a few years, followed by growing inequalities between the schools for the two racial groups. Separate schools were finally abolished in Boston; they may be initiated there again, as a result of changing tides of racial adjustments. Separate schools in the South have no prospect of a near abolition; and the inequality for Negro schools which seems to be an almost inevitable feature of a separate school system, shows no relative sign of disappearing. The causes for this consistent inferiority of Negro schools in a separate system are inherent in the very reason for their being. The inauguration of separate schools, the motivation of the crises which force Negroes to accept, or even to ask for them, are not original with Negroes. The basis for the separate school is apparently an unwillingness of the white population to accept the Negro as a full participant in the life of our Democracy. Fundamentally, what this means is that, in the words of an old Indiana decision on the question, "This [exclusion] has not been done because they do not need any education, nor because their wealth was such as to render aid undesirable, but because black children were deemed unfit associates of white, as school companions."[51]

Apart from Massachusetts, northern states would not take official action to end school segregation until after the Civil War: Connecticut in 1868 and 1872, Iowa in 1872, New York and Minnesota in 1873, and Illinois and Michigan in 1874. "By 1880, 18 Northern states had passed civil rights laws that in effect wiped out the racial school-segregation laws that they had passed earlier in the nineteenth century. True, these laws were not always well enforced."[52]

In the first decades of the twentieth century, northern school segregation became all the more entrenched in fact, if not always in law or policy, in response to a steady growth in Black population by migration from the South. Concern was expressed by James Weldon Johnson on behalf of the national NAACP that "there is a seemingly general campaign at this time towards the establishment of segregated high schools in our northern cities. This campaign our branches must consistently oppose."[53] That opposition, however, was uneven and often ineffective.

A particularly interesting example, because it was so highly regarded by John Dewey, Randolph Bourne, and other Progressives, was Gary, Indiana. Gary was a new city, created to serve a giant steel mill in 1906, with its schools headed by a superintendent who soon achieved a national reputation for progressive innovation. As the school system started, the Black children were assigned to a rented Baptist church. "We believe," Superintendent Wirt wrote, "that it is only in justice to the negro children that they be segregated. There is naturally a feeling between the negroes and the whites in the lower grades and we are sure the colored children will be better cared for in schools of their own, and they will take a pride in their work and will subsequently get better grades."[54]

As the Gary system expanded, Black pupils continued to be housed in a separate school, and those in the high school in separate classrooms. According to a report on the "Gary System" to the federal Bureau of Education, Wirt explained that "this is not due to the preference of the colored children themselves or their parents. The other patrons of the school, most of whom are foreigners, strenuously object to mixing colored children with the others." By 1915, all of the Black pupils were segregated with their own teachers and excluded from many of the school activities; in response to an inquiry from the national office of the NAACP, Wirt insisted that Gary would continue this practice.[55] It did so. In the 1920s,

> segregation, fueled by rampant white racism and reinforced by a separationist strain within the black community, was barely challenged by black integrationists and their few white allies. The number of black children...shot up from eleven hundred in 1920 to over four thousand ten years later, about 15 percent of the total child census.... Black teachers increased from fourteen to over eighty at the end of the decade; virtually all taught in the black schools.[56]

The relatively high number of Black teachers in Gary compared with other northern cities may help to explain why deliberately segregated schools—which provided jobs for those teachers—continued longer in Gary than elsewhere. In 1956, there were six Black teachers for every thousand Black residents in Gary, compared with 2.4 in Chicago, 2.3 in Detroit, and 1.1 in Milwaukee.[57] Support for separate schools in Gary came from the local chapter of Marcus Garvey's Black nationalist United Negro Improvement Association, which argued that "establishment of a school for both white and colored students...would tend to destroy the 'race consciousness' of the Negro children." The Black principal of two buildings serving over sixteen hundred Black pupils was convinced, according to one of his friends, that "public schools are already segregated throughout the nation. Would it not be better to have good black schools, completely segregated for the present, than to sit in the back of white classes, or to attend segregated classes in a white school?" In separate schools, "Negro children could develop dignity, pride, and self-respect." Reinforcing such attitudes was a walkout of more than six hundred White students from one Gary school to protest the assignment of additional Black students.[58]

Even before the "Great Migration" started during the First World War, Philadelphia was enrolling some of its Black pupils in "separate buildings...in which colored children have been placed under colored teachers," while others were attending the racially mixed schools closest to their homes, staffed by White teachers only. The school superintendent presented separate schools as a way to "provide employment to a group of deserving members of the colored race" who could not be assigned to teach White pupils; thus he proposed in 1907 that "wherever the colored parents will join in petition to the Board for a school organized on this basis, I earnestly recommend that such schools be established." There was another reason, as well, and no doubt more important in his mind, for creating segregated schools: "The fact is," he continued, "that when the percentage of colored children reaches thirty or more the other children begin gradually to withdraw from the school."[59] Over the next decades Philadelphia, like other cities, used what its Educational Equity League called "skillful zoning maneuvers" as well as permits for White pupils to flee racially mixed schools to keep White voters happy.[60]

Canada was, in this period, even less friendly toward Black migrants, taking official action to bar them from emigrating to the prairie provinces even as it was actively recruiting White Americans and Europeans to settle there. Blacks whose families had been in Canada for several generations found themselves forced to send their children to separate Black schools, and indeed in many communities this was apparently their preference. In Nova Scotia, in 1960, there were still seven Black school districts and three other exclusively Black schools, while it was not until 1964—ten years after the *Brown* decision in the United States—that Ontario repealed the law authorizing separate schools on the basis of race. Admittedly, most had been closed decades before, but the last racially segregated school in Ontario closed in 1965.[61]

It was only when the First World War and subsequent legislation cut off immigration that northern industry began to recruit labor—both White and Black—from the South, and a great internal migration occurred of Whites from Appalachia and of Blacks from Mississippi and Alabama to Chicago, Detroit, and other northern cities. Despite discrimination in employment—"the occupational rewards for Blacks with a given level of education were less than those obtained by other groups"—and the pressures of urban life, few of the migrants were willing to return to the South, and Blacks took over large areas of generally substandard housing that was being abandoned by the European immigrants who had come before them. "Black isolation in the average major urban center of the North in 1930 was about 4.5 times greater than it had been in 1890,"[62] and of course this led to racially segregated schools as well.

In 1908, only 31 percent of the Black pupils in Philadelphia were attending such separate schools, but as Black population grew there was an increasing residential and—even more—school isolation. State law prohibited forcing Black children to attend segregated schools, but it did not forbid operating public schools that were segregated voluntarily. The fact that segregated schools offered the only job possibilities for Black teachers weakened the efforts of the NAACP and other groups to oppose segregation. The Pennsylvania Association of Teachers of Colored Children passed a resolution, in 1925, "in favor of the continuation of segregation in public education in the state," arguing that it was supportive of "race development."[63]

The stronger force for continued and growing segregation, however, was the resistance of White parents to having Black children in classrooms with their own children. Black historian and social scientist Horace Mann Bond described, in 1935, a school in New Jersey where Black and White pupils were housed in the same school but in separate classrooms. The Black pupils were required to use a separate entrance, and "the play space for Negro children was carefully fenced off from that for white children by a high wire fence, at the top of which were several strands of barbed wire. The teacher of the Negro children had a standard degree, and was paid the same salary paid to the teachers of the white children. Their room was quite as adequate as any in use by the white children. Structurally, those children were receiving an equal educational opportunity—an American chance.... Imagine the dozen or so Negro children fenced away from a hundred or more white children—and why? Perhaps black is catching..."[64]

In Chicago, despite an active Black community and decades of effort, Black activists "had relatively little influence in school affairs."[65] In Detroit, school authorities regularly took measures to segregate schools as racially changing neighborhoods led to conflict, especially in high schools and junior high schools. As in Philadelphia, in the 1940s, Detroit school authorities assigned all of the Black teachers to the twenty-four elementary schools and three secondary schools that were heavily Black. The proportion of the total enrolment consisting of Black pupils increased rapidly, as it did in other northern cities: from 4.4 percent in 1921 to 17.3 percent in 1946 (when White enrolment was at its peak), 45.8 percent in 1961, and 85.5 percent in 1980.[66] The change, as elsewhere, was a result of both White movement to the suburbs and Black migration from the South.

In Indianapolis, there had been a mix of all-Black elementary schools and others with a mixed enrolment until the late 1920s, when assignments were made consistently on the basis of race and an all-Black high school was opened. Springfield, Ohio, established an all-Black elementary school in 1922, while Dayton placed Black pupils in separate classrooms.[67] Even in the cities like Chicago and New York that did not formally segregate Black pupils at this time, the effect of residential segregation and carefully drawn attendance zones had much the same effect.

In protest against the many formal and informal means employed to keep the races separate in their schooling, Black parents and students boycotted segregated schools in Alton, Illinois, in 1897–1908; in East Orange, New Jersey, in 1899–1906; and in Springfield, Ohio, in 1922–1923.[68] The protest in East Orange was led by an elite of middle-class Black long-time residents of the area, while recent migrants from the South were more willing to accept school segregation.[69] Segregation was in fact a reality in every sector of American life, as W. E. B. Du Bois pointed out in looking back, in 1934, at the minimal results of decades of effort by the NAACP and other organizations: "This situation has in the last quarter century been steadily growing worse."[70]

There were also boycotts in some cases by White students to protest the presence of Black students in their schools.[71] In Philadelphia in 1938, parents of hundreds of White pupils at one school petitioned for transfers on the grounds that "racial tensions" were harming their children.[72] As late as 1944, the New Jersey Supreme Court found that the city of Trenton—the state capital—was segregating junior high school students on the basis of race, and a succession of later cases, of which that in Boston, decided in 1974, was perhaps most controversial, found that various school-system policies had a segregating effect and required remedies. The Boston School Committee had manipulated attendance zones, grade structures, feeder patterns from lower to higher levels of schooling, and an "open enrolment" policy to satisfy the demand of White parents in racially changing neighborhoods that their children be able to escape to all-White schools, and continued to do so into the 1970s.

Such legal barriers were gradually removed, though generally the North remained an unwelcoming environment for Blacks. A survey in 1939 found that only 19 percent of residents of New England and the Middle Atlantic states, and 12 percent of Midwesterners, agreed that Blacks "should be allowed to live wherever they want to live, and there should be no laws or social pressures to keep them from it."[73] Partly this was the result of the very heavy European immigration of this period, which provided an ample labor supply for the positions that Blacks might otherwise have filled. It was not that the Blacks were less qualified for these positions: "The new European groups came from nations where illiteracy was far more widespread than among Blacks living in the North, and, indeed, many of the nations had higher illiteracy rates than those found among Blacks living in the South." Race became a social problem in the North in part because the White majority did not react to Blacks as they had to immigrants. "The emphasis called for Blacks to remain in their station whereas for immigrants it was on their ability to leave their old-world traits and become as much as possible like the older White settlers."[74]

After the Second World War, there was increased pressure to set a good example of "Americanism" by dismantling segregation in Gary and other northern cities, though Gary's new superintendent warned that "if we make a move to open all schools to Negroes, it may mean we'll have complete segregation instead." While by this point Black leadership was supporting desegregation, and had significant allies among the White elite, there was strong opposition from Gary's working-class immigrant population. Continuing residential segregation led to increasing segregation of schools, with 83 percent of Black pupils in all-Black schools in 1951. Cautious measures taken to end the dual segregated system had little effect because of the policy of assigning pupils to their neighborhood schools that continued to grow more racially distinct. A suit brought by the NAACP in 1962, charging that authorities had a "constitutional duty to provide and maintain a racially integrated school system," was lost by the plaintiffs.[75]

Jim Crow seemed as well established in the North as in the South.

CHAPTER 6

"Uplifting the Race"

So far, most of our emphasis has been on what the White majority, and government, did to and sometimes for Black Americans. We have also noted, however, that free Negroes created a number of schools in the North and even in the South before emancipation, and that Black churches were very active during the Reconstruction period in starting schools and even colleges. As W. E. B. Du Bois wrote in an influential essay, "The Talented Tenth," in 1903,

> They founded colleges, and up from the colleges shot normal schools, and out from the normal schools went teachers, and around the normal [school] teachers clustered other teachers to teach the public schools; the colleges trained in Greek and Latin and mathematics, 2,000 men; and these men trained full 50,000 others in morals and manners, and they in turn taught thrift and the alphabet to nine millions of men, who today hold $300,000,000 of property. It was a miracle—the most wonderful peace-battle of the nineteenth century.[1]

And, famously, he insisted that "the Negro race, like all races, is going to be saved by its exceptional men."

In the effort to produce such exceptional men (and women), three Black colleges had been established in border states before 1860, and another thirteen were set up by the Freedmen's Bureau before 1870. Subsequently, according to Du Bois's essay "The Talented Tenth,"

> nine were established between 1870 and 1880 by various church bodies; five were established after 1881 by Negro churches, and four are state institutions supported by United States' agricultural funds. In most cases the college departments are small adjuncts to high and common school work.... Six institutions—Atlanta, Fisk, Howard, Shaw, Wilberforce and

Leland, are the most important Negro colleges so far as actual work and number of students are concerned. In all these institutions, seven hundred and fifty Negro college students are enrolled. In grade, the best of these institutions are about a year behind the smaller New England colleges and a typical curriculum is that of Atlanta University.... One-fourth of this time is given to Latin and Greek; one-fifth, to English and modern languages; one-sixth, to history and social science; one-seventh, to natural science; one-eighth to mathematics, and one-eighth to philosophy and pedagogy.[2]

Even making allowances for a very considerable amount of exaggeration in this account of Black colleges whose academic standards and financial situation were equally weak, the accomplishment was significant and led to the creation of an educated Black middle class. By the end of the nineteenth century, as Du Bois wrote in 1930, "there had arisen in the South...a Black man who was not born in slavery. What was he to become? Whither was his face set? How should he be trained and educated?... The small New England college had been transplanted and perched on hill and river in Raleigh and Atlanta, Nashville and New Orleans, and a half dozen other towns."[3] Research by Carter Woodson estimated that, by the mid-1920s, there were about ten thousand African-Americans in middle-class employment, including 1,748 physicians, 1,230 lawyers, and 2,131 academics and educational administrators. While "in 1917 there were 2,132 African Americans in college; a decade later there were 13,580, with 200 to 300 in White institutions."[4]

Many of this growing group of Black professionals and businessmen, whose income derived almost exclusively from the services they provided to the Black community, believed strongly in the importance of creating their own institutions. Foremost among these, of course, were churches and the Black-controlled denominations that linked them together; there were also Black college fraternities and sororities that played—and continue to play—an important role for many college graduates throughout their lives, as well as fraternal orders, newspapers, and other institutions. In Chicago, during the last decades of the nineteenth century, the resources of Black churches "were devoted to erecting large impressive buildings and to undermining notions of Black inferiority. Countering these notions became a critical concern for many Blacks in the late nineteenth century in light of the spread of scientific racism." These efforts were an expression of "the primary racial ideology many Black Chicago Protestant churches followed...the doctrine of self-help, which had by the second decade of the twentieth century become the standard creed throughout most sectors of the Black community."[5]

In Selma, Alabama, in 1888 a local Black minister and newspaper editor called upon the Black community to "build schools everywhere, controlled and taught by yourselves, where true manhood and womanhood are taught. You need never expect a Negro child to be properly taught in a schools which Southern White people control. His education and training and avarice disqualify him for this work.... The colored people are waking up.... Give us all our rights, not social equality..."[6] Such invocations of self-help became increasingly common.

While Du Bois, in *The Souls of Black Folk* (1903), commended the work of Booker T. Washington at Tuskegee and in preaching "Thrift, Patience, and Industrial Training," he charged that Washington "withdraws many of the high demands of Negroes as men and American citizens," and had contributed to a decline of support for the liberal education of Black future leadership. "Neither the Negro common-schools, nor Tuskegee itself," Du Bois wrote, "could remain open a day were it not for teachers trained in Negro colleges, or trained by their graduates."[7] His essay "Of Mr. Booker T. Washington and Others" begins with an elegant judgment on the man who was then widely regarded as the spokesman for 9 million Black Americans:

> Easily the most striking thing in the history of the American Negro since 1876 is the ascendancy of Mr. Booker T. Washington. It began at a time when war memories and ideals were rapidly passing; a day of astonishing commercial development was dawning; as sense of doubt and hesitation overtook the freedmen's sons,—then it was that his leading began. Mr. Washington came, with a simple definite programme, at the psychological moment when the nation was a little ashamed of having bestowed so much sentiment on Negroes, and was concentrating its energies on Dollars. His programme of industrial education, conciliation of the South, and submission and silence as to civil and political rights, was not wholly original.... But Mr. Washington first indissolubly linked these things.[8]

The heart of Du Bois's argument with Washington is evident in his emphasis upon the liberal arts curriculum provided by the Black colleges. "The matter of man's earning a living, said the college," Du Bois would write in 1930, "is and must be important, but surely it can never be so important as the man himself. Thus the economic adaptation of the Negro to the South must in education be subordinated to the great necessity of teaching life and culture."[9] While Washington and his supporters denounced liberal college education as inappropriate given the low social and economic situation of post-emancipation

Blacks—"one of the effects," Du Bois charged, "of Mr. Washington's propaganda has been to throw doubt upon the expediency of such training for Negroes"—Du Bois insisted in 1903 that "knowledge of life and its wider meaning has been the point of the Negro's deepest ignorance, and the sending out of teachers whose training has not been simply for bread winning, but also for human culture, has been of inestimable value in the training of" Black community leaders such as ministers and teachers. After all, he insisted in the opening lines of his essay, "the Negro race, like all races, is going to be saved by its exceptional men. The problem of education, then, among Negroes must first of all deal with the Talented Tenth.... The Talented Tenth rises and pulls all that are worth the saving up to their vantage ground."[10]

In the concrete efforts made by Black educators to "uplift the race," as many thought of their mission, the choice between the approaches urged by Washington and by Du Bois seemed fundamental. One of the pioneers was Mary Jane Patterson, the first Black woman to graduate from college (Oberlin 1862) and in the 1870s principal of M Street High School for Blacks in Washington, D.C., which later became the celebrated Dunbar High School. When the controversy over strategy came to a head early in the twentieth century, the then principal, Anna Cooper, "aligned herself with the Du Bois group and succeeded in keeping M Street's curriculum that of the standard college preparatory school of the time."[11]

Du Bois cited a 1900 study of Black college graduates, which found that 53 percent were teachers or educational administrators at some level, 17 percent clergymen, and another 17 percent "in the professions, chiefly as physicians. Over six percent were merchants, farmers, and artisans, and four percent were in the government civil service."[12] This seemed a vindication of the effort to create and preserve these institutions as alternatives to those offering a training to fill humbler positions in society. For Du Bois, and to many Black and White educators committed to the higher education of Black youth, "the New England classical liberal curriculum" offered "access to the best intellectual traditions of their era and the best means to understanding their own historical development and sociological uniqueness." From this perspective, which Carter Woodson and others would later criticize, "the classical course was not so much the imposition of an alien White culture that would make Blacks feel inferior as it was a means to understanding the development of the Western world and Blacks' inherent rights to equality within that world."[13]

In 1918, responding to a federal government report on "Private and Higher Schools for Colored People," Du Bois returned to this theme, pointing out the prevalent belief that "the present tendency toward academic and higher education among Negroes should be restricted and replaced by a larger insistence on manual training, industrial education, and agricultural training." In fact, Du Bois pointed out, that tendency was a very mild one; there were only 1,643 students in Negro colleges, and there were "(in proportion to population) ten times as many Whites in the public high schools as there are colored pupils." Against the conclusion of the report, that the desire of Black leadership to provide its children with college education was inappropriate, Du Bois argued that "the object of a school system is to carry the child as far as possible in its knowledge of the accumulated wisdom of the world."[14]

In fairness to Booker T. Washington, he had pointed out in 1890 that "no one understanding the real needs of the race would advocate that industrial education should be given to every Negro to the exclusion of the professions and other branches of learning. It is evident that a race so largely segregated as the Negro is, must have an increasing number of its own professional men and women."[15] Similarly, fifty years later, Du Bois wrote of "the Hampton-Tuskegee ideas of Negro education," that "I would have said in 1900 that I believed in it, but not as a complete program. I believed that we should seek to educate a mass of ignorant sons of slaves in the three R's and the technique of work in a sense of the necessity and duty of good work. But beyond this, I also believed that such schools must have teachers, and such a race must have thinkers and leaders, and for the education of these folk we needed good and thorough Negro colleges."[16]

Du Bois sought to link the situation of Blacks with the triumphant capitalism and imperialism—expressed in occupation of the Philippines and Puerto Rico after the Spanish-American War—of the post-Reconstruction period. "The tendency is here," he pointed out, "born of slavery and quickened to renewed life by the crazy imperialism of the day, to regard human beings as among the material resources of a land to be trained with an eye single to future dividends.... Above all, we daily hear that an education that encourages aspiration, that sets the loftiest of ideals and seeks as an end culture and character rather than bread-winning, is the privilege of White men and the danger and delusion of Black."[17]

Despite all discouragements, and they were legion, the early twentieth century saw the steady growth of a Black middle class, who clung to the status that they had achieved with such difficulty, and which was called into question so constantly in their encounters with Whites, even those of far less accomplishment in every respect. For this emerging Black middle class, North and South, the migration of Blacks from the rural South "posed a threat to their own status and represented the antithesis of Black progress and respectability"; they formed a "Black leadership class unable to sympathize with destitute or ambitious Blacks' flight from misery and repression in the rural South."[18] Social and occupational stratification in the Black community, often extended over several generations, was more and more significant, with markers of color, occupation, education, wealth, and dignified behavior, but "the increasingly complex Negro status system, though faithfully duplicating that of whites, was steadfastly ignored by the latter, for they were disinclined to see differences between one Negro and another."[19] Individuals who had achieved middle-class status, often through painful self-denial and self-discipline, were humiliated to find themselves lumped in the eyes of the White majority with the newly-arrived southern sharecropper. The reaction was not unique to middle-class Blacks, but has been documented, for example, among well-established German Jews appalled by the arrival of Jews from Eastern Europe, and among other immigrant communities.

A study for the national government by Black educator Doxey Wilkerson, in 1939, concluded that "differences between the achievement of White and Negro pupils in Northern school systems are attributable almost entirely to scholastic deficiencies on the part of Negro migrants from impoverished school systems in the South."[20]

Developments in the organization of public-school systems may have made it especially unlikely that the migrants from the South would receive an appropriately challenging and supportive education.

> Black Americans arrived in northern cities in large numbers at a time when centralization had undermined ward school politics, when educators were increasingly empowered to make classifications of pupils according to their notion of what was best for the client, when the results of biased tests were commonly accepted as proof of native ability, when those in control of schooling generally agreed that the function of schools was to sort and train students to fit into the existing order, and when much writing in education and social science tended to portray Black citizens as a "social problem."[21]

Not all successful Blacks sought to separate themselves from the uneducated masses of Blacks moving up from the South. "Throughout the 1890s, and continuing through the first decade of the new century, altruistic uplift efforts among Blacks coincided with the urban progressives' similar efforts to alleviate class and cultural divisions through the Americanization of immigrants within such moral reform crusades as temperance, the settlement-house movement, and other forms of social and charity work."[22] Indeed, it is fair to say that "the institutions created or consolidated after the Civil War—the Black family, school, and church—provided the base from which the modern civil rights revolution sprang."[23]

Black Ambivalence about Integration

With these self-created institutions providing the only sphere within which most Black Americans and Canadians could be confident of being treated with respect, it is not surprising that there was considerable ambivalence on their part about integration in the majority White society, even to the extent that this was possible. A determination to build a parallel Black economy—in some respects a logical sequel to the strategy advocated by Booker T. Washington—was articulated with particular force and short-term though fragile results by Marcus Garvey, a Jamaica-born orator who made his base in Harlem in the 1920s. Garvey revived the long-discredited idea that Blacks should return to Africa, insisting that there was "no hope for the American Negro ... [because] this is a white man's country, and he will be pushed harder than ever against the wall. ... Africa is still the one land where it is possible to build a Negro state."[24]

While only a handful even attempted that migration, tens of thousands of Black Americans and Canadians formed local branches of Garvey's Universal Negro Improvement Association, and many of them bought shares in the shipping line that Garvey promised would trade between Africa, the West Indies, and North America and bring prosperity to its investors. Du Bois was appalled, and attempted to counter the widespread influence of Garvey on Blacks nationwide, warning (correctly) in 1921 that Garvey's "methods are bombastic, wasteful, illogical and ineffective and almost illegal."[25]

On the other hand, Du Bois came to understand the frustrations that lay behind the popularity of Garvey among the Black masses and even some of the Black middle class and intelligentsia. Writing in 1919, he suggested that Negroes were beginning to practice self-segregation rather than to insist—vainly—upon access to White institutions.

> They have welcomed separate racial institutions. They have voluntarily segregated themselves and asked for more segregation. The North is full of instances of practically colored schools which colored people have demanded and, of course, the colored church and social organization of every sort are ubiquitous. ... If the Negro is to develop his own power

and gifts; if he is not only to fight prejudices and oppression successfully, but also to unite for ideals higher than the work has realized in art and industry and social life, then he must unite and work with Negroes and build a new and great Negro ethos.[26]

The profound disagreement that led to his break with the NAACP and his resignation as editor of *The Crisis* occurred over the organization board's refusal to adopt a resolution that he proposed that, while condemning "segregation of human beings purely on a basis of race and color" as "stupid and unjust" as well as a cause of conflict, also recognized the need of Negroes as a group to "make up its mind to associate and cooperate for its own uplift and a defense of its self-respect." The resolution went on to contend that "the Negro church, the Negro college, the Negro public school, Negro business and industrial enterprises... should be made the very best and most efficient institutions of their kind judged by any standard... with the distinct object of proving Negro efficiency, showing Negro ability and discipline, and demonstrating how useless and wasteful race segregation is." His resolution was rejected, and the board adopted a briefer resolution condemning all forms of enforced segregation that "carries with it the implication of a superior and inferior group and invariably results in the imposition of a lower status on the group deemed inferior."[27] The board's resolution made no mention of voluntary self-segregation but it was clear that the organization did not want to lend the slightest encouragement to the idea that "separate but equal" was acceptable.

As he grew increasingly alienated, Du Bois abandoned his earlier optimism about the role of the liberal arts program of the Black colleges, concluding that they had failed to produce graduates capable of effective criticism of an unjust capitalist society, just as the industrial institutions—the Hamptons and Tuskegees—had failed to produce graduates prepared to enter modern industry. "Both types of teacher failed.... Our educational institutions must graduate to the world men fitted to take their place in real life by their knowledge, spirit, and ability to do what the world wants done."[28]

In a 1933 essay Du Bois had to admit, with a sort of grudging respect, that Garvey had "discovered that a black skin was in itself a sort of patent of nobility and that Negroes ought to be proud of themselves and their ancestors."[29] When Du Bois himself resigned from his position editing the NAACP's journal, it was because of his growing conviction that "the only thing that we not only can, but must do, is voluntarily and insistently to organize our economic and social power, no matter how much segregation it involves.... Run and support our own institutions." Sounding more than a little like Garvey, though with a very different rhetorical tone, Du Bois wrote in *The Crisis* that "segregation ... is today and in this world inevitable ... because without it, the American Negro will suffer evils greater than any possible evil of separation: we would suffer the loss of self-respect, the lack of faith in ourselves, the lack of knowledge about ourselves, the lack of ability to make a decent living by our own efforts and not by philanthropy."[30]

It was not an imagined return to Africa or creation of a physically separate territory within the United States, as proposed by the American Communist Party, but an altogether reasonable self-interest that led much of the Black middle class to be hesitant to press for school desegregation in northern cities, even to some extent after the *Brown* decision in 1954. Teaching was one of the few careers that college-educated Blacks could aspire to; it was no accident that, according to Superintendent Wirt of Gary in 1931, the Black teachers in his system were on average more academically qualified than the White teachers.[31] Far more than among Whites, schoolteachers represented the backbone of the Black middle class (perhaps more accurately the lower middle class) and, along with postal and other low-level government workers, the great majority of those whose employment—unlike that of ministers and funeral directors—did not depend on the meager resources of the Black community itself. Thus in Milwaukee in the early 1930s, the priority of Black leadership was to obtain teaching positions rather than school desegregation. "In order to advance the race, Black leaders sought ways to gain more influence over public education to create better Black employment opportunities. The solution, at least temporarily, would be white political patronage,"[32] which, in turn, required not raising issues that would upset White voters.

This process had begun long before in Atlanta and other southern cities. One result of the creation, by Black churches and northern missionary organizations, of a number of colleges providing teacher-training courses was that, a decade after the Civil War, there were a growing number of Black college graduates looking for work. Four experienced Black teachers petitioned the Atlanta Board of Education for jobs in 1876, while a group of Black ministers requested that the northern missionaries be replaced by Black teachers in Atlanta's Black public schools.

> These efforts were resisted by school board members, who opposed the loss of white jobs in the schools and feared that black teachers would

teach social equality to black students. In 1877, however, after unsuccessful attempts to replace the missionaries with southern whites, board members began to reconsider the possibility of hiring black teachers. Letters from other southern school systems attested to black teacher performance, while board members were attracted by the knowledge that black teachers could be paid lower salaries than whites. Atlanta's first black teachers were hired in 1878, with the stipulation that only blacks born and educated in the South should be eligible for employment.... Black teachers were employed in black schools because of the financial savings to the school board and not because blacks exercised real power or influence."[33]

In Philadelphia, where there was a long-established Black community that began to grow rapidly in the early twentieth century through migration from the South, the school system adopted an informal policy that a credentialed Black teacher, if there were no jobs available in the separate Black schools, "could go into the black neighborhood and gather together a group of children who were not already in school. After the number of children exceeded fifty or sixty, the teacher could go to the chairman of the local ward school board and request that a school be opened. The ward school board secured a building for the school, and the teacher who had found the children became the principal teacher, and then hired other black teachers as the need arose."[34] Obviously, under such an arrangement the convention that Black teachers would staff schools with no White pupils had the effect of reducing demand for integration. In fact, when the efforts of the Educational Equity League succeeded, in 1937, in persuading the Philadelphia School Board to merge the lists of Black and White teachers eligible for appointment, "the black teachers dropped precipitously in their standings for appointment. For example, the black teacher who was first on the black eligibility list dropped to number 300 on the merged list.... This virtually precluded the possibility that a black teacher would be appointed to a position in the public elementary schools in the near (or distant) future."[35]

In fact, the northern cities that had abandoned the practice of assigning Black pupils to separate schools had a significantly lower proportion of Black teachers, in relation to total Black population, than those that had not, like Gary and Dayton. "In 1930, in five cities with formal school segregation, there were on the average 323 black teachers for every 100,000 black inhabitants, more than triple the rate in nine systems with supposedly integrated schools (97 per 100,000).... Among officially integrated systems, Pittsburgh had only three Negro faculty members in 1930, Newark eleven, and Buffalo twelve (1927)."[36]

In the South, where there was no pretense of school integration, many Blacks "viewed their schools and colleges with pride; built at great personal cost, they provided jobs, leadership, and community facilities. For black southerners, integration was a leap in the dark. The NAACP promised to do everything in its power to prevent teachers from being intimidated and dismissed, but it was uncompromising in its view that the elimination of segregated schools should take priority over the career interests of black educators. Thousands of black teachers might indeed lose their jobs when integration occurred."[37]

The *Journal of Negro Education* sought to assure its readers that desegregation of public schools in the South would not displace Black teachers and administrators (though in fact it would do so on a massive scale), but added that "the elimination of legally-enforced segregated schools should outweigh in importance the loss of teaching positions even by a majority of the 75,000 Negro teachers who might conceivably be affected."[38] One doubts that this was altogether comforting to those directly affected; a study in four border states found that "a sizeable number of Negro teachers lost their jobs in the change to biracial schools."[39]

In addition to the direct concern about jobs, many Black teachers believed that they were more sympathetic toward and effective in teaching Black pupils, and that school integration subjected the latter to insensitive White teachers who treated them in degrading ways. "In the separate public schools, the incompetent teacher or insensitive educator was dealt with by the black principal and staff. It was only the rare educator who openly protested against the bigotry, insensitivity, and incompetence to which black children were subjected in many newly desegregated classrooms. Segregation had its drawbacks, but desegregation was 'no crystal stair.' "[40] Similarly, there were concerns that White teachers assigned to predominantly Black schools had low academic expectations; the Chicago Commission on Race Relations charged, in 1922, that Black pupils "are given handicraft instead of arithmetic, and singing instead of grammar." A White high-school teacher is reported to have said, "if you want to take it easy and not work too hard, you teach at [a Black school]...they just try to keep the kids busy and out of trouble. They give everyone in the room some kind of little job—one takes care of this, another takes care of that." This could, of course, be a misinterpretation of the pedagogy of Progressive Education, for which Chicago was a center, but there were regular complaints in the Black press about low standards. The *Defender* declared, in 1930, that "many are yearly graduated who have not mastered the grades."[41]

It was in response to this widely perceived reality that Du Bois wrote, in his autobiographical *Dusk of Dawn* (1940), that "most Negroes would prefer a good school with properly paid colored teachers for educating their children, to forcing their children into white schools which met them with injustice and discouraged their efforts to progress."[42] He had noted in 1934, when articulating the case for Black self-segregation that led to his departure from the NAACP, that a group of "excellent young [Black] gentlemen in Washington" who had criticized his position were in fact the beneficiaries of segregation, since "if most of them had been educated in the mixed schools in New York instead of the segregated schools of Washington, they never would have seen college, because Washington picks out and sends ten times as many Negroes to college as New York does."[43]

Even the NAACP had, before the Second World War, focused much of its effort on improving segregated schools rather than desegregating them. In Atlanta, where in 1916–1917 it had only 139 paid-up memberships among the 60,000 Black Atlantans, the NAACP "shied away from abstract concepts of human rights or equality; instead, the pitch was mainly along middle-class, moderate lines of the inequity of denying colored taxpayers their fair share of school funds."[44] Plank and Turner have identified four distinct stages in the demands made by Blacks upon the Atlanta school system: the period from 1872 and 1943, when Black leaders sought marginal improvements in the schooling provided to Black pupils, the period from 1943 to 1954 when they sought truly "separate but equal" schools, the period from 1954 to 1973 when they pressed for desegregation, and the period since 1973 when, in exchange for dropping desegregation demands, they have exercised control over the public-school system, including many highly-paid administrative positions.[45] In other words, the period during which racial integration of schools defined the Black agenda in Atlanta lasted only about twenty years.

When, in the 1950s, the national strategy of the NAACP shifted from equalizing resources and job opportunities to integration, many Black educators—among the most loyal members of the local NAACP branches, had serious misgivings. In his 1936 article "A Philosophy of Race Segregation," Du Bois had predicted, accurately as it too often turned out, that "if any outside power forced white and colored children in the same schools, the result would be turmoil and uprising as would utterly nullify the process of education."[46] It was only after the Second World War that desegregation—not just the dismantling of official segregation, but actual integration of schools—rose to the top of the civil rights agenda. In a sense, this "represented a sharp break with the past—a repudiation of existing black leadership rather than an extension of it."⁴⁷ It seemed to many to threaten to undo much that had been accomplished through patient effort and sacrifice over nearly a hundred years. As late as 1957, a Black community in Ontario sought to maintain its racially separate public schools, "arguing that their children were not prepared to compete with whites."⁴⁸ Similar doubts about replacing schools dedicated to the interests of Black children alone—however inadequate those schools may have been—with schools where those children were unwelcome or at least undervalued must have arisen in hundreds of other communities, North and South.

Education as the Solution

Some Black communities in the South, in fact, defended their separate schools even long after the 1954 *Brown* decision, and "local support for Black teachers—often recognized as pillars of their communities—sometimes outweighed or counterbalanced support for the national NAACP desegregation campaigns."⁴⁹ This reality "on the ground" reflected not only the desire to protect what were perceived as good jobs, but also a belief in the unique, almost magical, power of education, even if received in a segregated school. As we have seen, this confidence was often expressed in the efforts by Black communities to start their own schools during and after the Civil War, and by their eager response to the efforts of the White missionary teachers, and it continued even under the discouraging effects of Jim Crow. Often the segregated "public" schools that served Blacks in the South operated in facilities provided by Black churches or created by Black community initiatives supported by the Rosenwald Fund.

The education provided in those schools was inadequate in the ways that we have described, but they served an important function that would be in large part lost as Black pupils were grudgingly inserted into White schools, and Black teachers and especially Black principals lost the jobs that had been provided by the segregated schools. "What, exactly, was wrong with the old black public schools that for years served their constituencies so well despite the deprivations and the isolation of segregation?" the Black writer and "cultural activist" Tom Dent asked in 1997. "There is inescapable irony in the fact that those older schools provided much of what is lacking in today's post-segregation schools: the desperately needed psychological support...[and] a sense of the historical continuity of the educational experience of their race through the existence of the school itself."⁵⁰

This commitment to schooling was often expressed in the North as well. Headlines in the Black press in Chicago in the first decades of the twentieth century would proclaim "Education Most Important Thing in Life," with editorials promising that "education is the secret of all successes."[51] It was natural for Marcus Garvey, despite his limited schooling (though he had read widely), to wear a doctoral gown in many of his public appearances.

There was also disillusionment, of course. The belief in the potency of schooling to overcome every barrier seemed to fade more quickly under the conditions of northern urban life. "By the 1930s, black Chicagoans had shed much of their traditional optimism about education and had begun to realize that the schools were simply part of the problem."[52] Black high-school graduates, even college graduates, were still excluded from most desirable jobs and from almost all social contact with Whites of similar education; indeed, as Du Bois pointed out, the more education a Black man received, the more isolated he became. "The higher the Negro climbs or tries to climb," he wrote in *The Crisis* in 1934, "the more pitiless and unyielding the color ban."[53]

In the 1960s, Horace Mann Bond conducted a government-funded study of African-Americans who had earned doctorates, at a time when there were an estimated 1,500 alive; he was able to obtain detailed personal information from 517. In general, he found, they had behind themselves several generations of relatively advanced education, parents with high expectations and determination, and what was often the good fortune to live near one of the private schools sponsored and staffed by northern educational missionaries.

> At Emancipation and up to the last two decades, the public school instruments designed to repair a state of almost universal illiteracy were of a disgracefully inadequate and ineffective kind. For a scholar to emerge from such a social and educational system would be unlikely; Negro scholars did not. They have emerged where, almost fortuitously, an unusual social setting and unusual formal educational institutions—such as those provided by the "Yankee schoolmarm"—provided an educational foundation in earlier times to some few scholars themselves, or to the grandparents and parents of the prospective scholar.[54]

The underlying premise of these efforts was that mere instruction was not enough; that the advancement of "the race" required education that transformed attitudes, habits, and life goals. As Du Bois put it, "we look most anxiously to the establishment and strengthening of the home among members of the race, because it is the surest combination of real progress."[55] When an academic turned government official named Daniel Patrick Moynihan made much the same point, several generations later, it was no longer politically correct to suggest that there was any problem with Black family patterns, and he was fiercely criticized.[56]

It was a matter of acute concern that, as Black sociologist E. Franklin Frazier found in his studies of family structure among Blacks displaced from the land into cities like Baltimore, the rate of illegitimacy among Blacks was much higher than that among Whites. Despite the strong desire of many freed slaves to secure their marriages and families against the disruptions always potential under slavery, the new forms of insecurity created by the move to cities and the exclusion from skilled employment worked against the maintenance of stable families. As with other models of family life, the pattern thus established by default tended to perpetuate itself across generations.

As the crisis of African-American families has become undeniable, it has been common to attribute this to the fractured families created by slavery. Without denying the cruelty of an institution that gave no guarantee to marriage or the parent-child relationship, there is good evidence that slaves and freedmen valued their families highly and did everything possible to maintain them. "While Gutman estimates that 'one in six (or seven) slave marriages were ended by force or sale,' he maintains and documents the fact that 'the characteristic, or typical domestic arrangement' was a long-standing male-present or double-headed household established at the Black parents' own choice and supported by extended kin networks."[57] Similarly, after the war, "the attempts freedmen made to relocate loved ones forcefully belied the commonly held theories about a race of moral cripples who placed little value on marital and familial ties."[58]

More recently, "the vast majority of African-American families remained intact during the worst economic catastrophe in all of American history, during the 1930s. The rise in illegitimate births and single-parent families has largely taken place since 1960, a period in which Black people have made major economic gains."[59]

As we have seen, there is a long tradition in North America of attributing the inferior status of Blacks, whether held in bondage or competing unequally in freedom, to inherent qualities derived from their African past, whether as the result of origin as a separate species or through the influence of a thousand generations of ancestors. Under the influence of Franz Boas and other cultural anthropologists, the "liberal environmentalist" position gained ground in the 1920s and 1930s, finding expression in Gunnar Myrdal's *American Dilemma* in 1944. This denied any inherent racial characteristics, attributed differences to the circumstances in which children and their immediate forebears lived, and held out the promise of full social integration.

In the 1920s, however, the influence of "social Darwinism," with its emphasis upon the competitive struggle and the validation offered by economic success, was still much stronger among the general public, and to a considerable extent the emerging Black elite adopted elements of this theory and applied it to confirm their own achievements and to distance themselves from Blacks who had not been as successful.

> The self-help component of uplift increasingly bore the stamp of evolutionary racial theories positing the civilization of elites against the moral degradation of the masses.... It signaled the move from anti-slavery appeals for inalienable human rights to more limited claims for Black citizenship that required that the race demonstrate its preparedness to exercise those rights.... With Black political leadership in retreat, elite Blacks' use of uplift ideology to forge a sense of personal worth and dignity in an antiBlack society pointed to intraracial division along class lines virtually as an end in itself, as a sign of race progress.[60]

Some protested against this separation of the Black elite from the "masses." One of the most significant voices during the period between the world wars was that of Carter Woodson, who published in 1933 a study—really a polemic—on the *"Mis-Education of the Negro."* While many had pointed out that illiteracy and semiliteracy were prevalent among rural and even to some extent urban Black Americans, Woodson criticized the effects of the education provided to that small minority that had been able to attend college. "The 'educated Negroes,'" he wrote, "have the attitude of contempt toward their own people because in their own as well as in their mixed schools Negroes are taught to admire the Hebrew, the Greek, the Latin and the Teuton and to despise the African.... If after leaving school they have the opportunity to give out to Negroes what traducers of the race would like to have it learn such persons may thereby earn a living at teaching or preaching what they have been taught but they never become a constructive force in the development of the race. The so-called school, then, becomes a questionable factor in the life of the despised people."[61]

This was the case, Woodson argued, because schools were not making their pupils proud to be Black; after all, "to handicap a student by teaching him that his Black face is a curse and that his struggle to change is hopeless is the worst sort of lynching. It kills one's aspirations and dooms him to vagabondage and crime." As a result of such an education, "when a Negro has finished his education in our schools, then, he has been equipped to begin the life of an Americanized or Europeanized White man, but before he steps from the threshold of his alma mater he is told by his teachers that he must go back to his own people from who he has been estranged by a vision of ideals which in his disillusionment he will realize he cannot attain.... While being a good American, he must above all things be a 'good Negro'; and to perform this definite function he must learn to stay in a 'Negro's place.' "[62]

On the other hand, as historian Diane Ravitch has pointed out, "Blacks were more often oppressed by the education that they did not receive than by the education that they did receive."[63]

Woodson insisted that the lack of control, by Blacks, over the schools that educated their children made those schools unfit to be an instrument of their advancement. "The education of the Negroes, then, the most important thing in the uplift of the Negroes, is almost entirely in the hands of those who have enslaved them and now segregate them.... The present system under the control of the Whites trains the Negro to be White and at the same time convinces him of the impropriety or the impossibility of his becoming White. It compels the Negro to become a good Negro for the performance of which his education is ill-suited."[64]

The only institution that was created and sustained entirely by the Black community, Woodson pointed out, was the church, which, "although not a shadow of what it ought to be, is the great asset of the race. It is a part of the capital that the race must invest to make its future. The Negro church has taken the lead in education in the schools of the race, it has supplied a forum for the thought of the 'highly educated' Negro, it has originated a large portion of the business controlled by Negroes, and in many cases it has made it possible for Negro professional men to exist."[65]

Woodson was here identifying an aspect of Black community life that was almost entirely ignored by Myrdal's massive study, published in 1944: the crucial role of churches as the most dynamic and enduring institution created and supported by Black communities. "As a class," Myrdal wrote, "Negro preachers are losing influence, because they are not changing as fast as the rest of the Negro community.... It is difficult to see how the continuing decline of the minister's prestige and leadership can be stopped."[66] Someone with no other knowledge of the inner life of those communities than could have been derived from

Myrdal's account would have had no way of anticipating the crucial role that would be played in the Freedom Movement of the 1950s and 1960s by the southern Christian Leadership Conference and clergymen like Martin Luther King, Jr., or that Black churches and their pastors continue to occupy in their communities.

Although segregated schooling was in some respects a refuge from the insults encountered so often in situations of racial contact, as well as an institutional support for the modest development of a Black middle class, it was also—because imposed rather than chosen voluntarily—a standing insult. In 1956, the poet and novelist Robert Penn Warren, a White Southerner, published a sensitive "travel diary" of his journey of inquiry through a South faced with the legal requirement to desegregate its schools. An "eminent Negro scholar" told him that the most important issue was not that the Black child had poor school facilities, but "that he must endure a constant assault on his ego. He is denied human dignity."[67] Or, as Woodson had put it two decades before,

> If you can control a man's thinking you do not have to worry about his action. When you determine what a man shall think you do not have to concern yourself about what he will do. If you make a man feel that he is inferior, you do not have to compel him to accept an inferior status, for he will seek it himself. If you make a man think that he is justly an outcast, you do not have to order him to the back door. He will go without being told; and if there is no back door, his very nature will demand one.[68]

Frank Tannenbaum wrote, in 1946, that "the shadow of slavery is still cast ahead of us, and we behave toward the Negro as if the imputation of slavery had something of a slave by nature in it. The Emancipation may have legally freed the Negro, but it failed morally to free the white man, and by that failure it denied to the Negro the moral status required for effective legal freedom."[69]

It was this sense that segregated public schools and other legally- or socially-established forms of separation conveyed an insistent message of inferiority that made the demand for desegregation so powerful...and, perhaps, made the disappointments that followed so bitter.

To those in the White majority who were sympathetic to the demands of Black organizations like the NAACP for desegregation of every dimension of American life, it was easy to miss what was occurring in parallel, the continuing development of institutional life and of racial pride within the Black community, which would produce the apparently paradoxical emphasis, in the late 1960s, on Black separatism just as the legal barriers to integration were falling.

The period of the Great Migration into northern cities, starting with the First World War and continuing into the 1960s, was one of institution-building within Black communities. A study of Chicago churches during this period points out that "unlike the religious community of the last decades of the nineteenth century, few in migration-era Black mainstream churches put faith solely in the demonstration of respectability and middle-class decorum as a viable format for racial and social change. Integrationist impulses made way for a new confidence in the development of an institutionally parallel, self-sustaining Black community."[70] During the Second World War, many thousands of Black servicemen served in segregated units, and they were demobilized into a society that, for all of the rhetoric about "democracy," which had been used so freely during the war, was still segregated not only socially but also institutionally. Separate development must have seemed to many, as it did to Du Bois, the only viable response.

This belief in education, and in a distinctive Black approach to education, took a new form as the first, optimistic phase of the Freedom Movement of the 1950s and the 1960s, with its emphasis on breaking down racial barriers, was replaced by a determination to find ways to promote self-awareness and efficacy on the part of Black youth. Young activists in the Student Non-violent Coordinating Committee (SNCC) and its counterpart the Northern Student Movement (NSM) were convinced that Black youth had a distorted consciousness through living in a society and culture premised on their inferiority. Through creating "Freedom Schools"—usually short-term or even one-day events—SNCC sought to "fill an intellectual and creative vacuum in the lives of young Negro Mississippians, and to get them to articulate their own desires, demands and questions." Volunteer teachers (often White college students at first) were told that the "value of the Freedom School will derive from what the teachers are able to elicit from the students in terms of comprehension and expression of their experiences." In a typical expression of Progressive Education, volunteers were told that the SNCC curriculum

> begins on the level of the students' everyday lives and those things in their environment that they have already experienced or can readily perceive, and builds up to a more realistic perception of American society, themselves, the conditions of their oppression, and alternatives offered by the Freedom Movement. It is not our purpose to impose a particular set of conclusions. Our purpose is to encourage the asking of questions, and the hope that society can be improved.

The purpose of the Freedom School was not to convey facts but to explore "connections and associations which will be able to cross-cut the political, economic, and social elements of a given problem. We hope that the creativity of the class sessions will be mirrored by the creativity of the research as the students associate and pull incidents from their own experiences." This would require "very active participation" by the youth as they considered their own "experiences and life situation" in Mississippi. In this way they would "develop a new way of thinking and be awakened to their powers of analytic reasoning." Thus the volunteer teachers should above all "stimulate latent talents and interests that have been submerged too long,...causing...youth in Mississippi to QUESTION."[71]

A strategy that produced gratifying results under the exciting conditions of a Mississippi Freedom Summer in 1964, when White college students and Black youth could discuss the obvious instances of injustice on every side was less successful when translated to northern urban ghettoes. For inner-city Black youth, the nature of oppression was unclear and even to some extent self-imposed; guided discussion of their "experiences and life situation" did not produce the sort of consciousness that could lead to focused and effective action under conditions where the challenge was far more complex than to register to vote or drink a Coke at a drugstore soda fountain. By the late 1960s, Black activists—with Whites increasingly excluded—had abandoned the belief that integration was the answer. SNCC rejected integration as a goal in 1966, and urged "black Americans to begin building independent political, economic, and cultural institutions that they will control and use as instruments of social change in this country."[72] In a sense, they were recapitulating the change of direction that Du Bois had made three decades before. As a result, in the educational programs organized (as SNCC faded away in 1967, "bankrupt and reduced to some twoscore nihilists"[73]) by the Black Panthers a "progressive pedagogy that trusted students to discover the truth gave way to one in which students were informed about politics and culture.... The Panthers did not believe they could rely on Blacks living in darkness to discover the path to liberation. It was up to their teachers to light the way."[74]

The Panthers opened their first "Liberation School" in Berkeley in 1969. Black elementary- and middle-school students learned to

> march to songs that tell of the pigs running amuck and Panthers fighting for the people. Employing a curriculum "designed to...guide [youth]

in their search for revolutionary truths and principles," the Panthers taught the children "that they are not fighting a race struggle, but, in fact, a class struggle... because people of all colors are being exploited by the same pigs all over the world." The children learned to work for the "destruction of the ruling class that oppresses and exploits,... the avaricious businessman,... and the racist pigs that are running rampant in our communities." At the Panthers' San Francisco Liberation School, "everything the children do is political.... The children sing revolutionary songs and play revolutionary games." The entire curriculum contributed to students receiving a clear and explicit ideology. Teachers avoided lessons "about a jive president that was said to have freed the slaves, when it's as clear as water that we're still not free." Instead, students learned the origins and history of the Black Panther Party and could "explain racism, capitalism, fascism, cultural nationalism, and socialism. They can also explain the Black Panther Party Platform and Program and the ways to survive."[75]

The Panthers followed this up, in 1971, by starting a full-time elementary school in Oakland for the children of Party members. The Oakland Community School (OCS) provided instruction in Panther ideology and fieldwork "distributing the *Black Panther* newspaper, talking to other youths in the community, attending court sessions for political prisoners and visiting prisons." In a "conservative" move that Antonio Gramsci would have approved of, by 1974 the school leadership began to criticize the Oakland public schools not only for being repressive but also for failing "to adequately teach English or grammar." Mastery of traditional skills came to seem more truly liberating than consciousness-raising. At OCS, students "recite[d] consonant blends and studied word endings, diacritical marks, and alphabetization... as the radical hopes of the late 1960s faded, the school abandoned the idea that students could either make meaning of their world or be instructed so as to understand their oppression."[76]

The shift from the high hopes and the "we'll walk hand-in-hand" of 1963 to the disillusionment several years later, despite the passage of strong federal laws responding to the injustices of official segregation, was stunning in its speed and its apparent completeness. "Apparent" because to some extent this may have been a mood among a few thousand mostly young activists who failed to see how deep and permanent were the changes that in fact had occurred. These "young militants abandoned their former beliefs and ideals. Continued school and residential segregation convinced the disenchanted blacks that King's goal of an integrated society was an impossible dream. Embittered, they took the growth of the white backlash as proof of the hopeless position of blacks in America. SNCC [Student Nonviolent Coordinating Committee] and CORE [Congress of Racial Equality] began to believe they had to transform the struggle for desegregation into a battle for self-determination."[77]

Meanwhile, however, the process of integration—economic and residential if not necessarily social—continued among the growing Black middle class, in the process ironically (as William Julius Wilson has shown) depriving many Black communities of what had been their leadership.

CHAPTER 7

Integration and Its Disappointments

By the early twentieth century, alongside the comfort that many Black teachers and others took in the existence of a separate system of schooling that was, to some extent at least, theirs to control and to derive material benefits and status from, there was a growing demand on the part of some Black leaders and intellectuals for elimination of official segregation of schools, and "the idea of a voluntary Negro community virtually disappeared from respectable discussion."[1] This derives in part from decades of experience that "Black" schools would always be neglected and provided with inadequate resources. In 1915, William Pickens wrote an overview of "the Negro question" for the National Conference of Charities and Correction, arguing that the

> Negroes in Northern communities are generally opposed to the separate school idea and face the usual accusation that they "do not want to associate with their own people," which ignores the more positive reason which the Negro himself advances—the universal temptation and tendency of the school authorities to degrade the Negro schools wherever they have been successfully segregated...whenever retrenchment was necessary the Negro's share was always trimmed down first.... [The Negro] knows that where Black and White attend the same school this discrimination is forever impossible.... Cincinnati, Washington and St. Louis have the best separate schools for the Negro in the United States, and it is significant that the percentage of attendance of colored children at these schools is lower than at the mixed schools of Boston, Cleveland and New York.[2]

Horace Mann Bond, in 1935, criticized the self-segregation that was attracting Black intellectuals like Du Bois, writing that "southern

[White] nationalism has been irrational; Negro nationalism is no less so, and can be defended only on the ground that it intends itself to be an antidote to the prevailing lack of reason, and thus may aid the child, placed between two irrationalities, to select the middle course of 'true reason,' whatever that may be."[3]

In some complex manner, the experience of national mobilization and its accompanying rhetoric about democracy during the Second World War, and the worldwide move toward national liberation movements and toward the definition of universal human rights, made a segregated existence less and less acceptable to Black Americans and Canadians. Bond wrote much more forcefully, in 1962, that

> we need, I think, to sue, and sue, and sue, for access to every opportunity available to every other American citizen. We need, I think, to plan, for a genuine integration—on our terms—and to fight for it. We need to struggle to open all doors now closed; to integrate Negro students into all schools, and Negro teachers into all faculties, and Negro board members into all private and public, local, state, and national boards. We need to press—to press, I say—with all of the force of persuasion and law, to arrive at integration beyond the scope of mere physical occupancy of space within an institution. We need to hope for the admission of Negroes to the normal intimacies that comprise so large a portion of modern education. I think, also, we need not feel ashamed, and convinced of our minority inferiority, as to think of integration as a one-way street, leading only by the door of the majority into final unity.[4]

And sue they did. The brief filed by the NAACP, in October 1953, in the cases that led to the Supreme Court's historic *Brown v. Board of Education* decision of May 1954, argued that "the Fourteenth Amendment prevents states from according differential treatment to American children on the basis of their color or race." In school assignments, "the racial classifications here have no reasonable relation to any valid legislative purpose"; in fact, "candor requires recognition that the plain purpose and effect of segregated education is to perpetuate an inferior status for Negroes which is America's sorry heritage from slavery." Earlier decisions of the Supreme Court in the law school cases had recognized "the educational detriment involved in racially constricting a student's associations," and the Court was now asked to apply this logic to school experiences.[5]

There can be no question that the Court was influenced, in its decision, by changes in the world that would not have seemed relevant at the time of the *Plessy v. Ferguson* decision in 1896 upholding "separate but equal" treatment of Blacks, or even during the 1930s. In its earlier decisions, "the Supreme Court had, in effect, told the Negro to seek solace not in the law of the land but, like Stephen Foster's Old Black Joe, in cotton fields, mournful song, darkey friends, and the hereafter."[6] But after the Second World War, revulsion against Nazi racism, the adoption of the Universal Declaration of Human Rights in 1948, and the worldwide competition with the Soviet Union all made it clear that the United States needed to address at least the more egregious examples of its own official racism. A brief filed on behalf of the federal government by the attorney general, in 1952, in relation to the school cases quoted the secretary of state as saying that the

> segregation of school children on a racial basis is one of the practices in the United States which has been singled out for hostile foreign comment in the United Nations and elsewhere. Other peoples cannot understand how such a practice can exist in a country which professes to be a strong supporter of freedom, justice, and democracy.[7]

As an indication of what national policy makers thought was at stake in the *Brown* decision, the result was broadcast by the *Voice of America* in thirty-five languages within hours of its release!

Chief Justice Warren, delivering the opinion of the Court, noted that each of the cases that had been consolidated in *Brown* involved "minors of the Negro race" who had been "denied admission to schools attended by White children under laws requiring or permitting segregation according to race." Lower courts had refused to strike down these laws, citing the principle of "separate but equal" that had been the basis of the *Roberts* case in Massachusetts, many years before, and had been used by the Supreme Court in deciding *Plessy v. Ferguson* in 1896. However, Warren noted, "the plaintiffs contend that segregated public schools are not 'equal' and cannot be made 'equal,' and that hence they are deprived of the equal protection of the laws" guaranteed by the Fourteenth Amendment since 1868. Review of the "circumstances surrounding the adoption of the Fourteenth Amendment" had not proved helpful, Warren pointed out, but there had been recent decisions involving graduate school admissions in which "inequality was found in that specific benefits enjoyed by White students were denied to Negro students of the same educational qualifications."

In the school cases consolidated in *Brown* decision, however, there was evidence that "the Negro and White schools involved have been equalized, or are being equalized, with respect to buildings, curricula, qualifications and salaries of teachers, and other 'tangible' factors." These efforts were being made by southern states and local governments precisely to lend credence to the "separate but equal" doctrine, after decades of grossly unequal treatment of the schools attended by Black pupils. The Supreme Court's decision, Warren wrote, "cannot turn on merely a comparison of these tangible factors in the Negro and White schools involved in each of the cases. We must look instead to the effect of segregation itself on public education." The Court here anticipated by several decades the more recent trend in education reform, which focuses less on the inputs of education and more on its outcomes.

"In approaching this problem," Warren wrote, "we must consider public education in its full development and its present place in American life throughout the Nation. Only in this way can it be determined if segregation in public schools deprives these plaintiffs of the equal protection of the laws." In effect, he was saying, it was irrelevant that Congress, in the 1860s and 1870s, had considered and rejected a requirement that schools be racially integrated; the important question was whether racial segregation could be justified as providing equal education under the conditions of the 1950s.

Then, in one of the most famous passages in American jurisprudence, Warren wrote:

> Today, education is perhaps the most important function of state and local governments. Compulsory school attendance laws and the great expenditures for education both demonstrate out recognition of the importance of education to our democratic society. It is required in the performance of our most basic public responsibilities, even service in the armed forces. It is the very foundation of good citizenship. Today it is a principal instrument in awakening the child to cultural values, in preparing him for later professional training, and in helping him to adjust normally to his environment. In these days, it is doubtful that any child may reasonably be expected to succeed if he is denied the opportunity of any education. Such an opportunity, where the state has undertaken to provide it, is a right which must be made available to all on equal terms.
>
> We come then to the question presented: Does segregation of children in public schools solely on the basis of race, even though the physical facilities and other 'tangible' factors may be equal, deprive the children of the minority group of equal educational opportunities? We believe that it does.

In the graduate school cases, the Court had noted "those qualities which are incapable of objective measurement but which make for greatness in a law school" and the importance, for a graduate student, "to study, to engage in discussions and exchange views with other students, and, in general, to learn his profession." Warren pointed out that "such considerations apply with added force to children in grade and high schools. To separate them from others of similar age and qualifications solely because of their race generates a feeling of inferiority as to their status in the community that may affect their hearts and minds in a way unlikely ever to be undone." He cited with approval the conclusion of one of the lower courts in the case, that "the policy of separating the races is usually interpreted as denoting the inferiority of the negro group. A sense of inferiority affects the motivation of a child to learn, segregation with the sanction of law, therefore, has a tendency to [retard] the educational and mental development of negro children and to deprive them of some of the benefits they would receive in a racial[ly] integrated school system." The Supreme Court had concluded that "whatever may have been the extent of psychological knowledge at the time of *Plessy v. Ferguson*, this finding is amply supported by modern authority. Any language in *Plessy v. Ferguson* contrary to this finding is rejected. We conclude that in the field of public education the doctrine of 'separate but equal' has no place. Separate educational facilities are inherently unequal."[8]

Horace Mann Bond had made the same point two decades before, pointing out that "when we think of 'separate' schools, we think of Negro, and not of white schools. The 'white' school is the norm, the standard, in fact, 'the school'; the 'separate' school is the Negro school." Nor was this a mere verbal convention:

> the separate school is an instrument of policy in the hands of the dominant group, with a foundation upon the concept of racial inequality and unassimilability. It has been suggested that the structural inferiority of the system that is actually "separated"—the Negro system—must be regarded as an inevitable concomitant of such a system. There are considerations involved in separate schools for Negroes other than those of material and physical equality. These conditions involve the outcomes of the policy of separation, and the consequent effect upon the minds of the segregated Negro children, who are separated from the white children as one would take from a school those with measles, or chicken-pox, or diphtheria. The structural inequality of the separate Negro school is warrant of an inferior educational process; and there are subtle shadings to the effect of segregation which need to be carefully balanced regardless of the maintenance of physically equivalent opportunities for both races.[9]

Bond saw that clearly in 1935; the Supreme Court would recognize it and make it the basis of a fundamental constitutional protection in

1954. While it has frequently been pointed out that the social science evidence used in this case, and indeed the practice of educing such evidence in resolving legal questions, is rather shaky, it enabled the Supreme Court to forbid a practice that, on its face, was a fundamental insult to Black Americans.

Wilkinson points out that the Court could have upheld the plaintiffs on the narrow ground that in fact the schools provided for Black pupils were not equal in various measurable ways, such as the qualifications of teachers, the condition of facilities, or the amount spent on books and supplies. Such inequities did indeed continue to exist, and if the Court had ruled on that basis "a century of petty law might have begun to build over the issue of what was equal and what was not. Yet through all the din over questions of mortar, size of playgrounds and salaries of teachers, the hurt and degradation would have persisted."[10] By venturing onto the legally shaky ground of psychological damage caused by official segregation, the Court recognized that hurt and degradation; and committed the country to removing its causes. The position taken was noble, but its translation into concrete and effective measures would prove frustrating.

Although by the summer of 1955 the NAACP had filed desegregation petitions signed by local residents with 170 school boards in seventeen states, the pace of actual implementation was glacial for nearly a decade. In a number of southern states, legislatures declared that—in the words of the Alabama vote—the Supreme Court's decision was "null, void, and of no effect" because of the "interposition" of state authority. Mississippi stated that the *Brown* decision was "unconstitutional and of no lawful effect," while four states adopted penalties against local officials who dared to comply with the Court. Two states amended their constitutions to allow public schools to be abolished altogether, and South Carolina repealed compulsory school attendance. Alabama enacted a law providing for dismissing teachers who advocated desegregation, allowed the state government to close the schools whenever "necessary to avoid friction or disorder," and allowed public funds to be used for substitute private schools. While there was full or partial compliance in the District of Columbia and some border states, in the eight states of the "solid South" there was no compliance at all. By 1958, eleven states had enacted 145 laws intended to protect segregated education and, after the initial burst of compliance in some areas, there was almost no additional progress during the late 1950s. By 1962–1963, nine years after *Brown*, "fewer than 13,000 Negro public school pupils out of 2,803,882 were in school with Southern whites."[11]

National leadership in support of school desegregation was half-hearted. This was true even among the Black clergy, with their strong influence on local communities and national perceptions. The Rev. J. H. Jackson of Chicago, leader of the (Black) National Baptist Convention, and an opponent of Martin Luther King, Jr., told *Jet* magazine that some Negroes "talk too much about racial integration and not enough about racial elevation."[12] President Eisenhower, in his annual State of the Union Message of January 1957, urged the Congress to enact laws to protect voting rights and give the federal government authority to protect civil rights. A bill was duly filed that would become the Civil Rights Act of 1957; its preamble pointed out that "any intolerance or discrimination or deprivation of our constitutionally guaranteed rights and privileges resound and reverberate throughout the globe" in a time of competition with the Soviet Union. While the scope of the bill was very limited, and it was further weakened during the legislative process, it marked the first engagement of Congress with the civil rights of Black Americans, and was followed by more significant civil rights acts in 1960, 1964, 1965, and 1968.

Not all were convinced that Congress should concern itself with what they insisted with internal matters for the individual states. Senator Sam Erwin called it a "queer concoction of constitutional and legal sins" and a "cunningly conceived and deviously worded bill," while a Mississippi congressman charged that "members of both political parties who are so intent on currying the favor of the Negro and left-wing voters have succeeded in bringing to this floor...a bill...obviously designed to heap vindictiveness upon the Southern states." The bill represented, from a southern White perspective, "un-American fanaticism" that would revive "sectional animosities" and was "motivated solely by a cynical greed for capturing the votes of easily misled, highly sensitive, and often emotionally unstable minorities" in the districts of northern politicians.[13]

The Civil Rights Act of 1964, in response to intense national concern about the Freedom Movement in the South, from the Montgomery bus boycott to the televised use of fire hoses and police dogs against demonstrating Black students in Birmingham in 1963, would be far more significant. The assassination of President Kennedy in November 1963 created a strong desire to "do something," and adoption of a strong law protecting civil rights would, President Johnson told Congress less than a week later, be the best possible memorial. Title VI of the law that was enacted prohibited racial discrimination in any activity receiving federal funding, which would give the national administration great leverage over schools that received national government support.

Despite the strong support of President Johnson, and the national mood, enactment of this law was by no means easy. Debate in the Senate "lasted over eighty days and took up some seven thousand pages in the Congressional Record. Well over ten million words were devoted to the subject by members of the upper house. In addition, the debate produced the longest filibuster in Senate history." In the course of the debate, supporters of the legislation pointed out that, despite the decision in *Brown v. Board of Education* ten years before, "there still remain...more than 2,000 school districts which require that White and Negro pupils attend separate schools. Many Negro children who entered segregated grade schools at the time of the 1954 Supreme Court decision entered segregated high schools this past year."[14]

However, there was strong opposition and predictions that "this so-called Civil Rights Act would cause strife and chaos among our people.... It will be resisted and contribute to violence in every State of this Union wherein the Federal Government intervenes.... It would rob all Americans of precious freedom on the theory that this can give economic, cultural, and social equality to a minority of Americans who, let us face it, have failed to achieve such equality on their own initiative.... The present Negro leadership blames every ill on racial discrimination. Every Negro failure, every Negro fault, every Negro crime, every Negro hurt, every Negro childhood trauma, is blamed on the White man's racial discrimination against the Negro.... They are deluding themselves and their followers, too." Segregation, the opponents argued, was often voluntary, as when "in one area there may be people of German ancestry who enjoy being among their own kind," or when "those who organize Episcopalian, Presbyterian, or Methodist schools tend to segregate to some extent, and to be selective in permitting those of another religion to attend."[15]

Despite such opposition, the bill was passed in the House of Representatives with 59 percent of the Democrats and 78 percent of the Republicans voting for it and, after a much longer process permitted by the Senate's rules, it was adopted by the Senate as well, in what Senator Russell of Georgia called "the greatest tragedy ever played out in the Senate of the United States." Russell predicted that it would be followed by other legislation "to use the Federal power to enforce absolute conformity of thought and action by every one of our citizens." Similarly, a senator from South Carolina called it "the Blackest day in the U.S. Senate since 1875, when the Congress passed a civil rights bill similar to this one," which was later declared unconstitutional. "I predict," he told the Senate, "that this bill will never be enforced without turning our Nation into a police state and without the cost of bloodshed and violence." He predicted with some complacency that one of the results would be to make the "racial situation in the North...so explosive as to be intolerable." "Already," a Virginia senator announced, "the second invasion of carpetbaggers of the Southland has begun. Hordes of beatniks, misfits, and agitators from the North, with the admitted aid of the Communists, are streaming into the Southland on mischief bent, backed and defended by other hordes of Federal marshals, Federal agents, and Federal power."[16]

Although official or de jure segregation was banned by the *Brown* decision and subsequent decisions required many school districts to take positive measures to bring Black and White pupils together in the same schoolhouses, school authorities found a variety of effective means of minimizing the actual racial mixing at the classroom level. One of the means by which southern states evaded the implications of the *Brown* decision was by adopting "pupil placement" laws that allowed school boards to assign pupils "on the basis of such factors as psychological aptitude for types of teaching and association involved, effects of the pupil's admission upon the prevailing standards of the school, and the possibility of threat or friction or disorder among pupils and others." A Florida law permitted the assignment of students to the school "for which he is best fitted." In 1955, Alabama adopted a pupil assignment law that provided sixteen factors that could be used to place pupils in schools or classrooms, including "the adequacy of the pupil's academic preparation for admission to a particular school and curriculum" and "the scholastic aptitude and relative intelligence or mental energy or ability" of the pupil.[17] The constitutionality of such laws was upheld by the Supreme Court in 1958.

The Charleston, South Carolina school authorities, seeking a way to avoid desegregation, were advised by their attorney that "we need to press for a state-wide I.Q. and Achievement test administered in all our schools. This difference in achievement between the two races may be our last line of defense."[18] Tracking became an increasingly common practice, and reached down from secondary to intermediate and even elementary schools, as a way to assure White parents that their children would not be placed in classes with low-performing and possibly disruptive Black pupils, even in desegregated schools.[19] Washington's high schools used IQ test scores to assign students to college preparatory (87 percent White and 13 percent Black), regular, general, or basic (89 percent Black and 11 percent White) programs.[20]

"Moderate" southern leaders "recognized that token desegregation could limit federal intervention and allow southern school officials to control the process. Moderates accomplished this by broadening testing and tracking within schools, requiring that applicants to southern colleges submit test scores, and expanding use of the [National Teacher Examination]. Well before the courts swept away the paraphernalia of massive resistance and required widespread desegregation, educational authorities rationalized restrictions limiting access to middle-class blacks." Paradoxically, then, "by fueling the advancement of some African Americans, desegregation heightened the isolation of others. Even more so than in the past, desegregation created the greatest opportunities for the most affluent and educated segments of the black population."[21]

Testing was also used as an "objective" way to continue the long-standing pattern of discrimination in salary and placement against Black teachers. Ironically, southern school systems had adopted the National Teacher Examinations (NTE) under pressure to equalize teacher salaries. This did in fact benefit the best-educated Black applicants, generally from middle-class families, but it

> heightened class divisions among African Americans...as new, more rational restrictions replaced those once required by law, the legacies of caste—and the class divisions that developed within the black caste—shaped educational opportunities and outcomes. While advantaged blacks entered schools, colleges, and universities, most African Americans, handicapped by generations of segregation and discrimination, were not prepared to compete educationally with whites and remained cloistered in predominantly African-American institutions. Desegregation, then, has been both a triumph and a tragedy, expanding opportunities for advantaged blacks without ending the isolation of most African Americans.[22]

In a pattern that sociologist William Julius Wilson would detail on a larger scale in *The Truly Disadvantaged* (1987), the growing opportunities for the Black elite on the basis of educational achievement and social connections left other Blacks in some ways even more deprived of leadership based on racial solidarity.

Despite all the predictions of disaster, enactment of the Civil Rights Act of 1964 created momentum for changes in education that had only been promised by the *Brown* decision ten years before. This was reinforced by the decision of the Supreme Court in *Green v. County School Board* in 1968 "the burden on a school board today is to come forward with a plan that promises realistically to work, and promises realistically to work *now*."[23] The pace of school desegregation throughout the

South accelerated. Whereas only 1.2 percent of the Black students in the South attended schools with White students in 1965, the proportion had grown to 39 percent five years later, and other school districts were in the process of developing or implementing desegregation plans, usually in response to pressure from the courts or from the federal Office for Civil Rights.[24] By 1972, 91 percent of the Black students in the South were in school with White students, even as the number of all-Black schools in northern cities was increasing rapidly.[25] Much more progress in desegregation was made in the South than in the North. A comparison over the years can be seen in table 7.1.

During the 1970s, a series of cases in northern states where school segregation had never been official concluded that actions of state or local government that had the predictable effect of promoting racial isolation could be the basis for ordering desegregation plans, some of which also included extensive—and very expensive—requirements for educational measures to compensate minority youth for the harm done to them by previously attending segregated schools. The effects of these cases was largely undermined by the continuing effects of movement of White families out of the cities where Blacks were increasingly concentrated. In fact, the "slow retreat of *de jure* [official] segregation in the South had been paralleled by a rapid advance of *de facto* [unofficial] segregation of residence and schools in the North. The increase of black population in northern cities was accompanied by a panic of white retreat to the suburbs and an acceleration of urban decay, crime, and delinquency."[26] Cities that undertook to desegregate their schools often found that those schools were resegregated as the number of White pupils available for assignment declined.[27]

Table 7.1 Progress of School Desegregation

	South	*Northeast*	*Midwest*
Percent Black students in schools over 90 percent minority			
1968	77.5	42.7	58.0
1980	24.6	48.7	43.6
1992	26.5	49.9	39.4
Percent White students in schools over 90 percent White			
1968	68.8	82.5	89.4
1980	32.2	79.5	81.0
1992	26.0	66.7	71.9[28]

One of the northern cities most affected was Detroit, where Black public school enrollment had grown from 5,680 after the First World War to 38,529 after the Second World War, as a result of the expansion of manufacturing jobs for war industry, and then leapt to 168,299 twenty years later. Even more dramatic was the change in racial proportions, from 4.4 percent Black in 1921 to 17.3 percent Black in 1946 to 56.7 percent Black in 1966. By 1980, the school system was 85.5 percent Black; White enrollment had dropped from 183,862 in 1946 to 26,230 in 1980. The fact that private and parochial school enrollment also fell indicates that White families were actually leaving the city, not just switching schools. With this enrollment change came a hollowing-out of the school system's tax base as industry as well as middle-class home owners abandoned the city. When, in the 1960s, the school system began to take steps to reduce the racial segregation of its schools, it encountered opposition and school boycotts from White parents who were already feeling under siege.[29]

More frustrating to most Black parents in Detroit (and other northern cities) than the failure or very moderate success of desegregation efforts was a perceived decline in the quality of schooling provided to their children. This was not so much a case of inferior resources devoted to the schools attended by Black pupils—though it was very common for them to have less experienced teachers and more staff turn over as a result of seniority rights under union contracts—as it was of lowered expectations about what pupils could learn.

> In predominantly black schools, the dilution of the curriculum proceeded at a faster rate and with a broader stroke than in white schools. Black high school students were channeled more frequently than whites into the insubstantial general track and they were virtually denied apprenticeship opportunities in the most promising vocational programs.[30]

Such programs, in most cases, were partially controlled by the conditions set by trade unions for admission to apprenticeship; conditions designed to favor the relatives of union members and often functioning to exclude potential apprentices of color. As a result, most of the predominantly Black high schools in Detroit had, by the mid-1960s, "become 'general track' institutions dominated by the philosophy that the less teachers demanded of students the more tractable the students would be." Community activists charged that the "continuing failure to educate inner city children reflects a deliberate policy of racial discrimination," and that the public schools were engaged in the "systematic destruction of the Afro-American child's self-image and racial pride."[31]

While school and teacher union officials argued that what was required to solve all the problems was more funding from the state, outspoken Black leaders insisted that the only answer was control of the schools by the Black community. The effect, as in New York City and elsewhere at the same period, was to break apart the political coalition between organized labor and Black organizations, with the third party, middle-class liberals, often withdrawing entirely from engagement with issues of urban education. In ongoing escalation of rhetoric, some Black spokesmen insisted that school integration was "a form of genocide."[32]

This new voice that began to be heard with increasing urgency in the 1960s was that of "Black Power," rejecting integration into the majority society as a primary goal. Although there is abundant evidence that this was very much a minority view in the wider Black community (in Detroit, a 1971 survey found that 81 percent of Black respondents favored racially integrated schools[33]), it proved seductive to many young activists. With bewildering speed, organizations like the Congress of Racial Equality went from being an interracial proponent of integration to a self-described "Black Nationalist Organization" seeking racial separation...and promptly collapsed. With the wave of urban riots—Watts, Detroit, Newark, altogether 150 officially identified as "major"—it seemed for a time that the country was indeed moving toward being, in the words of the President's Commission on Civil Disorders in 1968, "two societies, one black, one white—separate and unequal."[34]

Kenneth Stampp suggests that, both under slavery and during the difficult ninety or one hundred years that followed of an ambiguous and contested freedom, Blacks were "obliged to wear the mask of Sambo, whatever they may have been inside...[and] troubled to an extraordinary degree by the problem of role conflict. To escape this problem seems to have been one of the aims of the black revolution of the 1960s and 1970s, for the search for black identity is in part a search for role clarity. To end the dissembling, to be all of one piece, to force the white community to accept them as they really are, not as it so long wanted to see them, is quite obviously one determined goal of the new generation of blacks."[35]

New York City, like Detroit, experienced a rapid growth in Black (and Puerto Rican) school enrollment during the 1950s and 1960s, and this in turn tended to drive White families out of the areas and schools that were becoming racially mixed. An attempt to respond to demands for "community control" by creating several districts with decentralized authority to manage their schools led to the crisis that began in

1967 in Ocean Hill-Brownsville (Brooklyn) and diverted energies and resources away from concrete school improvement for several years. Critics "alleged that parent leadership had been usurped by representatives of activist poverty agencies...and that this had been accomplished with the covert assistance of Ford Foundation personnel." By the close of that school year, in April 1968, the local board "was increasingly embittered by its inability to have the powers it demanded and increasingly caught up in its own revolutionary aspirations. The union, defensive of its members and its contract, was dead set against community control. " For those supporting the local board, the only possible reason for opposing its ability to replace teachers in the schools under its supervision was White racism.[36] Unfortunately,

> three years in, the reading test scores in Ocean Hill-Brownsville were lower than they had been before the experiment began. Ten years after decentralization was adopted, Kenneth Clark, one of its leading advocates, conceded that "the schools are no better and no worse then they were a decade ago. In terms of the basic objective, decentralization didn't make a damn bit of difference."[37]

There were no winners from this controversy, least of all the children and their parents.

Elijah Mohammad wrote, in the *Black Muslim* newspaper, in 1963, "we want equal education—but separate schools up to sixteen for boys and eighteen for girls on condition that the girls be sent to women's colleges and universities."[38] More recently, there has been a tendency for Black educators to argue, as an article in *Crisis*, the venerable publication of the NAACP, reported, that "the solution to the Black male's difficulties in the educational process lies with the development of separate Black educational facilities."[39] In 1991, the heavily Black Detroit school system sought to open three all-male "African-American academies"; under court order, a few girls were admitted as well, but the racial focus of the schools remained intact.[40]

Advocates continued to press their argument that this was the only solution for the catastrophic academic and social problems of Black youth, and vowed that their efforts would continue around the country.[41] Nor was this a fringe opinion; the Savannah, Georgia branch of the NAACP supported a local decision, in March 1993, to establish separate classrooms for African-American boys, taught by specially trained African-American men, though reserving judgment about the possible establishment of a separate Black school.[42]

Other cities across the United States have taken similar measures. Milwaukee, for example, designated two public schools as "African-American immersion schools... designed to eliminate the institutional and attitudinal influences that impede the academic success of African-American students."[43] Some of those advocating these schools argued that temporary segregation would be less devastating in its effects than the lifelong segregation from opportunities in a technologically advanced society that is the fate of many ill-educated Black youth.[44]

What Bullock wrote more than forty years ago remains, unfortunately, to some extent true today:

> The Negro's movement toward the status of desegregated citizen could not be matched by corresponding growth in individual achievement within the race itself. Negro education was strong enough to produce leaders who successfully directed the course of desegregation, but was too weak to produce students who, when placed within the mainstream of American life and education, would show no effect of having grown up outside of it. One of the subtle ironies of out day is the fact that the privileges that desegregation brings to Negroes expose their inadequacies with such force as to drive them back into the protection and security of the segregated world they have always known.[45]

This is not the place to review the extensive literature—and debate—over how and why Black youth, including many from privileged backgrounds, avoid the effort required for high academic achievement. John Ogbu, Signithia Fordham, Ronald Ferguson, Claude Steele, and other Black social scientists have advanced competing theories but all have noted the self-limiting pattern of self-segregation by Black youth in both high schools and colleges. John McWhorter, in an eloquent and angry book, has condemned the "self-sabotage in Black America."[46] As Sigmund Freud said about dreams, it seems likely that the achievement gap is "overdetermined" with a variety of causes, any one of which would be sufficient.

This "achievement gap" has, a half-century after *Brown v. Board of Education*, resisted all efforts to eliminate it, though individual schools and instructional strategies have achieved promising—but difficult to replicate—results.

In casting her deciding vote in favor of racial preferences in admission to law school, in 2003, Supreme Court Justice Sandra Day O'Connor insisted that affirmative action was still needed in America, but affirmed that "we expect that 25 years from now, the use of racial preferences will no longer be necessary to further the interest approved today." The same wan hope was expressed by many twenty-five, and thirty-five, years ago, but the remedies no longer seem obvious. In the words of the introduction to an important collection of studies on *The Black-White Test Score Gap* (1998),

> In the 1960s, racial egalitarians routinely blamed the test score gap on the combined effects of Black poverty, racial segregation, and inadequate finding for Black schools. That analysis implied obvious solutions: raise Black children's family income, desegregate their schools, and equalize spending on schools that remain racially segregated. All these steps still look useful, but none has made as much difference as optimists expected in the early 1960s.... The average Black child and the average White child now live in school districts that spend almost exactly the same amount per pupil.

The result is that "the number of people who think they know how to eliminate racial differences in test performance has shrunk steadily since the mid-1960s."[47] This remains the great unfinished business of the American educational system.[48]

CHAPTER 8

Have We Learned Anything?

As I wrote in the concluding chapter of my book about the schooling of American and Canadian Indian children and youth,[1] there is no satisfactory solution to the complicated problem of educating children if they are considered by the dominant members of the society as *different* in ways that—explicitly or implicitly—are assumed to make them unable to benefit fully from the sort of education provided to children of the majority.

This is not a question of resources only, or of technique, or of the structure of schooling, but more fundamentally of the whole enterprise of "minority education." Inevitably, such education, even with the best of intentions, is a preparation to occupy (and to internalize) a separate and consequently inferior position. As a result, public schools, which Horace Mann and his allies saw as "the great equalizers of the conditions of men," have been reproducers and confirmers of inequality for Black pupils for well over a century. For many, their schooling has subtracted rather than added value, has sent them out into the world *less* competent and less capable of learning life's lessons, of functioning effectively in society, than they might have been without such schooling.

This is not to call for a "one-size-fits-all" education, or to ignore the fact that some pedagogical strategies are especially effective with pupils from one sort of background, with one set of childhood experiences, or with a particular set of interests and abilities. On the contrary, there is growing evidence that a flourishing diversity of approaches, determined at the school level in response to immediate challenges and the desires of parents, while informed by the shared experience of networks of schools committed to particular methods of instruction and school organization, is what is needed to confront the problems of educating poor children well.[2]

Fortunately, we now have hundreds of examples of schools that are doing so very well indeed. A hundred KIPP (Knowledge Is Power Program) schools across the United States, serving mostly Black and Latino pupils from low-income families, have produced remarkable results, recognized in 2010 by a $50 million grant from the federal government to expand its model. The instructional strategy "Success For All" has been implemented in thousands of schools with notable results. The Harlem Children's Zone in New York City, seeking to address the whole range of issues that affect children in an area of concentrated poverty and social dysfunction,[3] has inspired imitators across the country. Public charter schools, while of uneven quality, seem to produce positive results in measured achievement when serving low-income students.[4] Balanced against these results is the below-average measured achievement of charter schools in more affluent area that, it has been suggested, reflects their offering a form of Progressive Education with little concern for external accountability beyond satisfying progressive middle-class parents valuing other outcomes more than in scores on standardized tests.

Whatever the merits of charter schools as a reform movement—and this is much debated at present—it is clear that many individual urban charter schools serving Black pupils have produced remarkable results. Similar results have been achieved by urban Catholic schools, including such new developments as the Cristo Rey high schools and the Nativity Miguel middle schools.[5] The late James Coleman and others have noted the so-called Catholic school advantage for Black pupils. One study of nationwide data found that

> the achievement advantage of white over minority students... increases in public high schools during the last two years of schooling, whereas the minority gap actually decreases in Catholic schools.... Over the two years between sophomore and senior year, white students in the public sector gain 2.1 years in mathematics achievement. In the Catholic sector, white students gain somewhat more (2.5 years). For minority students the differences between the two sectors are bigger. In public schools, the average gain is 1.5 years. In Catholic schools, however, minorities are gaining 3.3 years—more than any other group, including their white classmates."[6]

The same positive effect for Black pupils has been found in evaluations of the private voucher programs in New York City and elsewhere.

There are many other examples of both public and private schools serving Black youth that have abandoned the racial essentialism that calls for distinctive educational approaches; approaches based on the assumption that they are somehow fundamentally different from their peers, schools that have instead insisted on high expectations, while providing the consistent support and constant encouragement necessary for at-risk youth to meet those expectations. What these schools have in common is that they are free from the constraints of bureaucracy with its pressure to implement a one-size-fits-all model of instruction, and that they refuse to hide behind—or let their students hide behind—excuses for why they can't be expected to achieve. They do not allow "rumors of inferiority" to hamper their students from full engagement with learning and with achievement.[7]

In other respects, in instructional methods and the structuring of school life, successful schools and programs differ greatly from one another, and that is as it should be, since only under such conditions can educators teach whole-heartedly in a manner that they believe in, and parents chose a school in which they have full confidence.

Education policy makers should abandon the harmful illusion that the diversity to which schooling should respond is a diversity defined by *race*. Attempts to define the appropriate education for *all* Black American and Canadian youth have been profoundly misguided. This has been true even when those attempts have been motivated by the most benevolent and sympathetic intentions. They rest, finally, on a form of racial essentialism, the assumption that racial differences "go all the way down," and that it is possible to generalize about members of those groups on the basis of what is, finally, an ascribed identity.

Black Americans and Canadians vary enormously in their interests, abilities, religious convictions, and everything else imaginable. Many take a keen interest in their African heritage, if something as wildly diverse as the hundreds of cultures and languages of West Africa can be said to constitute a single heritage, while for others that is something of little concern. Orlando Patterson, as we have seen, contends that "most of that the typical Afro-American does in daily life has little or nothing to do with being Afro-American."[8]

This is not, of course, to deny that racial discrimination still exists, or that any Black person may experience racially motivated snubs or barriers, but it is to suggest that most Black Americans and Canadians are primarily concerned with getting on with their lives, not defining themselves or allowing themselves to be defined by how they differ from the mainstream of society. It is perhaps only at the intensely self-conscious stage of late adolescence that these identity matters are at the forefront of consciousness. To quote Patterson again, "One has only to walk for a few minutes on any of the nation's great campuses to witness the extent of ethnic separation, alternating with periodic outbursts of ethnic, gender, and other chauvinistic hostilities. The thought that repeatedly haunts me as I travel the nation's campuses is that the South did indeed finally win the moral battle over integration, for no group of people now seems more committed to segregation than Afro-American students and young professionals."[9]

Unfortunately, consciousness of race as a defining—and often limiting—element of identity has been nourished by some who have a self-interest in the exploitation of that idea. Continuing to emphasize separateness benefits the racial virtuosi, those who make it their business to be accepted as ethnic leaders or spokesmen.[10]

This can have serious negative effects for those in whose interests these "ethnic leaders" allegedly speak. As Patterson has pointed out: "The comparative sociology of ethnic relations strongly suggests that separate always means unequal for the mass of minority group members. The only members of minority groups to benefit from such a system are leaders who enjoy the collective spoils permitted by the dominant group as a payoff for keeping the groups separate, ensuring the continuation of the deprived condition of the majority, a deprivation which, in turn, becomes the rhetorical fodder for the coopted separatist leadership."[11] The essence of such political agendas is their oppositional nature; they are premised upon a necessary conflict between the interests of ethnic minority groups and those of the host society.

The situation is much more serious when it comes to those who claim to speak for Black Americans and Canadians, because the demand for special treatment is often made not only on the basis of a deprived condition but also of what is represented to be a racially based and significantly distinct mode of functioning that only the racial virtuoso can prescribe for. This has the effect of reviving the assumptions about fundamental racial differences that, as we have seen, have been so profoundly harmful to the education of Black youth. "There is something terrifying," writes French anthropologist Emmanuel Todd, "in seeing black intellectuals championing the old association between a biological substratum and psychic organization which was the very heart of European [and American] racial doctrines from 1880 to 1945."[12]

Abandoning racial essentialism—the belief that there is a particular form of education especially suited to members of a racially identifiable group—does not mean we should continue to seek to impose a single model of schooling on every child. It is time to return to the wise conclusion of a landmark study of inequality of educational outcomes in

American society, forty years ago, that urged caution in forming generalizations about the ways in which Black pupils learn, or the pedagogies and forms of school organization that are best suited to their needs.:

> We will have to accept diverse standards for judging schools, just as we do for judging families. Indeed, we can even say that diversity should be an explicit objective of schools and school systems. No single home-away-from-home can be ideal for all children. A school system that provides only one variety of schooling, no matter how good, must almost invariably seem unsatisfactory to many parents and children. The ideal system is one that provides as many varieties of schooling as its children and parents want and finds ways of matching children to schools that suit them. Since the character of an individual's schooling appears to have relatively little long-term effect on his development, society as a whole rarely has a compelling interest in limiting the range of educational choice open to parents and students. Likewise, since professional educators do not seem to understand the long-term effects of schooling any better than parents do, there is no compelling reason why the profession should be empowered to rule out alternatives that appeal to parents, even if they seem educationally "unsound." ... The list of competing objectives is nearly endless, which is why we favor diversity and choice.[13]

For those concerned with educational policy, an historical perspective suggests that equity is best served by a flexible and empirical approach, paying close attention to what works in particular situations and with particular children and youth,; and always listening carefully to what parents and other caretakers tell us about who those children are and what dreams they have for their future. Nothing is more remarkable in this story than the faith that Black adults have had in the benefits of education, especially in view of the meager benefits that, too often, their children have actually received.

Policy makers should also learn from this history to treat with more respect the institutions that Black communities have always created for themselves—most of them religious—and to which they, even more than other Americans, have entrusted the formation of youth. Partnership with these community-based institutions in a variety of new ways—a civil society strategy in place of the drive for standardization and bureaucratic control that characterizes so much educational reform today—could bring a new dynamism into the education of those for whom the present system is failing.

Notes

Note on Terminology

1. Patterson (1998), xxii.

Introduction

1. Winks (1997), xvii.
2. See Glenn (1988).

1 Assumptions about Race

1. King (1981), 111.
2. See, for example, Cantor (1963); Cohn (1970); Desmond and Moore (2009); Dyer (1980); Frederickson (1987); Jordan (1969); Newby (1965); and Ruchames (1970).
3. Stampp (1980), 45.
4. Gossett (1965), 240, 242.
5. Tocqueville (2000), 304.
6. Gossett (1965), 262.
7. Williams (2005), 179.
8. Gossett (1965), 262–63.
9. Lyons (1975), 39; Jordan (1969), 253.
10. Jefferson (1984), 266–70.
11. Desmond and Moore (2009), 93, 161, 375, 289.
12. Jordan (1969), 478.
13. In Grant (2008), 300.
14. Lyons (1975), 44.
15. Ibid., 36.
16. In Jordan (1969), 259.
17. Ibid., 276.
18. Ibid., 283.
19. In Noll (2002), 104.
20. See Filler (1960), 23–24; Dumond (1959), 35.

21. Frederickson (1987), 29, 90.
22. Lyons (1975), 36.
23. In Butts (1978), 60–61.
24. Hinks (1997), xiii, 206, 210.
25. Frederickson (1987), 2, 4.
26. Ibid.
27. Tocqueville (2000), 348–49, 339, 326.
28. Desmond and Moore (2009), 196.
29. Frederickson (1987), 179.
30. In Kendrick and Kendrick (2004), xix; Desmond and Moore (2009), 232–33.
31. Lyons (1975) 57, 87, 89, 93, 110.
32. In Stampp (1980), 153.
33. Anderson (1988), 85.
34. Frederickson (1987), 235, 256.
35. Cornelius (1991), 115.
36. In Calhoun (1969), 336–39.
37. Stampp (1965), 12.
38. Frederickson (1987), 230–32, 235; King (1981), 128.
39. Frederickson (1987), 250–52.
40. In Gossett (1965), 281.
41. Willcox (1905), 567–70.
42. Frederickson (1987), 255.
43. Newby (1965), 66.
44. In Schwartz (1970), I, 403–4.
45. Newby (1965), 11.
46. In Wilkinson (1979), 18.
47. Bond (1972), 53.
48. In Bardolph (1961), 83.
49. Branch (1988), 31.
50. Buck (1959), 304, 306.
51. Grant (2008), 169, 259, 20, 116.
52. Grant and Osborn (1918), 16.
53. Ibid., 77.
54. In Morris (1981), 167.
55. Thernstrom and Thernstrom (1997), 364–65.
56. Patterson (1998), 77, 72.
57. Jencks and Phillips (1998), 9.
58. See Whitman (2008).

2 Enslaved and Free Blacks before 1862

1. In Raboteau (1978), 100.
2. Monroe (1971), 224.

3. Cornelius (1991), 13.
4. Sobel (1998), 65.
5. Kaestle (1983), 196.
6. Lyons (1975), 47.
7. Sobel (1998), 65.
8. In Calhoun (1969), 55.
9. Jordan (1969), 133, 207–8.
10. Selleck (1995), 21.
11. Berlin (1981), 74; Winks (1997), 57–59.
12. Freedman (1999), 13.
13. Cornelius (1991), 19.
14. Jordan (1969), 214.
15. Elkins (1963), 60.
16. In Calhoun (1969), 55–56.
17. Litwack (1980), xi.
18. Levine (1978), xi.
19. Du Bois (1986), 364–65.
20. Bullock (1967), 7–8.
21. Ibid., 13.
22. Raboteau (1978), 154–55, 158.
23. Cash (1941), 86.
24. Butler (1990), 248.
25. Bardolph (1961), 45.
26. Berlin (1981), 74.
27. Jordan (1969), 400.
28. In Cohen (1974), 3, 1622.
29. In Stampp (1964), 208.
30. Bowen (1981), 280.
31. Genovese (1975), 561–62.
32. Hinks (1997), 119.
33. Douglass (1963), 36.
34. Cornelius (1991), 105.
35. Bullock (1967), 10.
36. Hinks (1997), 156.
37. Cornelius (1991), 105.
38. Berlin (1981), 306.
39. Cornelius (1991), 34.
40. Olmstead (1959), 51, 88, 206.
41. Cornelius (1991), 79–80.
42. Bullock (1967), 12.
43. Payne (1968), 25, 27.
44. Cash (1941), 80.
45. Selleck (1995), 61.
46. In Butts (1978), 144.

47. In Freedman (1999), 6, 17.
48. In Raboteau (1978), 241.
49. Freedman (1999), 11.
50. Ibid., 8.
51. Ibid., 10.
52. Cornelius (1991), 126.
53. Ibid., 116.
54. Berlin (1981), 304.
55. Verba, Schlozman, and Brady (1995), 383.
56. Berlin (1981), 69.
57. Raboteau (1978), 178.
58. McLoughlin (1993), 159.
59. Hinks (1997), 39, 54–55, 59; Berlin (1981), 285.
60. Freedman (1999), 13.
61. Ibid., 10, 28, 33.
62. Butler (1990), 131.
63. Winks (1997), 46, 99, 110–11.
64. Cornelius (1991), 30.
65. Stampp (1965), 32.
66. Tocqueville (2000), 336n.
67. In Ruchames (1963), 56.
68. See Glenn (1988).
69. In Aptheker (1951a), 83, 141.
70. In Filler (1960), 70.
71. In Ruchames (1963), 61, 136.
72. Winks (1997), 149, 367–68.
73. Ibid., 370–71.
74. In Aptheker (1951a), 19.
75. In Hinks (1997), 173.
76. Meier and Rudwick (1970), 94.
77. Houston and Prentice (1988), 37.
78. Franklin (1979), 29; Monroe (1971), 82–87.
79. Selleck (1995), 21.
80. In Aptheker (1951a), 73.
81. Franklin (1979), 32.
82. Justice (2005), 31.
83. Kaestle (1973), 168–69.
84. Ravitch (1974), 26; Quarles (1969), 13.
85. In Aptheker (1951a), 117.
86. Bond (1972), 14.
87. Small and Small (1944), 506–29.
88. Wyatt-Brown (1969), 161; Filler (1960), 75.
89. In Cohen (1974), 3, 1702.
90. Stewart (2003), 323–24.
91. In Aptheker (1951a), 135.

92. Hinks (1997), 104, 85.
93. Quarles (1969), 109.
94. In Aptheker (1951a), 205.

3 Equipping the Freedman

1. Welter (1962), 142.
2. Olmstead (1959), 171.
3. Cash (1941), 105.
4. Woodward (1974), 20.
5. In Gossett (1965), 256.
6. Franklin (1961), 46.
7. In Stampp (1965), 78, 115–16.
8. Levine (1978), 142.
9. In Bullock (1967), 18–19.
10. In Cohen (1974), 3, 1411.
11. Litwack (1980), 452–53.
12. Williams (2005), 91.
13. Bond (1939), 269–70.
14. Payne (1968), 163n.
15. In Morris (1981), 187.
16. McAfee (1998), 11.
17. Freedman (1999), 2–4.
18. Williams (2005), 81.
19. Morris (1981), 1–2, 102.
20. Franklin (1961), 108.
21. Sherer (1977), 2.
22. In Aptheker (1951b), 546.
23. In Welter (1962), 145.
24. Anderson (1988), 7, 10–13.
25. Bullock (1967), 28.
26. Woodson (1922), 26.
27. Fairclough (2000), 66.
28. Cornelius (1991), 145.
29. Plank and Turner (1987), 589; Toppin (1967), 4.
30. Peterson (1985), 97.
31. In Ruchames (1963), 249.
32. Gaines (1996), 33.
33. McPherson (1975), 161.
34. Du Bois (1986), 380.
35. Foner (1988), 25.
36. Wesley (1957), 118.
37. Rose (1967), 333.
38. Williams (2005), 99.
39. Richardson (1986), 237, 247.

40. Morris (1981), 115.
41. Foner (1988), 97–99.
42. Sherer (1997), 3–4, 9.
43. Wesley (1957), 123.
44. West (1966), 13.
45. Ibid., 11.
46. West (1966), 4–7.
47. McPherson (1975), 152.
48. Selleck (1995), 47–48, 62, 80, 87.
49. Wyatt-Brown (1969), 292–93, 334.
50. Sherer (1997), 114.
51. Richardson (1986), 73–75.
52. Rose (1967), 387–88.
53. In McPherson (1975), 148.
54. Anderson (1988), 241.
55. Gaines (1996), 35.
56. Foner (1988), 28.
57. Bullock (1967), 24.
58. Cash (1941), 140.
59. Williams (2005), 182.
60. Wesley (1957), 121.
61. Williams (2005), 121.
62. Morris (1981), 54–84.
63. Jones (1979), 49.
64. Sherer (1997), 117.
65. Williams (2005), 185.
66. In Butts (1978), 148.
67. Bond (1972), 41.
68. Richardson (1986), 215, 250.
69. Anderson (1988), 281.
70. In Litwack (1980), 460.
71. Selleck (1995), 183.
72. Morris (1981), 85–130.
73. Sherer (1997), 115–16.
74. Morris (1981), 32.
75. Richardson (1986), 75, 81–82.
76. Morris (1981), 49.
77. Richardson (1986), 83.
78. In Cohen (1974), 3, 1642.
79. Richardson (1986), 83.
80. Morris (1981), 242–43.
81. Butts (1978), 150–51.
82. In Cohen (1974), 3, 1686–90.
83. Genovese (1975), 563.
84. Sherer (1997), 18.

85. In Cohen (1974), 3, 1640.
86. Rose (1967), 230–31.
87. In McPherson (1975), 170.
88. Washington (1965), 33.
89. Woodson (1922), 47.
90. Lincoln and Mamiya (1990), 251.
91. Wesley (1957), 123.
92. Du Bois in Genovese (1975), 564.
93. Du Bois (2003), 169.
94. Morris (1981), 105.
95. Franklin (1961), 141.
96. Lieberson (1980), 139.
97. In Cohen (1974), 3, 1642.
98. Selleck (1995), 94.
99. Wesley (1957), 121.
100. Franklin (1961), 46.
101. Foner (1988), 366.
102. Ibid., 366, 422, 589.
103. Anderson (1988), 23.
104. Butts (1973), 453.
105. In Morris (1981), 134.
106. Richardson (1986), 123.
107. Du Bois (1986), 430.
108. Morris (1981), 160.
109. McPherson (1975), 150.
110. Anderson (1988), 34.
111. Foner (1988), 145, 368.
112. Meier and Rudwick (1970), 164–65.
113. Du Bois (1986), 427.
114. Bardolph (1961), 100.
115. Anderson (1988), 238.
116. Herbst (1996), 71.
117. Bardolph (1961), 101.
118. Sherer (1997), 143, 65, 79, 97.
119. In Schwartz (1970), I, 263, 270–71.
120. Ibid., 288–89.
121. Ibid., 667.
122. McAfee (1998), 16–17.
123. In Bennett (1969), 142–43.
124. Ibid., 126.
125. West (1966), 16.
126. In Schwartz (1970), I, 687, 691.
127. Ibid., 696, 721–23, 733.
128. McAfee (1998), 129.
129. In Schwartz (1970), I, 697–702.

130. McAfee (1998), 126, 135, 143, 168.
131. See Justice (2005).
132. Murray (1960), 519.
133. Bennett (1969), 302.
134. West (1966), 14.
135. Buck (1959), 168–69.
136. Bond (1940), 480–81, 489.

4 Jim Crow South

1. Bullock (1967), 65.
2. In McAfee (1998), 164.
3. Buck (1959), 71.
4. Glenn (1988).
5. Tyack and Lowe (1986), 250.
6. In Gossett (1965), 276–77.
7. Buck (1959), 301.
8. Ibid., 299.
9. McPherson (1975), 143.
10. Reese (1986), 220.
11. Best (2005), 71.
12. Morris (1981), 228–29.
13. Reese (1986), 220.
14. In Cohen (1974), 3, 1651.
15. Bond (1935b), 322.
16. Butts (1978), 146, 152.
17. In Aptheker 1951b, 692–93.
18. Woodward (1974), 94–95.
19. Ibid., 102.
20. Ibid., 46.
21. In Noll (2002), 418–19.
22. Leloudis (1996), 181.
23. Newby (1965), 72.
24. Cash (1941), 178–79; note that, in his widely acclaimed book *The Mind of the South*, Cash did not think it necessary to explain that his "South" was the White South alone.
25. Newby (1965), 175.
26. In Cohen (1974), 3, 1698.
27. Frederickson (1987), 324, 269.
28. Baker (1964), 100, 246–47.
29. Myrdal (1962), 880.
30. Ibid., 895.
31. In Bond (1937a), 19.
32. In Cohen (1974), 3, 1653.

33. Williams (2005), 177.
34. Leloudis (1996), 182.
35. Anderson (1988), 34.
36. In Drost (1967), 41–42, 82.
37. Bond (1937b), 178–79.
38. Power (1996), 87.
39. Fraser (1985), 108–9.
40. Wyatt-Brown (1969), 98.
41. Stewart (2003), 337–38.
42. Morris (1981), 157.
43. Bullock (1967), 77.
44. Anderson (1988), 47, 54.
45. Ibid., 51.
46. In Bullock (1967), 76.
47. Bullock (1967), 78.
48. Anderson (1988), 33.
49. Kelley (1979), 152.
50. In Aptheker (1951b), 649.
51. Kelley (1979), 155.
52. Bond (1937a), 27.
53. Washington (1965), 151, 163.
54. Bond (1937a), 29.
55. In Calhoun (1969), 350–51, emphasis added; also in Washington (1965) and elsewhere.
56. In Calhoun (1969), 353.
57. Washington (1907), 49–50, 56.
58. Sherer (1997), 53, 145.
59. In Lazerson (1987), 59–61.
60. In Calhoun (1969), 356.
61. Bond (1937b), 182–83.
62. Fairclough (2000), 74.
63. Anderson (1988), 66.
64. In Cohen (1974), 3, 1682.
65. Foner (1988), 85.
66. In Cohen (1974), 3, 1682.
67. Cash (1941), 318.
68. Willcox (1905), 590, 592.
69. Myrdal (1962), 898.
70. Gaines (1996), 23.
71. Anderson (1988), 34.
72. Bullock (1967), 175.
73. In Myrdal (1962), 897.
74. In Morris (1981), 162.
75. Leloudis (1996), 182–83.

76. In Calhoun (1969), 357.
77. Leloudis (1996), 193–94, 228.
78. In Baker (1964), 285–86.
79. Anderson (1988), 101, 254.
80. Thernstrom and Thernstrom (1997), 39.
81. Leloudis (1996).
82. In Bullock (1967), 94.
83. McPherson (1975), 206.
84. In Toppin (1967), 4.
85. Ravitch (2000), 108–9.
86. Fultz (1995), 402.
87. Ibid., 403.
88. Thernstrom and Thernstrom (1997), 38.
89. Fultz (1995), 404.
90. Lieberson (1980), 141.
91. Toppin (1967), 3–5.
92. Bullock (1967), 139, 144–45.
93. Butts (1973), 456.
94. Plank and Turner (1987), 589.
95. Leloudis (1996).
96. Cash (1941), 201.
97. In Bullock (1967), 75–76.
98. Peterson (1985), 101.
99. Morris (1981), 246.
100. Frederickson (1987), 303.
101. Baker (1964), 293.
102. Bullock (1967), 149.
103. Best (2005), 7.
104. In Best (2005), 124.
105. In Aptheker (1951c), 165, 171, 175.
106. In Best (2005), 6.
107. In Sernett (1999), 365.
108. Leloudis (1996), 211–12.
109. In Cohen (1974), 5, 2998–99.
110. Myrdal (1962), 943.
111. Ibid., 949, 951.
112. Fairclough (2000), 73.
113. In Cohen (1974), 5, 3007.

5 Jim Crow North

1. Stampp (1980), 268.
2. Franklin (1979), 29; Jordan (1969), 133.
3. Jordan (1969), 417, 355.

4. Meier and Rudwick (1970), 94.
5. Ibid., 96.
6. MacMullen (1991), 55, 63.
7. Franklin (1979), 32.
8. Winks (1997), 135, 137, 144.
9. Handlin (1959), 31.
10. In Pease and Pease (1965), 197.
11. Winks (1997), 217, 248.
12. Ibid., 270, 289, 215.
13. Kaestle (1983), 173.
14. In Aptheker (1951a), 243; in Kendrick and Kendrick (2004), 164.
15. Mabee (1968), 343–44.
16. Aptheker (1951a), 298.
17. In Martin (1984), 135.
18. In Pease and Pease (1965), 282, 285.
19. Ibid., 288.
20. Ibid., 293, 295.
21. 59 Mass. (5 Cush.) 198 (1850), cited from http://brownvboard.org/research/handbook/sources/roberts/roberts.htm
22. Mabee (1968), 355–56.
23. Ibid., 358.
24. Tyack and Hansot (1982), 61–62.
25. Mabee (1968), 346.
26. Kaestle (1983), 89.
27. Desmond and Moore (2009), 164.
28. Kendrick and Kendrick (2004), 253.
29. Wyatt-Brown (1969), 117–21.
30. Stewart (2003), 329; Winks (1997), 155–56.
31. Ibid., 329.
32. In Kaestle (1983), 179.
33. Aptheker (1951a), 398–402.
34. in Filler (1960), 224.
35. Kaestle (1983), 186–87.
36. In Kendrick and Kendrick (2004), 119.
37. Voegeli (1967), 172.
38. Homel (1983), 1.
39. In Buck (1959), 83.
40. Homel (1983), 2–4.
41. Peterson (1985), 111, 113.
42. Homel (1983), 35, 40–41.
43. Ibid., 157.
44. In Cohen (1974), 3, 1712–13.
45. McAfee (1998), 160.
46. In Cohen (1974), 3, 1761–65.

47. McLoughlin (1993), 240–41.
48. In Aptheker (1951b), 609.
49. In Cohen (1974), 3, 1714–15.
50. In Aptheker (1951b), 624, 639.
51. Bond (1935b), 324.
52. Butts (1978), 142.
53. In Cohen (2002), 94.
54. Cohen (2002), 8.
55. Ibid., 36, 68.
56. Ibid., 92.
57. Dougherty (1998), 135.
58. Cohen (2002), 93–95, 99, 148.
59. Franklin (1979), 37.
60. Ibid., 191.
61. Winks (1997), 311, 367, 376, 386.
62. Lieberson (1980), 237, 258.
63. Franklin (1979), 71, 77.
64. Bond (1935b), 326.
65. Homel (1984), 177.
66. Mirel (1999), 188–89, 191.
67. Homel (1984), 189.
68. Cohen (1974), 4, xxxv.
69. Meier and Rudwick (1967).
70. Du Bois (1986), 1241.
71. Aptheker (1951c), 550.
72. Franklin (1979), 148.
73. Thernstrom and Thernstrom (1997), 60.
74. Lieberson (1980), 170, 35.
75. Cohen (2002), 184–85, 229, 232–33.

6 "Uplifting the Race"

1. Du Bois (1986), 848.
2. Ibid., 848–49.
3. Du Bois (2003), 86–87.
4. Gaines (1996), 237.
5. Best (2005), 185, 186.
6. In Aptheker (1951b), 674.
7. Du Bois (1986), 398–99.
8. Ibid., 392.
9. Du Bois (2003), 88.
10. Du Bois (1986), 852, 842, 847.
11. Bond (1972), 25.
12. Du Bois (1986), 433.

13. Anderson (1988), 29–30.
14. Du Bois (1986), 871–72.
15. In Cohen (1974), 3, 1668.
16. Du Bois (2003), 21.
17. Du Bois (1986), 428.
18. Gaines (1996), 89.
19. Bardolph (1961), 137.
20. In Lazerson (1987), 122.
21. Tyack (1974), 217.
22. Gaines (1996), 75.
23. Foner (1988), 612.
24. Grant (2008), 396.
25. Du Bois (1986), 979.
26. Ibid., 1178.
27. Ibid., 1252–53.
28. Du Bois (2003), 102–3.
29. Du Bois (1986), 1020.
30. Ibid., 1242–43.
31. Cohen (2002), 147.
32. Dougherty (1998), 125.
33. Plank and Turner (1987), 592–93.
34. Franklin (1979), 41.
35. Ibid., 146.
36. Homel (1984), 191.
37. Fairclough (2000), 87.
38. Fultz (1995), 421.
39. Ravitch (1983), 138.
40. Franklin (1979), 192.
41. Homel (1984), 110.
42. Du Bois (1986), 701.
43. Ibid., 1242.
44. Toppin (1967), 17.
45. Plank and Turner (1987), 585; Woodward (1974), 218.
46. In Fairclough (2000), 87.
47. Fairclough (2000), 88.
48. Winks (1997), 385.
49. Dougherty (1998), 122.
50. Fairclough (2000), 90.
51. Homel (1984), 88.
52. Ibid., 127.
53. Du Bois (1986), 1241.
54. Bond (1972), 29.
55. Gaines (1996), 78.
56. See Rainwater and Yancey (1986).

57. Sobel (1998), 173.
58. Litwack (1980), 230.
59. Thernstrom and Thernstrom (1997), 255.
60. Gaines (1996), 21.
61. Woodson (1933), 1–3.
62. Ibid., 3, 5–6.
63. Ravitch (1985), 203.
64. Woodson (1933), 22–24.
65. Ibid., 53.
66. Myrdal (1962), 2, 875.
67. In Warren (1956), 72.
68. Woodson (1933), 84–85.
69. Tannenbaum (1946), 42.
70. Best (2005), 89.
71. In Perlstein (2002), 253–54.
72. In Mirel (1999), 309; see Sitkoff (1981), 199–223.
73. Sitkoff (1981), 216.
74. Perlstein (2002), 259, 261.
75. Perlstein (2002), 262.
76. Ibid., 263, 267–68.
77. Sitkoff (1981), 210.

7 Integration and Its Disappointments

1. Woodward (1974), vii.
2. In Aptheker (1951c), 83.
3. Bond (1935b), 164.
4. Bond (1952), 249.
5. In Aptheker (1993), 129–31.
6. Wilkinson (1979), 11.
7. In Woodward (1974), 132.
8. In Schwartz (1970), I, 361–64.
9. Bond (1935b), 325.
10. Wilkinson (1979), 25.
11. Woodward (1974), 154–73; Ravitch (1983), 133; Bullock (1967), 258–59.
12. Branch (1988), 373.
13. In Schwartz (1970), II, 847–48, 859, 878–79, 881.
14. Schwartz (1970), II, 1089, 1109.
15. Ibid., 1133–34, 1155.
16. Ibid., 1395–96, 1404, 1414, 1421.
17. Bullock (1967), 258–59.
18. Baker (2001), 332–34.
19. Ravitch (1983), 149.
20. Baker (2001), 334.

21. Ibid., 332, 337.
22. Ibid., 322.
23. *Green v. County School Bd.*, 391 U.S. 430, 441 (1968).
24. Butts (1978), 332.
25. Ravitch (1983), 167.
26. Woodward (1974), 192.
27. Ravitch (1983), 132.
28. Thernstrom and Thernstrom (1997), 341.
29. Mirel (1999), 359, 258–60.
30. Ibid., 275.
31. Ibid., 300, 309–10.
32. Ibid., 341.
33. Ibid., 345.
34. Woodward (1974), 195–96.
35. Stampp (1980), 71.
36. Ravitch (1974), 340, 352.
37. Kahlenberg (2007), 121.
38. In Aptheker (1994), 186.
39. Hatchett (1986), 46.
40. *Education Week*, September 4, 1991; October 21, 1992.
41. Kunjufu (1991), 29.
42. *Education Week*, March 24, 1993.
43. Leake and Leake (1992), 785.
44. See Glenn (1995).
45. Bullock (1967), 279.
46. McWhorter (2001).
47. Jencks and Phillips (1998), 10.
48. See Kirp (2010) for an excellent recent discussion of causes and remedies.

8 Have We Learned Anything?

1. Glenn (2011).
2. Whitman (2008).
3. Tough (2008).
4. Institute of Education Sciences (2010).
5. Kearney (2008); Fenzel (2009).
6. Bryk, Lee, and Holland (1993), 247–48.
7. Hammond and Howard (1985).
8. Patterson (1997), 3.
9. Ibid., 157.
10. See the discussion in chapter 4 of Glenn with De Jong (1996).
11. Patterson (1997), 201.
12. Todd (1994), 99, my translation.
13. Jencks and others (1972), 256–57.

References

Alba, Richard D., *Ethnic Identity: The Transformation of White America*, New Haven: Yale University Press, 1990.

Anderson, James D., *The Education of Blacks in the South, 1860–1935*, Chapel Hill: University of North Carolina Press, 1988.

Aptheker, Herbert, editor, *A Documentary History of the Negro People in the United States: 1. From Colonial Times through the Civil War*, New York: Citadel Press, 1951a.

———, editor, *A Documentary History of the Negro People in the United States: 2. From the Reconstruction years to the founding of the N.A.A.C.P. in 1910*, New York: Citadel Press, 1951b.

———, editor, *A Documentary History of the Negro People in the United States: 3. 1910–1932, From the Emergence of the N.A.A.C.P. to the Beginning of the New Deal*, New York: Citadel Press, 1951c.

———, editor, *A Documentary History of the Negro People in the United States: 6. From the Korean War to the Emergence of Martin Luther King*, Jr., New York: Citadel Press, 1993.

———, editor, *A Documentary History of the Negro People in the United States: 7. From the Alabama Protests to the Death of Martin Luther King, Jr.*, New York: Citadel Press, 1994.

Baker, R. Scott, "The Paradoxes of Desegregation: Race, Class, and Education, 1935–1975," *American Journal of Education*, Vol. 109, No. 3 (May, 2001), pp. 320–343.

Baker, Ray Stannard, *Following the Color Line: American Negro Citizenship in the Progressive Era (1908)*, New York: Harper & Row, 1964.

Bardolph, Richard, *The Negro Vanguard,* New York: Random House Vintage Books, 1961.

Barton, Josef J., "Eastern and Southern Europeans," in *Ethnic Leadership in America*, edited by John Higham, Baltimore: Johns Hopkins University Press, 1978.

Bell, Derrick, "The Case for a Separate Black School System," *Urban League Review* 7, 1–2, Summer/Winter, 1987–1988.

Bennett, Lerone, Jr., *Black Power U.S.A.: The Human Side of Reconstruction 1867–1877*, Baltimore: Penguin Books, 1969.

Berlin, Ira, *Slaves Without Masters: The Free Negro in the Antebellum South*, Oxford: Oxford University Press, 1981.

Best, Wallace D., *Passionately Human, No Less Divine: Religion and Culture in Black Chicago, 1915–1952*, Princeton: Princeton University Press, 2005.

Bond, Horace Mann, "Negro Education: A Debate in the Alabama Constitutional Convention of 1901," *The Journal of Negro Education*, Vol. 1, No. 1 (Apr., 1932), pp. 49–59.

———, "The Curriculum and the Negro Child," *The Journal of Negro Education*, Vol. 4, No. 2 (Apr., 1935a), pp. 159–168.

———, "The Extent and Character of Separate Schools in the United States," *The Journal of Negro Education*, Vol. 4, No. 3, The Courts and the Negro Separate School (Jul.,1935b), pp. 321–327.

———, "The Influence of Personalities on the Public Education of Negroes in Alabama, I," *The Journal of Negro Education*, Vol. 6, No. 1 (Jan., 1937a), pp. 17–29.

———, "The Influence of Personalities on the Public Education of Negroes in Alabama, II," *The Journal of Negro Education*, Vol. 6, No. 2 (Apr., 1937b), pp. 172–187.

———, "Education in the South," *Journal of Educational Sociology*, Vol. 12, No. 5 (Jan., 1939), pp. 264–274.

———, "The Negro Elementary School and the Cultural Pattern," *Journal of Educational Sociology*, Vol. 13, No. 8, Contribution of Sociology to Elementary Education (Apr., 1940), pp. 479–489.

———, "The Present Status of Racial Integration in the United States, with Especial Reference to Education," *The Journal of Negro Education*, Vol. 21, No. 3, The Courts and Racial Integration in Education (Summer, 1952), pp. 241–250.

———, "The Origin and Development of the Negro Church-Related College," *The Journal of Negro Education*, Vol. 29, No. 3, The Negro Private and Church-Related College.(Summer, 1960), pp. 217–226.

———, *Black American Scholars: A Study of Their Beginnings*, Detroit: Balamp Publishing, 1972.

Bowen, James, *A History of Western Education, Volume Three3: The Modern West*, London: Methuen, 1981.

Branch, Taylor, *Parting the Waters: America in the King Years 1954–63*, New York: Simon & Schuster, 1988.

Bryk, Anthony S., Valerie E. Lee and Peter B. Holland, *Catholic Schools and the Common Good*, Cambridge, MA: Harvard University Press, 1993.

Buck, Paul H., *The Road to Reunion, 1865–1900*, New York: Random House Vintage Books, 1959.

Bullock, Henry Allen, *A History of Negro Education in the South from 1619 to the Present*, Cambridge: Harvard University Press, 1967.

Butler, Jon, *Awash in a Sea of Faith: Christianizing the American People*, Cambridge: Harvard University Press, 1990.

Butts, R. Freeman, *The Education of the West*, New York: McGraw-Hill, 1973.

——, *Public Education in the United States: From Revolution to Reform*, New York: Holt, Rinehart and Winston, 1978.
Calhoun, Daniel, *The Educating of Americans: A Documentary History*, Boston: Houghton Mifflin, 1969.
Cantor, Milton, "The Image of the Negro in Colonial Literature," *The New England Quarterly*, Vol. 36, No. 4 (Dec., 1963), pp. 452–477.
Cash, W. J., *The Mind of the South*, New York: Alfred A. Knopf, 1941.
Cohen, Ronald D., *Children of the Mill: Schooling and Society in Gary, Indiana, 1906–1960*, New York: RoutledgeFalmer, 2002.
Cohen, Sol, *Education in the United States: A Documentary History*, I–V, New York: Random House, 1974.
Cohn, Jay, "The Negro Character in Northern Magazine Fiction of the 1860's," *The New England Quarterly*, Vol. 43, No. 4 (Dec., 1970), pp. 572–592.
Coleman, James A., "The Concept of Equality of Educational Opportunity," in Levine and Bane, 1975, pp. 199–213.
Cornelius, Janet Duitsman, *When I Can Read My Title Clear: Literacy, Slavery, and Religion in the Antebellum South*, Columbia: University of South Carolina Press, 1991.
Cummins, Jim, "Minority Status and Schooling in Canada," *Anthropology & Education Quarterly*, Vol. 28, No. 3. (Sep., 1997), pp. 411–430.
Desmond, Adrian and James Moore, *Darwin's Sacred Cause*, Boston: Houghton Mifflin Harcourt, 2009.
Dougherty, Jack, "'That's when We Were Marching for Jobs': Black Teachers and the Early Civil Rights Movement in Milwaukee," *History of Education Quarterly*, Vol. 38, No. 2 (Summer, 1998), pp. 121–141.
Douglas, Davidson M., *Jim Crow Moves North: The Battle over Northern School Desegregation, 1865–1954*, Cambridge University Press, 2005.
Douglass, Frederick, *Narrative of the Life of Frederick Douglass, An American Slave, Written by Himself (1845)*, New York: Doubleday, 1963.
Drost, Walter H., *David Snedden and Education for Social Efficiency*, Madison: University of Wisconsin Press, 1967.
Du Bois, W. E. B., *Writings*, New York: Library of America, 1986.
——, *The Education of Black People: Ten Critiques, 1906–1960*, New York: Monthly Review Press, 2003.
Dumond, Dwight Lowell, *Antislavery Origins of the Civil War in the United States*, Ann Arbor: University of Michigan Press, 1959.
Dyer, Thomas G., *Theodore Roosevelt and the Idea of Race*, Baton Rouge: Louisiana State University Press, 1980.
Elkins, Stanley M., *Slavery: A Problem in American Institutional and Intellectual Life*, New York: Grosset & Dunlap, 1963.
Fairclough, Adam, "'Being in the Field of Education and Also Being a Negro…Seems…Tragic': Black Teachers in the Jim Crow South," *The Journal of American History*, Vol. 87, No. 1 (Jun., 2000), pp. 65–91.
Fenzel, L. Mickey, *Improving Urban Middle Schools: Lessons from the Nativity Schools*, Albany: SUNY Press, 2009.

Ferguson, Ronald, *Toward Excellence with Equity*, Cambridge: Harvard University Press, 2007.
Filler, Louis, *The Crusade Against Slavery, 1830–1860*, New York: Harper & Row, 1960.
———, editor, *Abolition and Social Justice in the Era of Reform*, New York: Harper & Row, 1972.
Foner, Eric, *Reconstruction, 1863–1877*, New York: Harper & Row, 1988.
Foner, Phillip, *Frederick Douglass: A Biography*, New York: Citadel Press, 1964.
Fordham, Signithia, *Blacked Out: Dilemmas of Race, Identity, and Success at Capital High*, Chicago: University of Chicago Press, 1996.
Franklin, John Hope, *Reconstruction After the Civil War*, Chicago: University of Chicago Press, 1961.
Franklin, Vincent P., *The Education of Black Philadelphia: The Social and Educational History of a Minority Community, 1900–1950*, Philadelphia: University of Pennsylvania Press, 1979.
———, "First Came the School: Catholic Evangelization Among African Americans in the United States, 1827 to the Present," in *Growing Up African American in Catholic Schools*, edited by Jacqueline Jordan Irvine and Michèle Foster, New York: Teachers College Press, 1996.
Fraser, James W., *Pedagogue for God's Kingdom: Lyman Beecher and the Second Great Awakening*, Lanham, MD: University Press of America, 1985.
Frederickson, George M., *The Black Image in the White Mind: The Debate on Afro-American Character and Destiny, 1817–1914*, Wesleyan University Press, 1987.
Freedman, David, "African-American Schooling in the South Prior to 1861," *The Journal of Negro History*, Vol. 84, No. 1 (Winter, 1999), pp. 1–47.
Fultz, Michael, "African American Teachers in the South, 1890–1940: Powerlessness and the Ironies of Expectations and Protest," *History of Education Quarterly*, Vol. 35, No. 4 (Winter, 1995), pp. 401–422.
Fuquay, Michael W., "Civil Rights and the Private School Movement in Mississippi, 1964–1971," *History of Education Quarterly*, Vol. 42, No. 2 (Summer, 2002), pp. 159–180.
Gaines, Kevin K., *Uplifting the Race: Black Leadership, Politics, and Culture in the Twentieth Century*, Chapel Hill: University of North Carolina Press, 1996.
Genovese, Eugene D., *The World the Slaveholders Made*, New York: Random House Vintage Books, 1971.
———, *Roll, Jordan, Roll: The World the Slaves Made*, New York: Random House, 1975.
———, *A Consuming Fire: The Fall of the Confederacy in the Mind of the White Christian South*, University of Georgia Press, 1998.
Glenn, Charles L., *The Myth of the Common School*, Amherst: University of Massachusetts Press, 1988.
———, "Minority Schools on Purpose," in *Changing Populations, Changing Schools: 94th Yearbook of the National Society for the Study of Education*, Part II,

edited by Erwin Flaxman and A. Harry Passow, Chicago: National Society for the Study of Education, 1995.

———, *Native American/First Nations Schooling: From the Colonial Period to the Present*, New York: Palgrave Macmillan, 2011.

——— with Ester de Jong , *Educating Immigrant Children: Schools and Language Minorities in 12 Nations*, New York: Garland Publishing, 1996.

Goffman, Erving, *Asylums: Essays on the Social Situation of Mental Patients and Other Inmates*, Garden City, NY: Doubleday Anchor, 1961.

Gossett, Thomas F., *Race: The History of an Idea in America*, New York: Schocken Books, 1965.

Grant, Colin, *Negro with a Hat: The Rise and Fall of Marcus Garvey*, Oxford: Oxford University Press, 2008.

Grant, Madison and Henry Fairfield Osborn, *The Passing of the Great Race Or the Racial Basis of European History*, New York: Charles Scribner's Sons, 1918.

Grasso, Christopher, "Skepticism and American Faith: Infidels, Converts, and Religious Doubt in the Early Nineteenth Century," *Journal of the Early Republic*, Vol. 22, No. 3 (Autumn, 2002), pp. 465–508.

Gross, Theodore L., "The Negro in the Literature of Reconstruction," *Phylon*, Vol. 22, No. 1 (1st Qtr., 1961), pp. 5–14.

Handlin, Oscar, *Race and Nationality in American Life*, Garden City, NY: Doubleday Anchor, 1959.

Hatchett, David, "A Conflict of Reasons & Remedies," *The Crisis* 93, 3, March 3, 1986.

Herbst, Jurgen, *The Once and Future School: Three Hundred and Fifty Years of American Secondary Education*, New York: Routledge, 1996.

Herskovits, Melville J., *The American Negro: A Study in Racial Crossing*, Indiana University Press, 1928.

Hinks, Peter P., *To Awaken My Afflicted Brethren: David Walker and the Problem of Antebellum Slave Resistance*, University Park: Pennsylvania State University Press, 1997.

Holley, I. B., "Schooling Freedmen's Children," *The New England Quarterly*, Vol. 74, No. 3 (Sep., 2001), pp. 478–494.

Homel, Michael B., *Down from Equality: Black Chicagoans and the Public Schools, 1920–1941*, Urbana: University of Illinois Press, 1984.

Houston, Susan E., and Alison Prentice, *Schooling and Scholars in Nineteenth Century Ontario*, University of Toronto Press, 1988.

Hovey, Alvah, *Barnas Sears: A Christian Educator, His Making and Work*, New York: Silver, Burdett, 1902.

Howard, Jeff and Ray Hammond, "Rumors of Inferiority," *The New Republic*, September 9, 1985, pp. 17–21.

Institute of Education Sciences, *The Evaluation of Charter School Impacts: Final Report*, Washington, DC: National Center for Education Evaluation and Regional Assistance, 2010.

Jefferson, Thomas, *Writings*, New York: The Library of America, 1984.

Jencks, Christopher and Meredith Phillips, editors, *The Black-White Test Score Gap*, Washington, DC: Brookings Institution Press, 1998.

——, Marshall Smith, Henry Acland, Mary Jo Bane, David Cohen, Herbert Gintis, Barbara Heyns and Stephan Michelson, *Inequality: A Reassessment of the Effect of Family and Schooling in America*, New York: Basic Books, 1972.

Jones, Jacqueline, "Women Who Were More Than Men: Sex and Status in Freedmen's Teaching," *History of Education Quarterly*, Vol. 19, No. 1., Women's Influence on Education (Spring, 1979), pp. 47–59.

——, *Soldiers of Light and Love: Northern Teachers and Georgia Blacks, 1865–1873*, Athens: University of Georgia Press, 2004.

Jordan, Winthrop D., *White Over Black: American Attitudes toward the Negro 1550–1812*, New York: Penguin Books, 1969.

Justice, Benjamin, *The War That Wasn't: Religious Conflict and Compromise in the Common Schools of New York State, 1865–1900*, Albany: State University of New York Press, 2005.

Kaestle, Carl F., *The Evolution of An Urban School System: New York City, 1750–1850*, Cambridge: Harvard University Press, 1973.

——, *Pillars of the Republic: Common Schools and American Society, 1780–1860*, New York: Hill and Wang, 1983.

Kahlenberg, Richard D., *Tough Liberal: Albert Shanker and the Battles Over Schools, Unions, Race, and Democracy*, New York: Columbia University Press, 2007.

Kearney, G. R.., *More Than a Dream: How One School's Vision Is Changing the World*, Chicago: Loyola Press, 2008.

Kelley, Don Quinn, "Ideology and Education: Uplifting the Masses in Nineteenth Century Alabama," *Phylon (1960-)*, Vol. 40, No. 2 (2nd Qtr., 1979), pp. 147–158.

Kendrick, Stephen and Paul Kendrick, *Sarah's Long Walk: The Free Blacks of Boston and How Their Struggle for Equality Changed America*, Boston: Beacon Press, 2004.

King, James C., *The Biology of Race*, Revised Edition, Berkeley: University of California Press, 1981.

Kirp, David L., "The Widest Achievement Gap," *National Affairs*, 5, Fall 2010, pp. 54–74.

Kunjufu, Jawanza, "Detroit's Male Academies: What the Real Issue Is," *Education Week*, November 20, 1991.

Lazerson, Marvin, editor, *American Education in the Twentieth Century: A Documentary History*, New York: Teachers College Press, 1987.

Leake, Donald and Brenda Leake, "African-American Immersion Schools in Milwaukee: A View from the Inside," *Phi Delta Kappan*, June, 1992.

Leloudis, James L., *Schooling the New South*, Chapel Hill: University of North Carolina Press, 1996.

Levine, Donald M. and Mary Jo Bane, editors, *The "Inequality" Controversy: Schooling and Distributive Justice*, New York: Basic Books, 1975.

—— and ——, "Introduction," in Levine and Bane, 1975, pp. 3–16.

Levine, Lawrence W., *Black Culture and Black Consciousness: Afro-American Folk Thought from Slavery to Freedom*, Oxford University Press, 1978.

Lieberson, Stanley, *A Piece of the Pie: Blacks and White Immigrants Since 1880*, Berkeley: University of California Press, 1980.

Lincoln, C. Eric and Lawrence H. Mamiya, *The Black Church in the African American Experience*, Durham: Duke University Press, 1990.

Litwack, Leon F., *Been in the Storm So Long: The Aftermath of Slavery*, New York: Random House, 1980.

Logan, Rayford W., *The Betrayal of the Negro: From Rutherford B. Hayes to Woodrow Wilson*, Cambridge, MA: Da Capo Press, 1997.

Luker, Ralph E., "Bushnell in Black and White: Evidences of the 'Racism' of Horace Bushnell," *The New England Quarterly*, Vol. 45, No. 3 (Sep., 1972), pp. 408–416.

Lyons, Charles H., *To Wash An Aethiop White: British Ideas about Black Educability, 1530–1960*, New York: Teachers College Press, 1975.

Mabee, Carleton, "A Negro Boycott to Integrate Boston Schools," *The New England Quarterly*, Vol. 41, No. 3 (Sep., 1968), pp. 341–361.

MacMullen, Edith Nye, *In the Cause of True Education: Henry Barnard and Nineteenth-Century School Reform*, New Haven: Yale University Press, 1991.

Magnuson, Katherine and Jane Waldfogel, editors, *Steady Gains and Stalled Progress: Inequality and the Black-White Test Score Gap*, New York: Russell Sage Foundation, 2008.

Martin, Waldo E., Jr., *The Mind of Frederick Douglass*, Chapel Hill: University of North Carolina, 1984.

McAfee, Ward M., *Religion, Race, and Reconstruction: The Public School in the Politics of the 1870s*, Albany: State University of New York Press, 1998.

McLoughlin, William G., editor, *The American Evangelicals, 1800–1900: An Anthology*, New York: Harper & Row, 1968.

———, *Cherokee Renascence in the New Republic*, Princeton University Press, 1986.

———, *After the Trail of Tears: The Cherokees' Struggle for Sovereignty, 1839–1880*, Chapel Hill: University of North Carolina Press, 1993.

McPherson, James M., *The Abolitionist Legacy: From Reconstruction to the NAACP*, Princeton: Princeton University Press, 1975.

McWhorter, John, *Losing the Race: Self-Sabotage in Black America*, New York: Harper Perennial, 2001.

Meier, August and Elliott Rudwick, "Early Boycotts of Segregated Schools: The East Orange, New Jersey, Experience, 1899–1906," *History of Education Quarterly*, Vol. 7, No. 1 (Spring, 1967), pp. 22–35.

——— and ———, *From Plantation to Ghetto*, Revised Edition, New York: Hill and Wang, 1970.

Mirel, Jeffrey, *The Rise and Fall of An Urban School System: Detroit 1907–81*, Second Edition, Ann Arbor: University of Michigan Press, 1999.

Mitchell, Mary Niall, "'A Good and Delicious Country': Free Children of Color and How They Learned to Imagine the Atlantic World in Nineteenth-Century Louisiana," *History of Education Quarterly*, Vol. 40, No. 2 (Summer, 2000), pp. 123–144.
Monroe, Paul, *Founding of the American Public School System*, New York: Hafner Publishing, 1971.
Morant, G. M., *The Significance of Racial Differences*, Paris: UNESCO, 1958.
Morgan, Harry, *Historical Perspectives on the Education of Black Children*, Westport, CT: Praeger, 1995.
Morris, Robert C., *Reading, 'Riting, and Reconstruction: The Education of Freedmen in the South, 1861–1870*, Chicago: University of Chicago Press, 1981.
Murray, Alex B., "Harriet Beecher Stowe on Racial Segregation in the Schools," *American Quarterly*, Vol. 12, No. 4 (Winter, 1960), pp. 518–519.
Myrdal, Gunnar, *An American Dilemma: The Negro Problem and Modern Democracy* (1944), volume 1 and 2, New York: Random House, 1962.
Newby, I. A., *Jim Crow's Defense: Anti-Negro Thought in America, 1900–1930*, Baton Rouge: Louisiana State University Press, 1965.
Newby, Robert G. and David B. Tyack, "Victims Without 'Crimes': Some Historical Perspectives on Black Education," *The Journal of Negro Education*, Vol. 40, No. 3, Strategies for Educational Change (Summer, 1971), pp. 192–206.
Noble, Stuart G., "Education of the Negro," in *Twenty-Five Years of American Education*, edited by I. L. Kandel, Freeport, NY: Books for Libraries Press, 1924.
Noll, Mark A., *America's God: From Jonathan Edwards to Abraham Lincoln*, Oxford University Press, 2002.
Ochiai, Akiko, "The Port Royal Experiment Revisited: Northern Visions of Reconstruction and the Land Question," *The New England Quarterly*, Vol. 74, No. 1 (Mar., 2001), pp. 94–117.
Ogbu, John U., "Immigrant and Involuntary Minorities in Comparative Perspective," in *Minority Status and Schooling*, edited by Margaret A. Gibson and John U. Ogbu, New York: Garland, 1991.
———, *Black American Students in an Affluent Suburb*, Mahwah, NJ: Lawrence Erlbaum, 2003.
Olmstead, Frederick Law, *The Slave States*, edited by Harvey Wish, New York: Capricorn Books, 1959.
Orfield, Gary, *Must We Bus? Segregated Schools and National Policy*, Washington, DC: The Brookings Institution, 1978.
Orr, Marion, *Black Social Capital: The Politics of School Reform in Baltimore, 1986–1998*, Lawrence: University Press of Kansas, 1999.
Patterson, Orlando, *The Ordeal of Integration: Progress and Resentment in America's 'Racial' Crisis*, Washington: Civitas/Counterpoint, 1997.
———, *Rituals of Blood: Consequences of Slavery in Two American Centuries*, New York: Basic Books, 1998.
Payne, Daniel A., *Recollections of Seventy Years*, New York: Arno Press, 1968.
Pease, William H. and Jane H. Pease, editors, *The Antislavery Argument*, Indianapolis: Bobbs-Merrill, 1965.

Perlstein, Daniel, "Minds Stayed on Freedom: Politics and Pedagogy in the African-American Freedom Struggle," *American Educational Research Journal*, Vol. 39, No. 2, Education and Democracy. ((Summer, 2002), pp. 249–277.

Peterson, Paul E., *The Politics of School Reform, 1870–1940*, University of Chicago Press, 1985.

Plank, David N. and Marcia Turner, "Changing Patterns in Black School Politics: Atlanta, 1872–1973," *American Journal of Education*, Vol. 95, No. 4 (Aug., 1987), pp. 584–608.

Power, Edward J., *Religion and the Public Schools in 19th Century America: The Contribution of Orestes A. Brownson*, New York: Paulist Press, 1996.

Poxpey, C. Spencer, "The Washington-Dubois Controversy and Its Effect on the Negro Problem," *History of Education Journal*, Vol. 8, No. 4 (Summer, 1957), pp. 128–152.

Quarles, Benjamin, *Black Abolitionists*, Oxford University Press, 1969.

Raboteau, Albert K., *Slave Religion: The "Invisible Institution" in the Antebellum South*, Oxford University Press, 1978.

Rainwater, Lee and William L. Yancey, *The Moynihan Report and the Politics of Controversy*, Cambridge, MA: The M. I. T. Press, 1986.

Ravitch, Diane, *The Great School Wars: New York City, 1805–1973*, New York: Basic Books, 1974.

———, "On the History of Minority Group Education in the United States," in *History, Education, and Public Policy*, edited by Donald R. Warren, Berkeley, CA: McCutchan, 1978.

———, *The Troubled Crusade: American Education, 1945–1980*, New York: Basic Books, 1983.

———, *Left Back: A Century of Failed School Reforms*, New York: Simon & Schuster, 2000.

Reese, William J., *Power and the Promise of School Reform: Grass-Roots Movements during the Progressive Era*, Boston: Routledge & Kegan Paul, 1986.

Richardson, Joe M., *Christian Reconstruction: The American Missionary Association and Southern Blacks, 1861–1890*, University of Georgia Press, 1986.

Rose, Willie Lee, *Rehearsal for Reconstruction: The Port Royal Experiment*, New York: Random House, 1967.

Ruchames, Louis, editor, *The Abolitionists*, New York: Capricorn Books, 1963.

———, *Racial Thought in America: I. From the Puritans to Abraham Lincoln*, New York: Grosset and Dunlap, 1970.

Schwartz, Bernard, editor, *Statutory History of the United States: Civil Rights*, volumes I and II, New York: Chelsea House Publishers, 1970.

Seifman, Eli, "Education or Emigration: The Schism within the African Colonization Movement, 1865–1875," *History of Education Quarterly*, Vol. 7, No. 1. ((Spring, 1967), pp. 36–57.

Selleck, Linda B., *Gentle Invaders: Quaker Women Educators and Racial Issues during the Civil War and Reconstruction*, Richmond, IN: Friends United Press, 1995.

Sernett, Milton C., editor, *African American Religious History: Documentary Witness*, Second Edition, Durham: Duke University Press, 1999.

Shapiro, Harry L., *Race Mixture*, Paris: UNESCO, 1953.
Shenton, James P., editor, *The Reconstruction: A Documentary History, 1865–1877*, New York: Capricorn Books, 1963.
Sherer, Robert G., *Subordination Or Liberation? The Development and Conflicting Theories of Black Education in Nineteenth Century Alabama*, University of Alabama Press, 1977.
Sitkoff, Harvard, *The Struggle for Black Equality, 1954–1980*, New York: Hill and Wang, 1981.
Small, Miriam R. and Edwin W. Small, "Prudence Crandall Champion of Negro Education," *The New England Quarterly*, Vol. 17, No. 4 (Dec., 1944), pp. 506–529.
Sobel, Mechal, *Trabelin' on: The Slave Journey to An Afro-Baptist Faith*, Princeton: Princeton University Press, 1988.
Stampp, Kenneth M., *The Peculiar Institution: Slavery in the Ante-Bellum South*, New York: Random House Vintage Books, 1964.
———, *The Era of Reconstruction, 1865–1877*, New York: Random House Vintage Books, 1965.
———, *The Imperiled Union: Essays on the Background of the Civil War*, New York: Oxford University Press, 1980.
Stewart, James Brewer, "The New Haven Negro College and the Meanings of Race in New England, 1776–1870," *The New England Quarterly*, Vol. 76, No. 3 (Sep., 2003), pp. 323–355.
Stuckey, Sterling, *Slave Culture: Nationalist Theory and the Foundations of Black America*, Oxford University Press, 1987.
Tannenbaum, Frank, *Slave & Citizen: The Negro in the Americas*, New York: Random House Vintage Books, 1946.
Thernstrom, Stephan and Abigail Thernstrom, *America in Black and White: One Nation, Indivisible*, New York: Simon and Schuster, 1997.
Thomas, William B., "Black Intellectuals' Critique of Early Mental Testing: A Little-Known Saga of the 1920s," *American Journal of Education*, Vol. 90, No. 3 (May, 1982), pp. 258–292.
Tocqueville, Alexis de, *Democracy in America*, translated by Harvey V. Mansfield and Delba Winthrop, Chicago: University of Chicago Press, 2000.
Todd, Emmanuel, *Le destin des immigrés: Assimilation et ségrégation dans les démocracies occidentales*, Paris: Éditions du Seuil, 1994.
Toppin, Edgar A., "Walter White and the Atlanta NAACP's Fight for Equal Schools, 1916–1917," *History of Education Quarterly*, Vol. 7, No. 1 (Spring, 1967), pp. 3–21.
Tough, Paul, *Whatever It Takes: Geoffrey Canada's Quest to Change Harlem and America*, Boston: Houghton Mifflin, 2008.
Tyack, David B., "Growing Up Black: Perspectives on the History of Education in Northern Ghettos," *History of Education Quarterly*, Vol. 9, No. 3 (Autumn, 1969), pp. 287–297.
——— and Elisabeth Hansot, *Managers of Virtue: Public School Leadership in America, 1820–1980*, New York: Basic Books, 1982.

———— and Robert Lowe, "The Constitutional Moment: Reconstruction and Black Education in the South," *American Journal of Education*, Vol. 94, No. 2 (Feb., 1986), pp. 236–256.

Verba, Sidney, Kay Lehman Schlozman, and Henry E. Brady, *Voice and Equality: Civic Voluntarism in American Politics*, Cambridge, MA: Harvard University Press, 1995.

Voegeli, V. Jacque, *Free But Not Equal: The Midwest and the Negro during the Civil War*, Chicago: University of Chicago Press, 1967.

Warren, Donald R., "The U.S. Department of Education: A Reconstruction Promise to Black Americans," *The Journal of Negro Education*, Vol. 43, No. 4 (Autumn, 1974), pp. 437–451.

Warren, Robert Penn, *Segregation: The Inner Conflict in the South*, New York: Random House, 1956.

Washington, Booker T., *The Future of the American Negro*, Boston: Small, Maynard, 1907.

————, *Up from Slavery*, New York: Dell, 1965.

Waters, Mary C., *Ethnic Options: Choosing Identities in America*, Berkeley: University of California Press, 1990.

Welter, Rush, *Popular Education and Democratic Thought in America*, New York: Columbia University Press, 1962.

Wesley, Edgar B., "Forty Acres and a Mule and a Speller," *History of Education Journal*, Vol. 8, No. 4 (Summer, 1957), pp. 113–127.

West, Earle H., "The Peabody Education Fund and Negro Education, 1867–1880," *History of Education Quarterly*, Vol. 6, No. 2 (Summer, 1966), pp. 3–21.

Whitman, David, *Sweating the Small Stuff: Inner-City Schools and the New Paternalism*, Washington, DC: Thomas B. Fordham Institute, 2008.

Wilkinson, J. Harvie, III, *From Brown to Bakke: The Supreme Court and School Integration, 1954–1978*, Oxford University Press, 1979.

Willcox, Walter F., "The Probable Increase of the Negro Race in the United States," *The Quarterly Journal of Economics*, Vol. 19, No. 4 (Aug., 1905), pp. 545–572.

Williams, Heather Andrea, *Self-Taught: African American Education in Slavery and Freedom*, Chapel Hill: University of North Carolina Press, 2005.

Williamson, Joel, *A Rage for Order: Black-White Relations in the American South Since Emancipation*, New York: Oxford University Press, 1986.

Winks, Robin W., *The Blacks in Canada: A History*, Second Edition, Montreal: McGill University Press, 1997.

Woodson, Carter G., "Early Negro Education in West Virginia," *The Journal of Negro History*, Vol. 7, No. 1 (Jan., 1922), pp. 23–63.

————, *The Mis-Education of the Negro*, Chicago: Associated Publishers, 1933.

Woodward, C. Vann, *The Strange Career of Jim Crow*, Third Revised Edition, New York: Oxford University Press, 1974.

Wyatt-Brown, Bertram, *Lewis Tappan and the Evangelical War against Slavery*, Baton Rouge: Louisiana State University Press, 1969.

Index

Abbott, Lyman 48
abolition of slavery in the North 36
abolitionists 11, 37, 42–3, 60, 114, 116
achievement gap 21, 132, 157, 163, 166
Adger, John B. 34
Agassiz, Louis 6, 13
Alabama 28–9, 54, 69–70, 93, 101, 154, 157
Alford, John W. 49
Alton, Illinois 123
American Freedman's Union Commission 56, 59, 61
American Missionary Association 49, 53–4, 56–61, 67, 69–70, 103
Anglican church and schools 24–6, 39, 109–10
Arkansas 82
Armstrong, Samuel 86–90
Atlanta 20, 51, 102–4, 135, 138
'Atlanta Compromise' speech 91–2

Baker, Ray Stannard 100, 103
Baltimore 25, 43, 52, 141
Barnard, Henry 110
Bell Curve, The 21
Berkeley, George 23
Bible reading as motivation for literacy 26, 33, 57
Black churches 28, 30, 33–5, 39, 41, 43, 50, 53, 58, 67–9, 97, 101, 109, 127–8, 139, 143–5
'Black codes' 46

Black colleges 31, 41–2, 48, 67–70, 82, 86, 92, 96–8, 102, 106, 127–31, 134, 137
Black middle class 69, 123, 128, 131–2, 135, 144–5, 148
Black Panthers 146–7
'Black Power' 161
Black self-help organizations 35, 39, 50, 53, 60, 128–9, 142
Black separatism 6, 72, 111–12, 122, 133–40, 144–6, 149, 161–3
Black teachers 32, 39, 41, 49–51, 53–4, 61–2, 65, 68, 70, 83, 85–7, 94, 96, 98–101, 109, 111, 120–3, 129–31, 135–9, 149, 158
Blair, Lewis Harvie 84
Blumenbach's racial categories 5
Bond, Horace Mann 47–8, 76–7, 83, 88, 92, 94, 101, 119, 122, 140–1, 153
Boston 39, 43, 109, 111–14, 124
boycott of school 123
Bray, Thomas 24, 39
Brown v. Board of Education 3, 79, 107, 112, 139, 150–1, 154, 157

Cable, George W. 102
Calhoun, John C. 18
California 117–19
Canada 3, 33, 36, 38, 56, 109–10, 114, 121
Canterbury, Connecticut 41–2
Catholic schools 113, 166

Catholic teaching orders 33
Charleston 25, 27, 29, 31, 35, 48–9, 66, 68, 157
Charlottesville 59
charter schools 166
Chavis, John 28
Cherokee Indians 34–5, 56, 118
Chicago 104–5, 116–17, 121–3, 128, 137, 140, 145
Child, Lydia Maria 38
Cincinnati 43, 52, 114, 149
Civil Rights Act
   of 1875 71, 73–4, 118
   of 1957 155
   of 1964 155–7
clandestine schooling of slaves 31–2
Cleveland, Grover 92
common school 3, 14, 37–8, 54, 68, 73–4, 112–15, 119
Congress of Racial Equality 148
Connecticut 110, 119
Constitution
   Fourteenth Amendment 70, 151
   Fifteenth Amendment 17, 116
Cooper, James Fenimore 6
Crandall, Prudence 41–2
Crandall, Reuben 42
Cuvier, Georges 12

Dabney, Charles W. 13
Darwin, Charles 13, 15
Democratic Party 46, 66, 75, 101, 116, 156
desegregation of schools 113–14, 124, 137–9, 144, 154–60
Detroit 123, 160–2
disparity in expenditures in public schools 99–102
Dixon, Thomas, Jr. 17–18, 102
Douglass, Frederick 29, 57, 90, 112
Du Bois, W. E. B. 2, 6, 52, 65, 68–9, 90, 92, 97, 100, 123, 127–40, 145
Dunbar High School 130
Dunning, William Archibald 17

East Orange, New Jersey 123
Eisenhower, Dwight D. 155
Eliot, Charles W. 97
Erwin, Sam 107, 155
Evangelical teachers from the North 51–3, 82

family instability 140–1
Florida 31, 75, 83–4, 157
Frazier, E. Franklin 141
Freedman's Aid Society 52, 70
Freedman's Bureau 48, 52, 61–6, 70–1
Freedom Movement 58, 92–3, 144–5, 155
Freedom Schools 145
Freedom's Journal 37
Frelinghuysen, Theodore 71
Fuller, Richard 14

Gardner, Anna 59–60
Gardner, Howard 20
Garrison, William Lloyd 51, 89
Garvey, Marcus 19, 121, 133–5, 140
Gary, Indiana 120–1, 124, 135
Georgia 27–8, 80, 99
Great Awakening 25–6, 55
Green v. County School Board 158
Grimké sisters 29

Hammon, Jupiter 39
Hampton Institute 86–90, 97
Harlem Children's Zone 166
Harris, William Torrey 90
Hartford 110
Hearst, William Randolph 19
Higginson, Thomas Wentworth 60
Hoffman, Frederick 15
Howard, Oliver O. 61
Hume, David 8
Hurston, Zora Neale 9
Huxley, Thomas H. 15

Illinois 36, 115–16, 118–19
immigrants in competition with Blacks 117, 122, 124

Indiana 36
Indianapolis 123
industrial education, *see* manual labor education
integrated schools 28, 38, 72, 75, 109, 111–12, 116, 136, 152, 161

Jackson, J. H. 155
Jefferson, Thomas 8–9, 11
Jensen, Arthur 21
Johnson, James Weldon 120
Johnson, Lyndon B. 155–6

Kentucky 50
King, William 110
KIPP schools 166

laws against teaching slaves 28–30
LeBon, Gustave 17
Lincoln Normal School 60
literacy rate 68, 79, 102, 124, 142
Louisiana 28, 35, 46, 54, 66–7, 72, 75, 82
Lyell, Sir Charles 12

Mann, Horace 37, 55, 114, 165
manual labor education 69–70, 86–91, 95–6
Maryland 35, 58
Massachusetts 36, 46, 101, 111–15
May, Samuel 41
Mencken, H. L. 19
Milwaukee 121, 135, 163
Mississippi 28, 46, 66, 73, 81, 103, 105, 145–6, 154
Mobile 12, 49
Mohammad, Elijah 162
Montgomery 53
Morton, Samuel 8
movement of Blacks to North 104, 145
Moynihan, Daniel Patrick 141
Myrdal, Gunnar 86, 106, 142–4

National Association for the Advancement of Colored People 18, 51, 120, 122–3, 125, 134, 137–9, 144, 150, 154, 162
National Colored Labor Union 49
National Education Association 63, 85, 90
National Freedman's Relief Association 47
Negro Convention Movement 41–2, 90
New Brunswick 110
New England Freedmen's Aid Society 52
New England values, attempt to impose 45, 47, 55–6, 60
New Haven 42, 110
New Jersey 109, 122, 124
New Orleans 32–3, 75
New York City 24, 36–8, 40, 114, 161, 166
New York State 110, 116–17
North Carolina 31, 83, 98
Northern Student Movement 145
Nott, Josiah 12–13
Nova Scotia 25, 39, 110

Oakland Community School 147
Ocean Hill-Brownsville 22, 162
O'Connor, Sandra Day 163
Ohio 50, 64, 89, 110, 115, 117
Olmstead, Frederick Law 30–2, 45
Ontario 38, 110, 122, 139

parents 17, 22, 34, 37–8, 54, 56, 61, 75, 107, 111, 116–17, 121–2, 124, 140, 157, 160, 165–9
Passing of the Great Race, The 19
Patterson, Mary Jane 130
Patterson, Orlando 20–1, 167
Paul, Nathaniel 89
Payne, Daniel Alexander 31, 48, 68
Peabody Fund 54–5, 72, 83
Peake, Mary 48–9
Pennsylvania 40, 110
Philadelphia 11, 36, 39–40, 43, 52, 109–10, 121–4, 136
Phillips, Wendell 114

Pickens, William 149
Plessy v. Ferguson 150–3
private schools 31, 38, 40, 50–1, 59, 69, 75, 100, 109, 140, 154, 168
Proctor, Jenny 32
Progressive Education 85, 93, 137, 145–6, 166
Purdy, Edwin 32

Quakers 10, 25, 39, 55, 109
qualifications of Black and White teachers 101, 151, 154
Quebec 89

race 5–22, 66–7, 70, 74, 81, 83, 85–6, 93, 97, 107, 112, 124, 127, 135, 142–3, 153, 167–8
 scientific understanding of 7–8, 12–17, 85
 theological understanding of 9–12, 15
Rainey, Joseph 73
Raleigh 31
Reconstruction
 Congressional 46
 Presidential 46
Republican Party 46, 49, 51, 66, 71, 75, 116, 156
resentment of northern teachers 58, 67
Richmond 53
Roberts case 14–15, 112–13, 151
Robinson, Clement 50
Rochester 110
Roosevelt, Theodore 40
Rosenwald Fund 100, 102, 139
Ryerson, Egerton 38

St. Louis 53, 149
San Francisco 43, 117, 147
Savannah 32, 50–1, 53–4, 65, 162
Schaff, Philip 84
Sea Islands 53

Sears, Barnas 54–5, 72, 83
segregation of schools
 de facto 71, 85, 109, 117, 119–20, 123, 147
 de jure 71, 73, 79–80, 82–3, 107, 110, 112
Selma, Alabama 70, 129
separate but equal 107, 119, 124, 138, 150–3
Shaler, Nathaniel Southgate 15
Sherman, William Tecumseh 48
Sinclair, William 97
Slater Fund 95
Smith, Samuel Stanhope 10
Social Darwinism 7, 142
Society for the Propagation of the Gospel (SPG) 24–6
South Carolina 25–30, 46, 49, 65–8, 72, 80, 83–4, 154, 157
Southern Educational Association 98
Spencer, Herbert 17
Springfield, Massachusetts 109
Springfield, Ohio 123
Stephens, Alexander 13
Stevens, Thaddeus 46
Stowe, Harriet Beecher 75, 90
Student Non-violent Coordinating Committee (SNCC) 145–6, 148
Sumner, Charles 14, 71, 74, 112–13
Sunday schools 33–4, 50

Talladega College 69–70
Tappan, Lewis 114
Tennessee 66, 82
Texas 58, 67, 82
Tillman, Benjamin 86
Tocqueville, Alexis de 7, 12
Tuskegee Institute 88, 90

Union Missionary Society 56
Universal Declaration of Human Rights 150–1
urban riots 161

Vardaman, James K. 81
violence against Black schools and churches 56, 66, 74
Virginia 28, 31, 34, 50, 58, 82
Voltaire (François-Marie Arouet) 8

Walker, David 11, 29, 43
Warren, Earl 151–3
Warren, Robert Penn 144
Washington, Booker T. 18, 46, 64, 88, 90–4, 129–31
Washington, D.C. 31, 130, 138, 149, 154, 157
Wells, Ida B. 51
Wesley, John 10
West Virginia 50, 64–5
White supremacy 18, 31, 46, 98, 100
Whitefield, George 11, 26
Whittier, John Greenleaf 36
Wickersham, James P. 63
Wilberforce, William 10
Wilkerson, Doxey 132
Willcox, Walter 16
Wilmington 43
Wilson, William Julius 148, 158
Wilson, Woodrow 75
Wirt, William Albert 120, 136
Woodson, Carter 50, 64–5, 128, 142–4
Wright, Theodore 38

GPSR Compliance

The European Union's (EU) General Product Safety Regulation (GPSR) is a set of rules that requires consumer products to be safe and our obligations to ensure this.

If you have any concerns about our products, you can contact us on

ProductSafety@springernature.com

In case Publisher is established outside the EU, the EU authorized representative is:

Springer Nature Customer Service Center GmbH
Europaplatz 3
69115 Heidelberg, Germany

www.ingramcontent.com/pod-product-compliance
Lightning Source LLC
LaVergne TN
LVHW011821060526
838200LV00053B/3856

9 781349 295784